# INFORMATION PROCESSING AND TECHNOLOGY

# INFORMATION PROCESSING AND TECHNOLOGY

NIKOS MASTORAKIS
STAVROS D. NIKOLOPOULOS
(EDITORS)

**Nova Science Publishers, Inc.**
*Huntington, New York*

**Senior Editors:** Susan Boriotti and Donna Dennis
**Office Manager:** Annette Hellinger
**Graphics:** Wanda Serrano and Dorothy Marczak
**Coordinating Editor:** Tatiana Shohov
**Book Production:** Matthew Kozlowski, Jonathan Rose and Jennifer Vogt
**Circulation:** Cathy DeGregory and Ave Maria Gonzalez
**Communications and Acquisition:** Serge Shohov

*Library of Congress Cataloging-in-Publication Data*
*Available Upon Request*

ISBN 1-59033-116-8


227 Main Street, Suite 100
Huntington, New York 11743
Tele. 631-424-6682 Fax 631-425-5933
e-mail: Novascience@earthlink.net
Web Site: http://www.nexusworld.com/nova



*Printed in the United States of America*

# CONTENTS

# PREFACE

Information Processing and Technology have known an impressive development recently and are poles of attraction for many engineers and scientists. These fascinating fields have also swayed all the aspects of modern life; today it is widely recognized the role of information processing and technology in various fields of every day life (education, health, management, banking sector, communication, commerce, animation and many others).

This volume contains the latest developments in information processing and technology and reflects the experience of many researchers working in these areas. It contains papers on object-oriented techniques in software developments, formal methods for specification and verification of systems such as network protocols, languages for implementing parallel systems, QoS for multimedia applications, software system design approaches with a wide range of applications.

We are grateful to all authors for the willingness with which responded to our invitation to submit their recent research results. A standard journal review process gave us the opportunity to collect the most important contributions and to include those in this special issue. We are sure that the authors' effort to provide high quality contributions will be appreciated by the computer science community.

We, as editors, hope that its readers will find the results reported here interesting and beneficial for their own work.

Last but not least, we want to take this opportunity to thank the many referees for their cooperative effort and constructive criticism, without which this volume would not have been possible.

Nikos Mastorakis
Stavros D. Nikolopoulos

*Chapter 1*

# AN OBJECT PATTERN FOR COMPUTER USER INTERFACE SYSTEMS

STANLEY Y.P. CHIEN
Department of Electrical Engineering
Purdue Sch8ool of Engineering and Technology
Indiana University-Purdue University at Indianapolis
723 West Michigan Street, Indianapolis, Indiana 46202, USA
*chien@engr.iupui.edu*

*Abstract:* As the real-time embedded systems become more complex, the advantages of using object-oriented analysis (OOA) in software development becomes more apparent. Since the learning curve of OOA is relatively long and OOA is still more a creative work than an engineering routine, it is desirable to capture the common features of a set of problems in such away that they can be reused as is or easily replaced as necessary. In this paper, a *message pattern*, which is applicable to many computer user interface systems, is proposed. The process of using the message pattern to model the system is also described. The message pattern and the associated development process have four advantages. (1) It separates the system requirement into passive data objects and the active program control objects. This separation enables the quick development and easy modification of OOA model according to the given specification. (2) The approach is systematic and can be scaled up to large systems. (3) It represents the information explicitly so that it is easier for the OOA model compiler to generate efficient code. (4) It is easy to learn and apply since it provides detailed steps for model development. The application of the message pattern is demonstrated through a voice-controlled telephone dialing system.

*Key-Words:* message pattern, object oriented analysis, Shlaer/Mellor method.

# 1 Introduction

Using object-oriented analysis (OOA) in software development has two main advantages. (1) It heavily emphasizes the analysis process during the software development. This emphasis tends to make a better design of the software. (2) It separates the software analysis from actual software design and development. This separation makes the OOA model more portable and reusable. There are several requirements to ensure the good result by using OOA: (1) a complete knowledge (and/or valid assumptions) of the whole system, (2) proper definition of objects and state machines, (3) proper division of the system into tasks and component modules and (4) efficient model compilation to low level code. The requirement (1) is important for any project. It requires a lot effort to satisfy and is time consuming to do so [1-3]. Requirement (2) is not straightforward to satisfy. There are no concrete rules to guide a person to define objects for a given project. Many literatures suggest that the OOA objects be defined according to physical entities, similar behavior and characteristics [4-7]. However, it is not easy to find similar behaviors and cannot reference to physical objects in many applications. If the objects are not defined properly in an analysis, the state machines in objects may become very complicated. The requirement (3) and (4) are design issues that determine the efficiency of the software [8].

Since the OOA process encourages the analyzer to ignore the design and implementation details during analysis, the final OOA models sometimes become difficult to be implemented efficiently without model modification. A more detailed OOA model tends to require the model compiler to be more intelligent in order to make the final code efficient. It is often the case that the object-oriented analyst and the object-oriented designer work together to simplify the particular model and modify the model compiler to generate efficient code. In order to translate the good experience and knowledge into a systematic modeling process, many OOA patterns have been proposed [9-11]. An OOA pattern can be considered as a model template that can be used in many different systems. It captures the common features of a set of problems in such away that they can be reused as is or easily replaced as necessary.

In this paper, a new object pattern, message pattern, is described. This pattern is suitable for many computer user interface applications. A process of using this pattern to define the objects, attributes, events and state machines according to the system requirement is also described. This pattern demonstrates four advantages: (1) It separates the system requirement as passive data objects and the active program control objects. This separation enables the quick development and easy modification of OOA model according to the given specification. (2) The approach is systematic and can be scaled up to large embedded systems. (3) It makes the OOA model explicit thus making the model compiler easier to generate efficient code. (4) It is easy to learn and apply since it provides a detailed process for model development. The paper is organized as follows. Section 2 describes the message pattern. Section 3 describes the process of applying the message pattern using an application example. Section 4 discusses the initialization of the message objects defined in the message pattern and the translation of the message objects into C language. Sections 5 and 6 are the discussion and conclusion, respectively.

# 2 Message Pattern

The computer user interface problem includes the graphical user interface and voice based user interface. This problem requires many rounds of user-computer interactions for each user initiated task. The user-computer dialog can be described by a graph. It is difficult to use the traditional approach to develop a computational and memory efficient OOA model for the application. The message pattern provides a number of advantages to such systems.

## 2.1 General System Structure

The message pattern is developed based on the following assumptions. It is assumed that the embedded system could be a multi-domain system. The domains may be decomposed into three domain layers: application domain layer, service domain layer, and implementation domain layer. The structure of the domain layers is depicted in Fig. 1. The arrows in Fig. 1 indicate the directions of the service requests. The interactions between domains are based on the message (event) passing. It is usually desirable to divide the domains in such a way that each domain interacts with only a small set of well defined domains [5, 12, 13]. Objects are defined within each domain. The messages and operations viewed from each domain can be described in a general form as depicted in Fig. 2. The outgoing arrows indicate that the object sends a message out without expecting a response. The incoming arrows indicate that objects receive messages. A double arrow indicates that the object sends a message out and expects a response message. The response can be either immediate (return from a function call) or delayed (receive an event). The object "Asynchronous event handler" is responsible for synchronizing the external events with the internal activities in the domain.

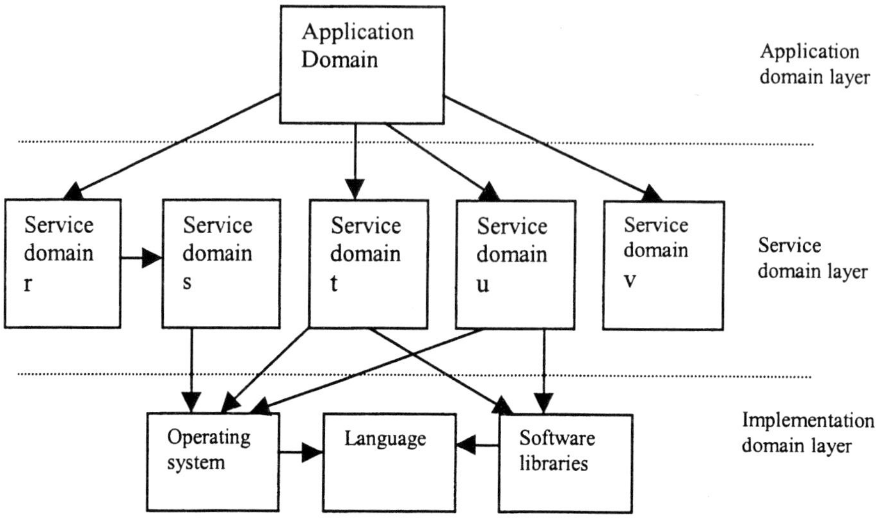


Fig. 1 Structure of domain layers in embedded systems.

To simplify the description, the messages viewed from an object or a domain are divided in two groups, send-messages and receive-messages:

Send messages include:

external events generated for triggering actions in other domains,
external functions to be called for obtaining service from other domains,
internal events generated for triggering actions in other objects within the same domain, and
internal functions to be called for obtaining services from other objects within the same domain.

Receive messages include:

external events received from other domains that triggers the actions in the current domain, and
internal events received from other objects that triggers the actions in the current object.

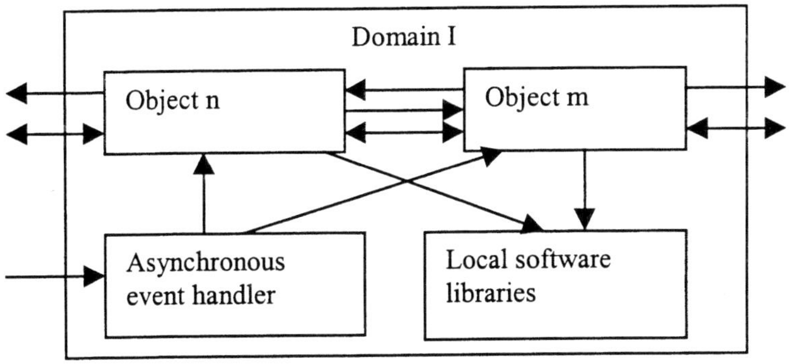


Fig. 2 A typical message passing structure of a domain.

## 2.2 Object Pattern

In a computer user interface application, the dialog process and contents are usually predefined. The information of all possible messages sent between different system components is also specified in the system requirement. From the view of the general system described in Fig. 1 and Fig. 2, it is observed that the set of received messages that responds to any particular sent message by a domain is small. For example, in a computer graphical user interface, the possible user input could only be one of the menu items provided by the computer. Based on this observation, a message pattern is described as follows. The object information model for the message pattern is depicted in Fig. 3.

The object information model consists of a message coordinator object, a set of message objects, and other supporting objects (Reset and exception handler, Error handler, User I/O interface, and Machine I/O interface). All message objects are passive objects that do not have states. The message coordinator object is an active object and has only one instance. It consists of at least three attributes: next_message_object, next_message, and current_state. Next_message_object indicates which message object is currently being accessed or to be accessed. Next_message indicates which message in the next_message_object may be sent. Current_state attribute contains the current state number of the message coordinator object (details see Section 2.3). More attributes may be added for specific application requirements.

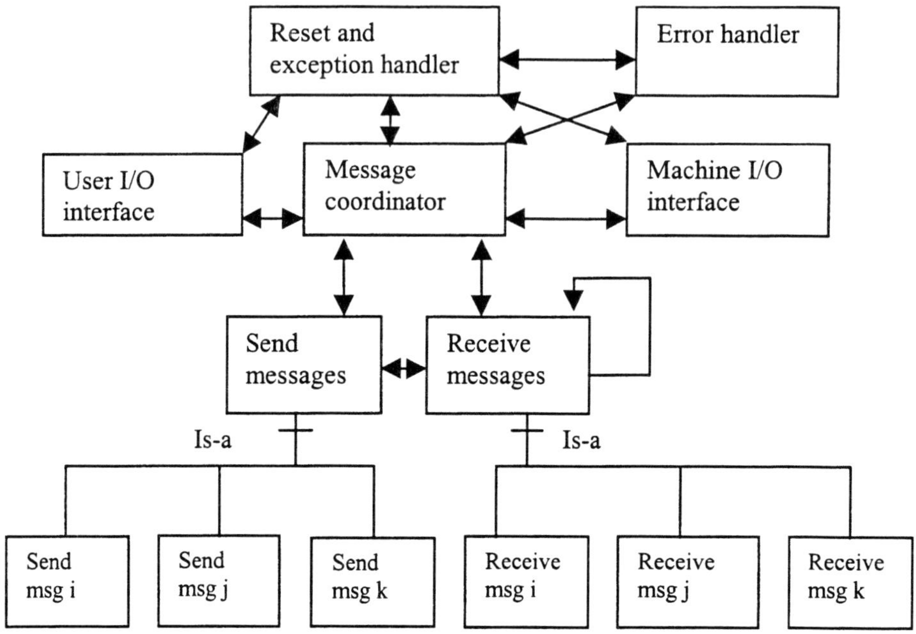


Fig. 3 Object information model of the message pattern.

Table 1. An example of a send_message object.

| *Instance (message) id* | *Message to be sent* | *Reference_object_id* | *Reference_message_id* |
|---|---|---|---|
| 0 | Message 1 | Message Object 1 | Message n |
| 1 | Message 2 | Message Object 2 | Message m |
| 2 | Error | Reset | 1 |

Table 2. An example of a receive_message object.

| *Instance (message) id* | *Message to be sent* | *Condition operator* | *Condition operand* | *Reference_ message_ id_ or_ condition _is_false* | *Reference_ object id_for_ Condition_ is_ true* | *Reference_ message_id_ for_ condition_ is_true* |
|---|---|---|---|---|---|---|
| 0 | Message 1 | Operator 1 | Operand 1 | 1 | Message Object 1 | Message n1 |
| 1 | Message 2 | Operator 2 | Operand 2 | 2 | Message Object 2 | Message m1 |
| 2 | Error Message | Operator 3 | * | N/A | Message Object 3 | Message p1 |
| 3 | Message 4 | Operator 4 | Operand 4 | 4 | Message Object 1 | Message n2 |
| 4 | Message 5 | Operator 5 | Operand 5 | 5 | Message Object 2 | Message m2 |
| 5 | Error Message | Operator 6 | * | N/A | Message Object 3 | Message p2 |
| | .... | | | | | |

Each message object has many instances. The message objects are divided into two types: send_message objects and receive_message objects. Each instance of the send_message objects is a command to the user or other system components. Each send_message object has two attributes: instance_id, and message. Each send_object also has two additional referential attributes that describe the relationship between the send_message object and receive_message objects. One referential attribute describes the id of the receive_message object. The other referential attribute describes the id of the message in the receive_message object. Each instance of the receive_message object is a possible input message or response message from other domains.

Each receive_message object has five attributes: the instance id, a binary condition operator, a condition operand and two response messages. One response message will be sent when the operation between the receive message and the condition operand is true. The other response message will be sent when the operation between the receive message and the condition operand is false. The message attribute contains the message name and associated parameters. The receive_object also has three additional referential attributes. Two attributes describe the relationship between this receive_message object and the send_message objects. The third attribute describes the relationship between this receive_message object and itself. Table 1 is an example of a send_message object and Table 2 is an example of a receive_message object. Each column is an attribute and each row is an instance of the object class. The message that has id equals to 2 in Table 2 is a special case. The values * of condition operand means that the condition is always true.

At any particular point of system execution, the message to be sent by the message coordinator object is precisely defined. The set of possible actions to be taken after receiving each message is also defined. Since the domain may receive one of several possible messages after sends out one message, a screening process is needed to understand what message is received and to what action to be taken. Such a screening process is described in the state model of the message coordinator object (see details in Section 2.3). The information for screening process is described by the instances of receive_message object. The receive_message object has many instances. All instances of a receive_message object that are possible responses to a send_message are linked together (as depicted by the self-relationship of object receive_message in Fig. 3). For example, the first three instances in Table 2 are linked (it is indicated by the column *Reference*_message_id_for_condition_is_false in Table 2). Each receive_message object may contain many linked instances. Since unexpected messages may be received, they are considered as error messages and be instances of receive_message objects. Each set of linked instances contains all possible expected message corresponding to the sent message. An error message is always attached to the end of the linked instances. When a message is received, an operation specified by the conditional operator between the message and the conditional operand is performed. If the result is true, the next action is specified by the attributes of *Referece_object_id_for_condition_is_true* and *Reference_message_id_for_condition_is_true.* If the result is false, the received message is checked with the condition attribute of the next instance in the linked instances. If the received message is being checked with the last instance of the linked instances, the received message is an unexpected message and an error message will be sent to the Error_handler object.

## 2.3 State Pattern

Each active object has a state model. Only the state model of the message coordinator object is described in this paper. The state models of other objects are not special and omitted here. The state pattern of the message coordinator object is depicted in Fig. 4. The state model has the following states and operation rules: a reset state, a wait_synchronous_event state, an Asynchronous_events_arbitration state, an object_transition state, and a set of message_object states (one state for each message object). All events with prefix Go_ are internal events generated within the object. Internal events are consumed before external events.

The operation in each message_object state can access only the instances of the corresponding message object. The reset state is generally the initial state. All states, except object_transition states, sets the next_object and next_message attributes of the message coordinator object. In Fig. 4, each arrow is a transition and the word beside the transition is the event that causes the transition. In each state that is associated with the message object, the object is waiting for an external event. If the received event is not an expected event, the event is ignored; otherwise, the object goes to the object_transition_state.

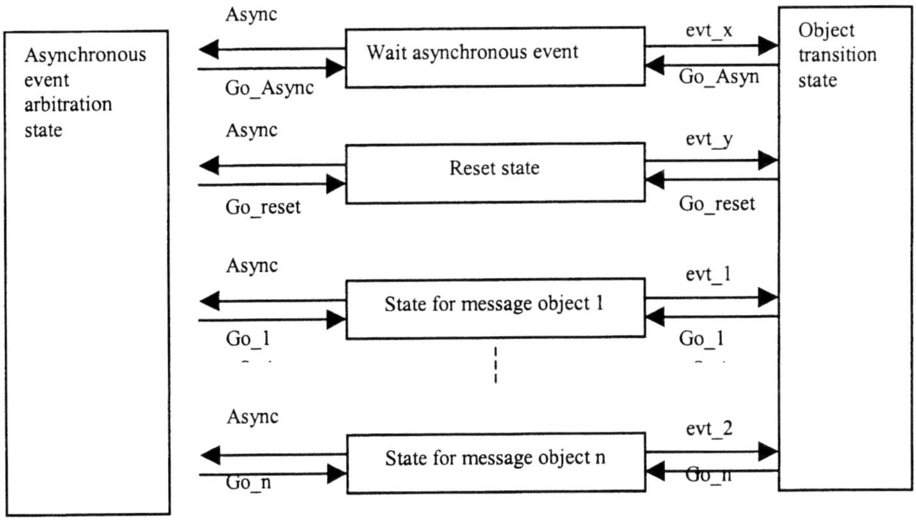


Fig. 4 The state pattern of message coordinator object.

The object_transition state generates a proper internal event based on the values of attributes next_object and next_message. This internal event causes the object to transit to another state. Certain system events, such as power up and reset, are not part of the normal system operation. This kind of events are called asynchronous events and denoted as Async. When an asynchronous event is received, the object goes to the state of asynchronous_event_arbitration. The asynchronous_event_arbitration state handles the asynchronous events and synchronizes the activities between this domain to other domains. Using this state pattern, the state model of the message coordinator object can be derived based on the definition of message objects.

# 3 Example

The purpose of developing object and state patterns is to change OOA modeling from the creative art to an engineering process. In the following example, the modeling process using the message pattern is presented using the Shlaer/Mellor methodology (the actions are executed in the state or in the entrance of the state) [5, 12]. However, this model is independent of the OOA methodologies. Other methodologies can also be used. In Shlaer/Mellor methodology, the condition attributes and message attributes of message objects are used to determine the next events to be generated in the message coordinator object. In Unified Model Language tools, the sequence diagram can be generated directly from the condition attribute, message attribute and next message attributes of the message objects.

A simplified voice-controlled telephone dialing system is used to demonstrate the application of the message pattern. The system consists of four functional blocks: (1) Voice_synthesis/recognition, (2) Telephone, (3) Interface_to_other_systems and (4) System_controller (see Fig. 5). Voice_synthesis/recognition block can be configured to recognize a subset of all recognizable words each time. It can also be configured to synthesize predefined words. The telephone block receives the command from the system controller block to dial the number and provides the phone status back to the system controller block. The block, Interface_to_other_systems, provides the system information, such as power on/power off/reset and abnormality. The system is reset when a voice cannot be recognized after being repeated 5 times in a row. The system controller block issues all voice recognition, module configuration and synthesis commands to the voice_synthesis/recognition block. The system_control block also commands the telephone for dialing operation and requesting the phone status. A voice-controlled phone dialing system can, based on user-machine conversation, (1) dial the telephone based on the given phone number, (2) dial the telephone based on the given name, (3) store/erase the name and phone number in the system, and (4) provide voice help to the user.

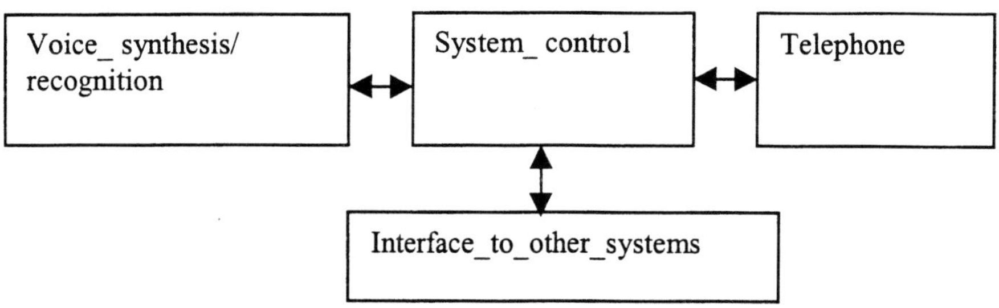


Fig. 5 The functional block diagram of an embedded system.

The voice-controlled telephone dialing system is modeled using the message pattern development process described as follows:

*Step 1. Divide the system into domains*

Divide the system into domains according to its hardware components or functional components. Each functional block is defined as a domain. To demonstrate the modeling process, only the details of the system_control domain is described.

*Step 2. Define coarse message object*

In each domain, define a set of send_message objects and a set of receive_message objects. Each send_message object consists of a set of messages that can be sent to the interface objects of another domains. Each receive_message object consists of a set of messages that the domain can be received from another domain. Since the system_control domain talks to Voice_synthesis/recognition, telephone, and interface_to_other_system domains. Six message objects are defined: voice_request, voice_response, phone_request, phone_response, other_system_request, and other_system_response.

*Step 3. Define actual message object*

Examine the message passing between the domains. Divide the message objects defined in step 2 into smaller message objects according to different message passing requirements (e.g., One way dialog – messages that do not need response, two way dialog - messages that need response, the relayed dialog - messages that need the response but the response is relayed from the third domain, etc.). For this example, since the system_control domain may send a message to control the voice synthesis/recognition hardware or send a voice prompt to the user through the voice synthesis/recognition hardware, the voice_request message object is divided into two message objects, prompt and dsp_request. Prompt object contains all voice messages to the user. Dsp_request object contains all messages for configuring the voice synthesis/recognition hardware. The voice_response object is also divided into two objects, promt_done and dsp_response. promt_done object contains the response messages to the prompt messages and the dsp_response object contains the response message to the dsp_request message. Other_system_request and other_system_response objects can also be divided into smaller objects. However, to demonstrate how to combine smaller objects into one object, these two objects are not divided. The other_system_request and phone_request are combined and called machine_request. The other_system_response and phone_response are also combined and called machine_response. Therefore, all sending and receiving messages in the system are divided into six message objects:

(1) Prompt - Send the voice prompt to the user.
(2) Prompt_done - Receive response for prompt done from the voice synthesis/ recognition domain.
(3) Dsp request - Configure the voice synthesis/recognition domain.
(4) Dsp_response - Receive user's voice from voice synthesis/recognition domain.
(5) Machine_request - Send messages to telephone or invoke software libraries.
(6) Machine_response - Receive messages from the telephone and software libraries.

The attributes of the send_message objects Prompt, Dsp_request, Machine_request are defined according to the format described in Table 1. The attributes of the receive_message objects Prompt_done, Dsp_response, Machine_response are defined according to the format described in Table 2.

*Step 4. Define message coordinator object, supporting objects and relationships*
The message coordinator object coordinates the event passing/function calling activities. Define the supporting objects for initialization, error handling, counting, timing and any other features needed by the system. In this example, the supporting objects include error_counter, reset_exeption_handler, user_IO_interface, and machine_IO_interface. The relationships between message objects and the message coordinator object are depicted in object information model in Fig. 6.

*Step 5. Define the attributes of message coordinator object*
The message_coordinator object should have at least three attributes. One attribute, next_id, contains the id of next message. The second attribute, next_object_id, indicates the corresponding object that contains the next message. The third attribute contains the current state number. Other attributes may be needed depending on the requirement of the system. In this example, the message_coordinator object has five attributes. The first attribute, next_message_id, is the id of next message. The second attribute, next_object_id, indicates the corresponding object that contains the next message. The third attribute indicates the current_state of the object. The fourth attribute is a message stack and the fifth attribute is an object stack (see the third paragraph of Section 5).

*Step 6. Define the state models for all active objects*
For the message coordinator object, assign
one message object state for each message object in the domain,
one reset state,
one object transition state,
one wait asynchronous event state, and
one asynchronous events arbitration state.
The state model for the message coordinator is depicted in Fig. 7. The state models for the other objects are very simple. They are omitted here.

*Step 7. Define all events for defined state transitions*
Each message state only accesses the message information from the corresponding message object. Therefore, the state transition can be directly obtained from the system requirement. If the state transition is difficult to specify, either the system specification is not clear or message objects are not defined properly. In this example, only the events of the message controller object are described. The names of all acceptable events are shown in Fig. 7. Internal events have a prefix Go_.

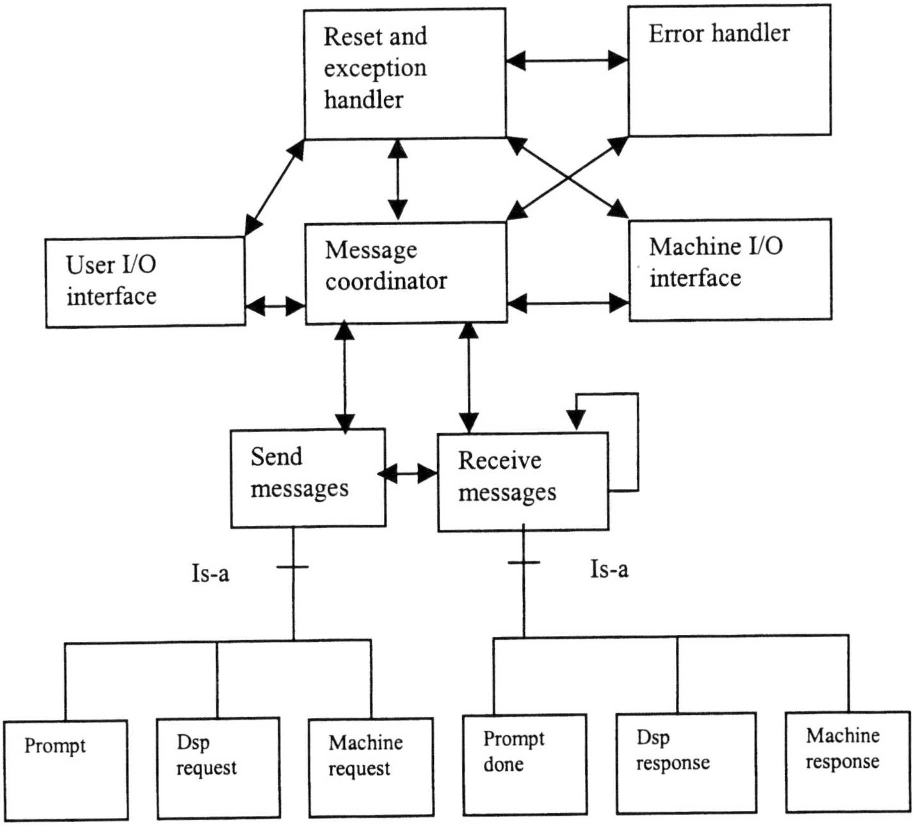


Fig. 6 The object information model of the system_control block in the voice-controlled telephone dialing system.

*Step 8. Define action in each state*

The action in each state is to generate events based on the following factors:

condition operator and condition operand attributes in the message object and parameters in the event.

The following pseudo code demonstrates the event generation in a send_message state.

O= the object whose id = the next_object_id of the message coordinator object;

P = the message whose id = the next_message_id of the message coordinator object.
X = the next_object_id attribute of P in O;
Y = the next_message_id attribute of P in O;
Z= the message attribute of P in O;
Set attribute next_object_id of the message coordinator object = X;
Set attribute next_message_id of the message coordinator object =Y;
Send message Z.

The following pseudo code demonstrates the event generation in a receive_message state. It is assumed that the received event has one discrete parameter and the condition operator is "=". The scope of the instruction is indicated by the indentation.

```
1.      O= next_object_id attribute of the message coordinator object;
2.      P = next_message_id attribute of the message coordinator object;
3.      U= the condition_operand attribute of P in O;
4.      V = parameter of the received event;
5.      If (U = V ) or (U=*)
            X = the Next_message_id for_condition_true of P in O;
            Y = the Next_object_id_for_ condition_true of P in O;
                Z= the message attribute of P in O;
                Set attribute next_object_id of message coordinator = X;
                Set attribute next_message_id of message coordinator =Y;
            Send message Z;
        Else
            Y = Next_object_id_for_condition_false of P in O;
            Go to 1.
```

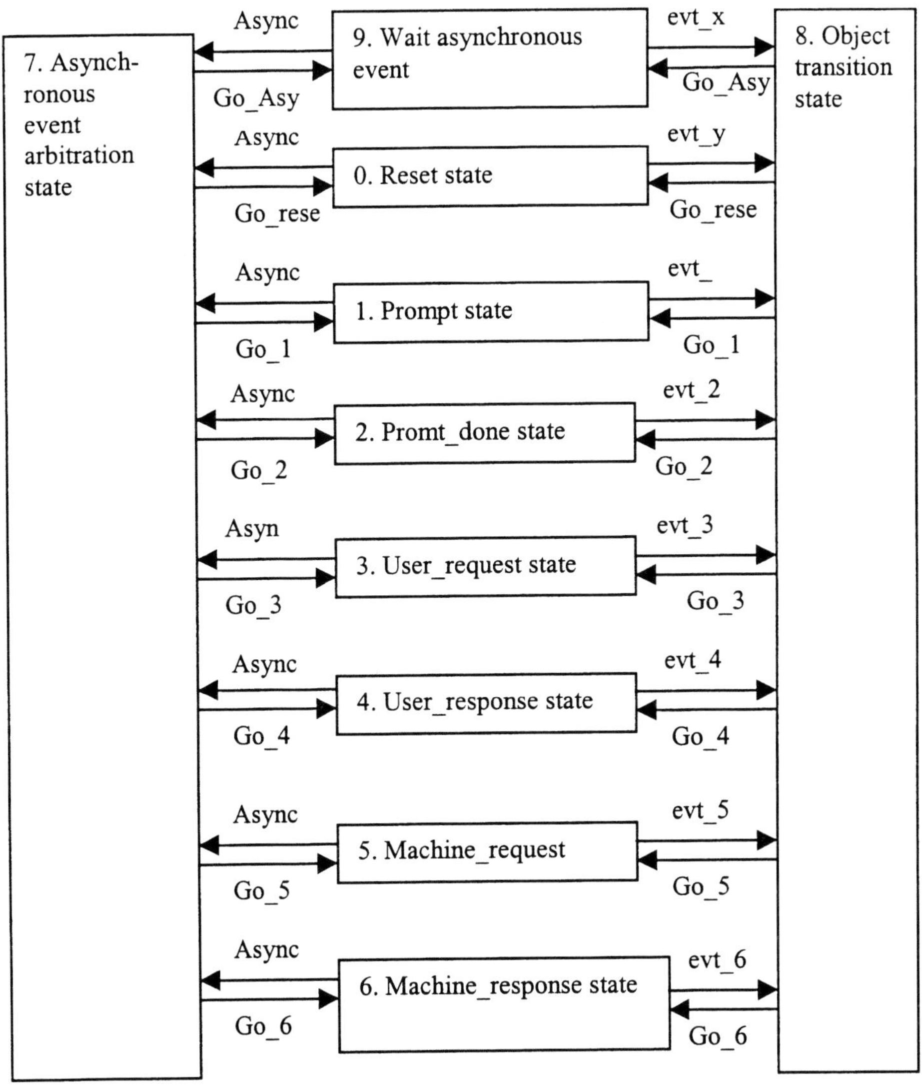


Fig. 7 The state model of the message-coordinator object.

*Step 9. Instantiate all message objects.*

It is convenient to identify all instances of the message objects before instantiating the message objects. All instances can be listed in a table with a format similar to that in Table 1.

Steps 1 to 5 in the modeling process essentially describe the system requirement. If the system requirement is well defined, steps 1 to 5 can be implemented easily. If there is difficulty to go through steps 1 to 5, more information about the system requirement should be collected and steps 1 to 5 should be iterated. Steps 6 to 9 are the detailed design of the model. All steps can be developed manually or automatically using software tools.

# 4 Instantiating Message Objects

There are several advantages of defining objects as messages between functional modules: (1) the behavior of the system can be easily captured, (2) the system requirement can be directly described by the model and (3) the translation of message objects to C program is straightforward. Although the implementation of object tables is conceptually simple, it is quite tedious. If it is not done properly, the modification of one object may require the modification of another objects. Here we describe a process that can conveniently initialize the message objects and translate the message objects into C-code. A software tool has been developed to support this process.

The basic idea is to describe each message object (see Table 1) into two parts: the definition part and the description part. The definition part of a message object includes a Message definition table, a Condition operator definition table and a Condition operand definition table (see Table 3 to 5). The first column of each table is the primary key of the table. The entries in the id columns in each definition tables should be unique unless two object names really mean the same instance (e.g., zero and 0). There is also an object definition table that defines all the message objects (see Table 6). The object description part of a message object includes a Next message table (see table 7 and 8). All entries of the Next message tables are defined in the definition tables.

Table 3. Message definition table.

| Message key (text) | Message id (number) | Actual message (text) |
|---|---|---|
| | | |

Table 4. Condition operator table.

| Condition operator key (text) | condition operator id (number) | Comments (text) |
|---|---|---|
| | | |

Table 5. Condition operand table.

| Condition operand key (text) | condition operand id (number) | Comments (text) |
|---|---|---|
| | | |

Table 6. Object definition table.

| Object key (text) | Object id (number) | Object name (text) |
|---|---|---|
| | | |

Table 7. Next message table for receive_message objects.

| Message Key (text) | Condition operator key (text) | Condition operand key (text) | Next message key if condition is false (text) | Next object key if condition is true (text) | Next message key if condition is true (text) |
|---|---|---|---|---|---|
| | | | | | |

Table 8. Next message table for send_message objects.

| Message Key (text) | Next object key (text) | Next message key (text) |
|---|---|---|
| | | |

The tables can be filled according to the following steps:

1. Define all entries of the object definition table.
2. Define all entries of the message definition tables.
3. Define all entries of the condition operator and condition operand definition tables.
4. Define the next message table. The values of message keys in next message tables are limited by the message names defined in the corresponding message definition tables. Keys defined in the condition tables limit the values of condition columns in next message tables.
5. If more messages are needed to complete the next message table go to step 2.

Note:
1. For the sake of efficient implementation in C language, the object id and message ids should be integers and be assigned in consecutive order start from 0.
2. The next message tables should be sorted in ascending order with respect to the message ids of message key column.
3. For easy translation of the tables into C program, the primary keys of the next message table, message definition table and condition operand and operator definition tables should be prefixed with the object key.
4. If the whole column in a table consists of the same value, the value can be used as the default value for the column and the column can be deleted.

## 4.1 An Example of Implementation of Message Objects

Part of a voice controlled telephone dialing dialog tree is as follows:

User says: Dial
System says: Number Please
User says: Zero
System says: Beep
User says: Nine
System says: Beep
......

The contents of tables for this part of the dialog are as follows:

Table 9. Object definition table.

| Object key (text) | Object id (number) | Object name (text) |
|---|---|---|
| U | 0 | User says |
| S | 1 | System says |
| Error | 2 | Error handling |

Table 10. Message definition table for object Error.

| Message key (text) | Message id (number) | Actual message (text) |
|---|---|---|
| Error_1 | 0 | Error handling |

Table 11. Message definition table for object S.

| Message key (text) | Message id (number) | Actual message (text) |
|---|---|---|
| S_NumPlease | 0 | Number please |
| S_Beep | 1 | Beep |

Table 12. Message definition table for object U.

| Message key (text) | Message id (number) | Actual message (text) |
|---|---|---|
| U_Dial | 0 | Dial |
| U_Nine | 1 | Nine |
| U_Zero | 2 | Zero |
| U_Error | 3 | Error |

Table 13. Condition operator definition table for object U.

| Condition key (text) | condition id (number) | Comments (text) |
|---|---|---|
| Equal | 0 | Input is equal to the message key |

Table 14. Condition operand definition table for object U.

| Condition key (text) | condition id (number) | Comments (text) |
|---|---|---|
| U_C_Dial | 0 | Dial |
| U_C_Nine | 1 | Nine |
| U_C_Zero | 2 | Zero |
| * | 3 | Always true |

Table 15. Next message table for object U.

| Message key (text) | Condition operand key (operator is = ) (text) | Next message key if condition is false (text) | Next object key (text) if condition is true | Next message key if condition is true (text) |
|---|---|---|---|---|
| U_Dial | U_C_Dial | U_Error | S | S_NumPlease |
| U_Zero | U_C_Zero | U_Nine | S | S_Beep |
| U_Nine | U_C_Nine | U_Error | S | S_Beep |
| U_Error | U_C_Star | U_Error | Error | Error_1 |

Table 16. Next message table for object S.

| Message key (text) | Next object key | Next message key |
|---|---|---|
| S_NumPlease | U | U_Zero |
| S_Beep | U | U_Zero |

The system requirement is essentially described in the message objects. The message objects can be considered as the data of the system. Since the message linking information is necessary for the proper program execution, it is either presented in the data form or hard coded in the program. If hard coded form is desired, all condition operations and next message information can be directly extracted from the message objects by the model compiler.

## 4.2 C Code Generation for Message Objects

The message objects can be implemented in a specific language directly from the tables and be linked to the active objects in the model later. The following C code for message objects is generated from the tables 9 to 16.

```
/* code generated from Table 9. Object definition table (O)*/
#define U          0     /*User says*/
#define S          1     /*System says*/
#define Error      2     /*Error handling*/
```

```
/* code generated from Table 10. Message definition table (Error)*/
#define Error_1            0

/* code generated from Table 11. Message definition table (S)*/
#define S_NumPlease              0
#define S_Beep             1

/* code generated from Table 12. Message definition table (U)*/
#define U_Dial  0
#define U_Zero  1
#define U_Nine  2
#define U_Error 3

/* code generated from Table 13. Condition operator definition table (U)*/
#define Equal    0

/* code generated from Table 14. Condition operand definition table (U)*/
#define U_C_Dial           0
#define U_C_Zero           1
#define U_C_Nine           2
#define U_C_Star           3

/* code generated from Table 15. Next message table of object U. */
  int nm_U[3][5] = {  U_Dial,    U_C_Dial,   U_Error,  S,        S_NumPlease,
                      U_Zero     U_C_Zero,   U_Nine,   S,        S_Beep,
                      U_Nine,    U_C_Nine,   U_Error,  S,        S_Beep,
                      U_Error,   U_C_Star,   U_Error,  Error,    Error_1        };

/*code generate from Table 16. Next message table of object S. */
int nm_S [2][2] = {   S_NumPlease,    U.                  U_Zero,
                      S_Beep,         U,                  U_Zero};
```

# 5 Discussion

There are several issues and possible problems for using the message pattern. One possible problem is that there may be too many objects and hence too many states in the message coordinator object. One solution is to divide the system into more domains. Another solution is to analyze the system and find the message objects that have few instances and not often invoked. These objects may be combined into one object in order to reduce the number of states in the message coordinator object. However, when several message objects are combined into one object, an interface object may need to be added to dispatch the message to proper objects. Fig. 8 depicts the process of combining objects.

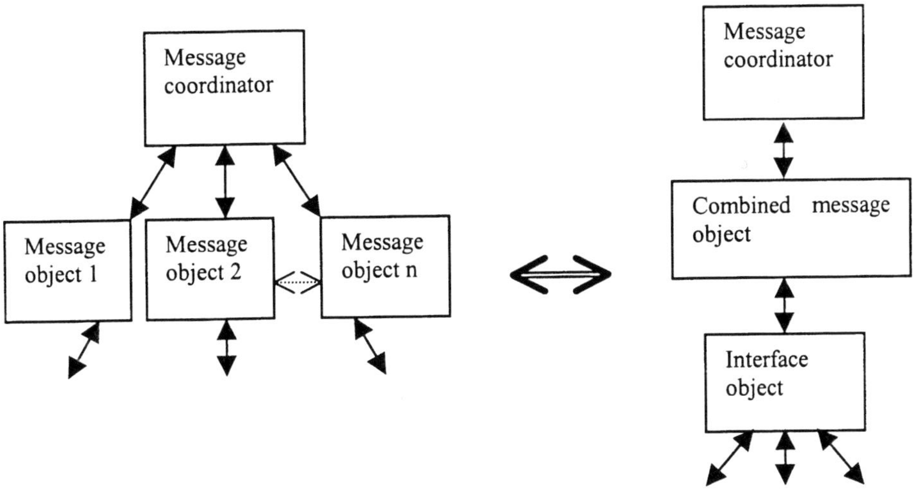


Fig. 8 Process for reducing the number of objects.

Another issue is related to the implementation of the model. A common message subsequence is defined as a sequence of messages that are part of more than one longer message sequences. A common message subsequence may involve many message objects (see Fig. 9). In Fig. 9, each block represents one message object. Blocks linked by dashed arrows and thick arrows represent a long message sequence. Blocks linked by dashed and thin solid arrows represent another long message sequence. Blocks linked by the thick solid arrows represent the common message subsequence. A mechanism is needed for indicating the path direction after exiting the common message sequence. There are two approaches to define such a mechanism.

The first approach is to disallow common message subsequence by duplicating common message subsequence. This approach is acceptable when the common message subsequence is short and not used by many message sequences. If a common message sequence is long and/or used by many message sequences, duplicating the common action sequence will use large memory space. The second approach is to implement a message stack. The implementation is as follows. (1) Create a stack attribute and corresponding push and pop operations in the message coordinator object. (2) Push the exit directions of the common message subsequence onto the stack before entering the common message subsequences. (3) Pop out the exit directions before exit the common message subsequence.

The message pattern can be used in various OOA methodologies. In Shlaer/Mellor methodology, the condition attributes and the message attributes of message objects determines the next events to be generated in the message coordinator object. Other methodologies can also be used. For example, the sequence diagram in Unified Model Language tools can be generated directly from the condition attributes, message attributes and next message attributes of the message objects. The message pattern is scalable. All domains of a system can follow the same modeling process. Since the proposed pattern is under the framework of OOA, all rules defined for the OOA development can be applied. Event synchronization is enforced in the state models and operating systems. The message pattern is a special case of the state pattern [9]. The message pattern defines the communication steps between different system modules as object states. Hence, the message pattern is applicable to communication and I/O intensive applications.

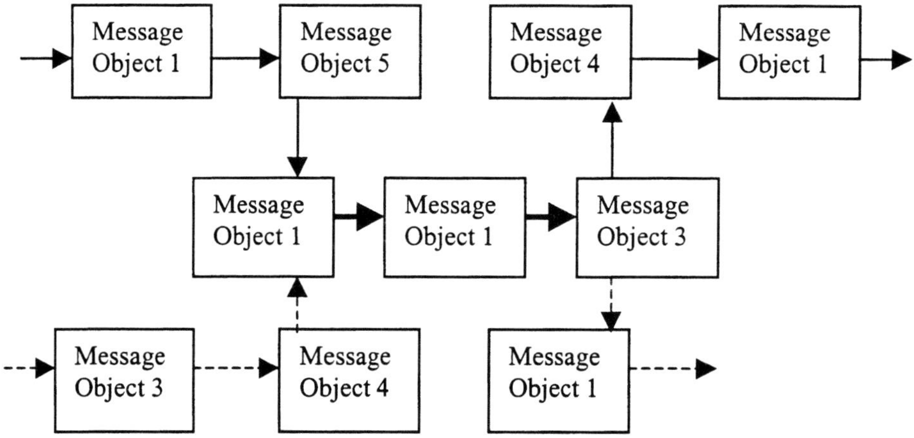


Fig. 9 Demonstration of common message subsequence.

# 6 Conclusion

A message pattern for user-computer interface applications is described. A process for applying the message pattern for developing an OOA model is also described. The advantage of the message pattern is that the description of the application problem is more related to hardware organizations and more systematic. It is less dependent on the analysist's preferences on object descriptions. This pattern will also support the generation of efficient code. The pattern can be applied to a variety of communication and I/O intensive embedded microcontroller applications.

## References

[1] X. Song and L. Osterweil, "Engineering Software Design Process to Guide process Execution," *IEEE Transactions on Software Engineering*, Vol. 24, No. 9, September 1999, pp. 759-775.

[2] S.M. Sutton, H. Ziv, H.E. Yessayan, D. Heimbigner, M. Maybee, L.J. Osterweil, and X. Song, "Programming A Software Requirements-Specification Process," *Proceedings of First International Conference Software Process*, IEEE Computer Society, October 1991, pp. 68-89.

[3] I. Vessey and S.A. Conger, "Requirements Specification: learning Object, Process, and Data methodologies," *Comm. ACM*, Vol. 37, No. 5, May 1994, pp. 102-113.

[4] P. Code and E. Yourdon, *Object-Oriented Analysis*, Englewood Cliffs, New Jersey:Prentice Hall, 1991.

[5]. S. Shlaer and S. Mellor, *Object-Oriented Systems Analysis: Modeling the World in Data*, Englewood Cliffs, New Jersey: Yourdon Press, 1988.

[6] J. Rumbaugh, M. Blaha, W. Premerlani, F. Eddy, and W. Lorenson, *Object Oriented Modeling and Design*, Prentice Hall International, 1991.

[7] G. Booch, *Object-Oriented Analysis and Design with Applications*, second edition, Redwood City, California: Benjamin/Cummings, 1994.

[8] B. Douglass, *Doing Hard Time: Developing Real-Time Systems with UML, Objects, Frameworks, and Patterns*, Massachusetts:AddisonWesley, 1999.

[9] E. Gamma, R. Helm, R. Johnson, and J. Vlissides, *Design Patterns-Elements of Reusable Object-Oriented Software*, Reading, Massachusetts: Addison-Wesley, 1995.

[10] F. Buschmann, R. Meunier, H. Rohnert, P. Sommerlad, and M. Stal, *A System of Patterns: Pattern-Oriented Software Architecture*, New York:John Wiley & Sons, 1996.

[11] J. Vlissides, J. Coplien, and N. Kerth, ed., *Pattern Languages of Program Design 2*, Reading, Massachusetts: Addison-Wesley, 1996.

[12] S. Shlaer and S. Mellor, *Object_Lifecycles: Modeling the World in States*, Englewood Cliffs, New Jersey: Yourdon Press, 1992.

[13] D. Harel and E. Gery, "Executable Object Modeling with State Charts," *IEEE Computer*, Vol. 30, No. 7, 1977, pp. 31-42.

*Chapter 2*

# A NEW FORMAL APPROACH FOR THE SPECIFICATION AND THE VERIFICATION OF MULTI-AGENT REACTIVE SYSTEMS OPERATING MODES

BOUCHAIB BOUNABAT[1, 2]
[1] LGI/IHM, ENSIAS, BP 713, Agdal Rabat, MAROC.
[2] Laboratoire des Mathématiques,
Faculté des Sciences Marrakech-Semlalia
bounabat@ensias.um5souissi.ac.ma

*Abstract:* A Reactive system is one that is in continual interaction with its environment, and executes at a pace determined by that environment. Examples of such systems are network protocols, industrial-process control systems etc. Reliability requirements are usually much more stringent for reactive systems than other computer systems. Fault tolerance technique is an approach to system design, which help that potential faults do not cause system failure, and increase system reliability.

Due to their complex nature, reactive systems are extremely difficult to specify and validate. In this paper, we propose a new formal model for the specification and the verification of such systems using several fault tolerance techniques. This approach considers a Reactive System as a Reactive Multi-Agent System consisting of concurrent reactive agents that cooperate with each other to achieve the desired functionality. In addition, this approach uses formal synchronous specification and verification tools in order to specify and to verify the systems behaviours. Finally an example of an application of the approach is mentioned.

*Keywords:* Reactive systems, Reactive agent, specification, formal methods, verification, fault tolerance modes.

# 1 Introduction

A Reactive system is one that is in continual interaction with its environment, and executes at a pace determined by that environment. Examples of such systems are network protocols, industrial-process control systems etc. Reactive systems are responsive systems consisting of two or more reactive parallel sub-processes that continuously cooperate to achieve a pre-defined goal [1]. In addition, such systems are intrinsically state based, and transition from one state to another is based on external and internal events. Another specificity of reactive system consists in taking into account a great number of events and temporal constraints. Thus, Reactive systems are complex computer systems, and may not be modeled by transformational techniques.

The use of rigorous formal methods in specification and validation, can help designers to limit the introduction of potentially faulty components during the construction of the system. Specification modeling is an important stage in reactive system design where the designers specify the desired properties in the form of a specification model that acts as the guidance and source for the implementation.

Validation of an abstract specification of a reactive system, is an important aspect of system design. The operational problem here is how to determine if a reactive system is successful. One approach for validation is to consider observable behavior as a criteria to determine success.

Due to their complex nature, reactive systems are extremely difficult to specify and validate. In this paper, we propose a new formal model for the specification and the validation of such systems. This approach considers a Reactive System as a Reactive Multi-Agent System, i.e. a distributed computing system consisting of several autonomous reactive agents (as computing units) that coordinate their action in order to fulfill usually joint but also sometimes competitive tasks. Concurrency is further characterized by the need to express communication and synchronization among concurrent agents.

When the behaviour of a system deviates from that which is specified for it, this is called a failure. It results from unexpected problems internal to the system, which eventually manifest themselves in the system's external behaviour. The paper presents a set of techniques dealing with the reactive system fault tolerance modes

This paper is organized as follows: Section 2 surveys the specification and verification used tools, Section 3 sets out the Reactive Decisional Agent model and its related temporal constraints, Section 4 describes how such Agent can manage its failures modes, Section 5 describes the proposed hierarchical structure of a Reactive System and its related failures modes. Section 6 mentions the example of a reactive system which has been specified and verified with the approach .

# 2 Specification and Verification Tools

This section will describe all the specification and verification tools used in this work.

## 2.1 STATECHARTS

STATECHARTS (SC) are introduced by Harel [2][3] like a visual formalism that provides a way to represent state diagrams with notions like hierarchy, concurrency, broadcast communication and temporized state. A SC can be seen like one or several automata which are labeled by ?event[condition]/!action. SC is said to be synchronous because the system reacts to events by instantly updating its internal state and producing actions, the actions produced can trigger in the same instant other transitions, this is named chain reaction causing a set of transitions, the system is always in a waiting state until the condition for a transition is true.

## 2.2 ESTEREL

To hit this target, the specified SC behaviors are automatically translated to the synchronous language ESTEREL [4][5][6]. It's a language, with precisely defined mathematical semantics, for programming the class of input-driven deterministic systems. The software environment of ESTEREL provides high-quality tools, including an editor, compiler, simulator (XES tool), debugger and verifier.

## 2.3 Real-Time Temporal Logic

Temporal logic has been widely used for the specification and verification of concurrent systems [7][8]. However, these temporal logics only allow qualitative reasoning about time. Several extensions have been proposed for expressing and reasoning about real-time systems. These include Real-Time Temporal Logic (RTTL) [9], which is based on linear time temporal logic, and allows in addition the expression of quantitative real-time properties (e.g. exact delays or event deadlines).

*Example of RTTL Formula*

$s_1 \wedge t = T \rightarrow \Diamond (s_2 \wedge t \leq T + 5)$ - If $s_1$ is true now and the clock reads T ticks, then within T + 5 clock ticks, $s_2$ must become true. Thus, once $s_1$ becomes true, $s_2$ must become true no more than 5 ticks later. This formula can be also written as follows: $s_1 \rightarrow \Diamond_{[0,5]} s_2$ or $s_1 \rightarrow \Diamond_{<=5} s_2$

The formula $s_1 \leftrightarrow s_3$ indicates that events $s_1$, $s_3$ are simultaneous. If C(w) is a RTTL formula defining a temporal constraint on an event w, then w $\Vdash$ C(w) means that w satisfies the formula C(w).

# 3 Reactive Decisional Agent

In this paper, the agents are classed as either deliberative or reactive [10][11]. Deliberative agents derive from the deliberative thinking paradigm: the agents possess an internal symbolic, reasoning model and they engage in planning and negotiation in order to achieve coordination with other agents. Reactive agents don't have any internal symbolic models of their environment, and they act using a stimulus/response type of behavior by responding to the present state of the environment in which they are embedded.

## 3.1 A Brief Critical Review of Reactive Agents Work

There is a yearning need for a clearer methodology to facilitate the development of reactive software agent applications. This requires the development of more associated theories, architectures and languages.

Among the few current approaches for specifying Reactive Agents: [12] describes agents, tasks and environments using the Z specification language [13]; [14] specifies the reactive agent behavior by Real Time Knowledge models; [15] describes agent using temporal logic tools.

All of these approaches lack of formal verification tools of the modeled behavior. Our purpose is to build a formal model of a reactive agent based on the decisional object concept [16]. The STATECHARTS models are used here in order to describe the reactive agent's behavior. These behaviors will be formally checked in a qualitative (respectively quantitative) way by the synchronous language ESTEREL (respectively by Real Time Temporal Logic deduction).

## 3.2 Formal Description

The proposed model of reactive agent consists in putting forward decisional models allowing the representation of objects according to their behavioral aspects and their degree of intelligence.

**Definitions.** A Reactive Decisional Agent (RDA) is 9-tuple noted < A, D, S, E', O, O', act, dec, sig > where:

- A: Set of actions exerted on the agent. Each action, undergone by an object, represents a possible operation to be carried out on this object in order to achieve a specific goal.
- D: Set of decisions generated by the agent. Each decision is a solution concerning process behavior in the future; each decision is characterized by its action horizon: Ha, the time during which this decision remains valid.

- S: Set of Signaling received by the agent. Each Signaling received by an object, reflects at any given time the state of the controlled tools used to achieve a specific goal.
- E': Set of external states delivered by the agent. Each one represents the object state emitted to the environment.
- E: Set of agent's internal states. Each one indicates the current state of the agent.
- O: Set of agent's internal objectives. Each decision is elaborated in order to achieve an internal objective according to the current external objective and the actual internal state.
- O': Set of agent's external objectives which can be achieved. These objectives represent the agent's interpreting of each action.

From a dynamic point of view, the sets above indicate the received events (A, S), the emitted events (D, E') and the internal events (E, O, O').

**Decisional Functions.** act, dec, and sig are three decisional functions that define the behavior of a RDA.

$$\text{act: } A \longrightarrow O'$$
$$a \longrightarrow o' \text{ with,} \qquad \forall\, a \in A,\ \exists!\, o' \in O' \,/\, o' = \text{act}(a) \Rightarrow a \leftrightarrow o' \quad (1)$$

(1) means that the occurrence of an action *a* implies instantaneously the occurrence of its associated external objective *o'* by the function *act*.

$$\text{dec: } O' \times E \longrightarrow D \times O$$
$$(o', e) \longrightarrow (d, o) \text{ with,} \qquad \text{dec}(o', e) = (d, o) \Rightarrow [o' \wedge e \leftrightarrow d \wedge o] \qquad (2)$$

(2) means that depending of the current external objective *o'* and as soon as the agent is in an appropriate internal state *e*, corresponding decision *d* an internal objective *o*, by the function *dec*, are instantaneously produced.

$$\text{sig: } O' \times O \times S \longrightarrow E \times E'$$
$$(o', o, s) \longrightarrow (e, e') \text{ with,} \qquad \text{sig}(o', o, s) = (e, e') \Rightarrow [o' \wedge o \wedge s \leftrightarrow e \wedge e'] \quad (3)$$

(3) means that that depending of the current external objective *o'* and the expected internal objective *o*, and as soon as the receipt of a signaling *s*, its associated external state *e'* is instantaneously emitted and the new agent internal state becomes *e*.

**Internal Architecture of an RDA.** This section presents a set of SC which describe the external objective of a RDA.

*External Objectives Manager.* A Reactive Decisional Agent has an External Objective Manager. It consists in a SC model of the function *act* described above (Fig.1).

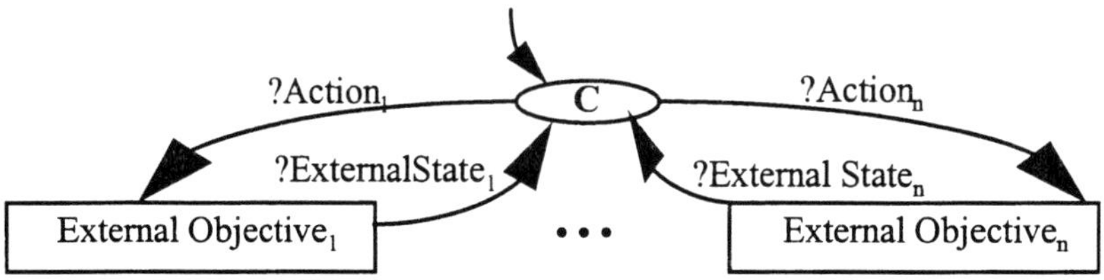


Fig. 1 This shows a figure consisting of a SC model of External objectives manager. Each state represents an external objective whose activation is started by the reception of a specific action (*?Action*), and terminated by the emission of the acknowledgment external state (*!ExternalObjective*).

In addition, each operating mode of the agent (normal mode, diagnostics modes, etc.) can be considered as an external objective to be reached. The objectives manager has to maintain the same objective or to change it, according to the occurred fault or failure.

*External Objectives Modeling.* An external objective is composed by many others SC states corresponding to the associated internal states and internal objectives that are deducted by the functions dec and sig definitions (Fig.2).

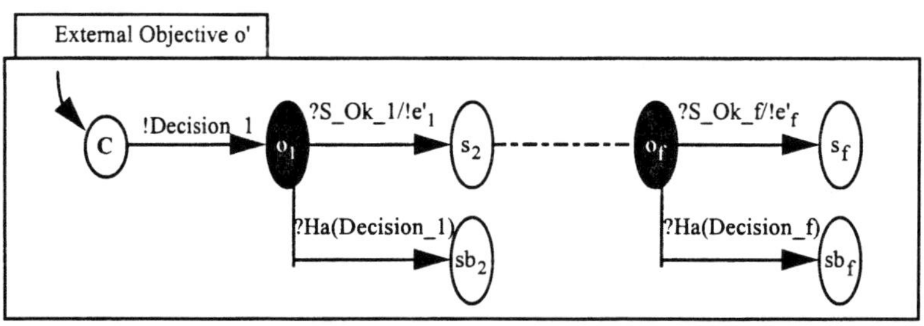


Fig. 2 This figure shows the general SC model of an External objective. The transition (*Internal state → Internal objective* ) is made by a decision emission (*!Decision*), and the transition (*internal objective → Internal state*) is made by a signaling receipt (*?S_OK*), and eventually an external state emission (*!e'*). Internal state C corresponds to the default initial state of a SC model. Internal state and Internal objective are indicated respectively by $s_i$ et $o_i$. In case of an action horizon exceeding without receiving any acknowledgment signaling, the agent's internal state changes from $s_i$ to $sb_i$ (*breakdown state*).

### 3.3 Temporal Constraints of an RDA

**Decision Temporal Constraints.** Each decision is characterized by its action horizon, Ha: the time during which this decision remains valid. So, an occurrence of a decision requires the occurrence of its corresponding acknowledgment signaling, in a delay that doesn't exceed its action horizon.

This defines the following function, acqDec:

$$\begin{aligned} \text{acqDec} : \quad & D \longrightarrow S \times \mathbb{N} \\ & d \longrightarrow (s, Ha) = \text{acqDec}(d), \text{ with acqDec}(d) = (s, Ha) \Rightarrow \\ & [\, d \rightarrow \Diamond_{<=Ha}\, s \,] \end{aligned} \tag{4}$$

In the following sections and for any decision d:

- acqDec(d) indicates the acknowledgment signaling of d,
- Ha(d) is the action horizon of d,
- C(d) points out the constraint $[\, d \rightarrow \Diamond_{<=Ha(d)}\, \text{acqDec}(d) \,]$

The temporal property that a RDA must verify:

$$\forall\, d \in D,\ d \,||\!\!= C(d) \tag{5}$$

**External Objective Temporal Constraints.** Each external objective o' is characterized by an acknowledgment specific external state e', that indicates the good ending of o'. this defines a function acq:

$$\begin{aligned} \text{acq} : O' & \longrightarrow E' \\ o' & \longrightarrow e' = \text{acq}(o') \text{ with,} \qquad \forall\, o' \in O', \exists!\, e' \in E' \,/\, e' = \text{acq}(o') \end{aligned} \tag{6}$$

Dynamically, the event acq(o') comes as early as the receipt of the acknowledgment of the last decision generated by o'.

Another function called durMAx is introduced in order to associate to each external objective o' the longest duration of its operations execution.

$$\begin{aligned} \text{durMax:} \quad O' & \longrightarrow \mathbb{N} \\ o' & \longrightarrow \sum_{i=1}^{\text{card}(D_{o'})} Ha(d_i), \text{ where } d_i \in D(o') \end{aligned}$$

By combining the two functions acq and **durMAx**, we can obtain the following constraint:

$$\forall\, o' \in O',\ o' \rightarrow \Diamond_{<=durMax(o')}\, \text{acq}(o') \tag{7}$$

i.e. after an occurrence of an external objective o', the agent must generate the corresponding acknowledgment, in a delay that does not exceed durMax(o').

**Action Temporal Constraints.** Another function rep is introduced in order to define the acknowledgment of an action received by the agent.

$$\begin{aligned} rep : A &\longrightarrow E' \\ a &\longrightarrow e' = acq(act(a)) \end{aligned}$$

C(a) indicates the constraint $[a \rightarrow \Diamond_{<=durMax(act(a))}\ rep(a)]$, the temporal property that a RDA must verify is:

$$\forall\, a \in A,\ a\ \|\!= C(a) \qquad (8)$$

The following assertion can be proved by deduction

$$\forall\, a \in A,\ [\forall\, d \in D(act(a)),\ d\ \|\!= C(d)] \Rightarrow a\ \|\!= C(a) \qquad (9)$$

# 4 Management of a Reactive Decisional Agent Failures Modes

Two approaches that can help designers improve the reliability of their systems can be distinguished [17]:

- The first is known as fault prevention; this attempts to eliminate any possibility of faults creeping into a system before it goes operational. This goal can be achieved by the use of formal requirements specifications.
- The second is fault tolerance; this enables a system to continue functioning even in the presence of faults. Both approaches attempt to produce systems which have well-defined failure modes. This section will focus on the second approach.

## 4.1 Full Fault Tolerance Operating Mode

**Principle.** The system continues to operate in the presence of errors, for a limited period, with no significant loss of functionality or performance.

This principle can be interpreted as if the agent is able to "delay" the deadlines waiting for the decision acknowledgement. These delays can be shown to the environment by sending a specific external state.

**STATECHARTS Specification.** The STATECHARTS corresponding to an external objective that verifies the full fault tolerance principle can be shown by Fig.3.

The exceeding of an action horizon ?Ha(d), generates the "empty" decision $\tau$ in order to expect the acknowledgement signalling (?SOk). This expectancy must not exceed a specified duration $\Delta t$, otherwise the agent internal state becomes sb. The internal state sd indicates a delay state.

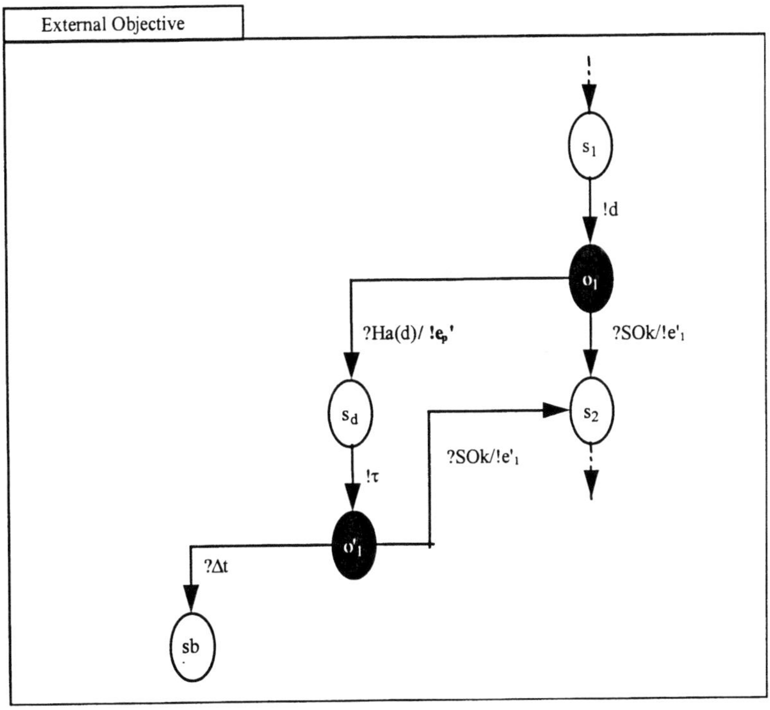


Fig. 3 STATECHARTS Model of an RDA Deadline Prolongation.

The agent reaction is to wait the acknowledgement signalling without changing the external objective, even if a failure had been detected.

## 4.2 Graceful Degradation Operating Mode

**Principle.** The system continues to operate in the presence of errors, accepting a partial degradation of functionality or performance during recovery or repair.

Each operating mode is considered here as an external objective to be reached by the agent. The objective manager has to maintain the same objective or to change it, according to the occurred fault or failure.

**STATECHARTS Specification.** The STATECHARTS corresponding to an external objective that verifies the graceful degradation principle can be shown by Fig.4.

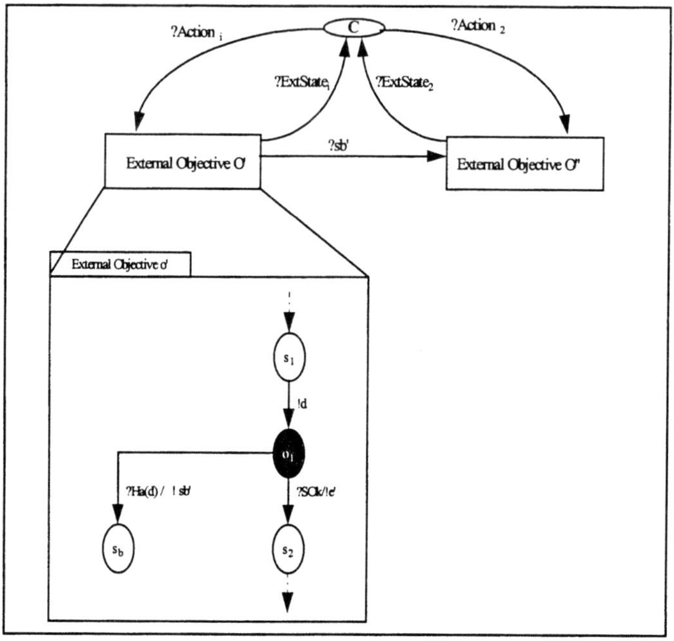


Fig. 4 SC Model of an RDA External Objective Change.

The exceeding of an action horizon generates an external state ($!s'_b$). It can be received by the objective manager ($?s'_b$) and used to change the current external objective, and then the current operating mode.

# 5 RDA Based Hierarchical Structure of Reactive Systems

We consider that a reactive system can be modeled as a distributed computing system consisting of several autonomous RDA.

## 5.1 Internal Organization of a Reactive System

A reactive system is defined by a set of agents, connected to each other by communication interfaces. Thus, its basic structure rests on a two levels tree (Fig. 5).

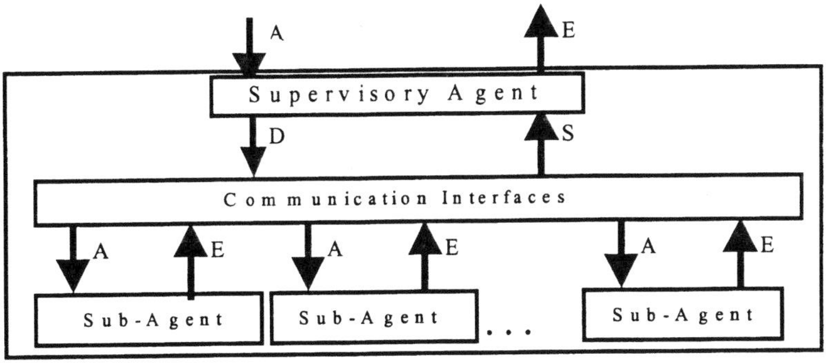


Fig. 5 The internal organization of a reactive system consists in a tree, that is made up in parallel of a supervisor (*Supervisory Agent*), of two or several sub-agents components, and two communication interfaces between the supervisor and the sub-agents. Such system interacts with its environment by the means of:
- Actions exerted by this environment.
- External States emitted to the environment.

**Supervisory and Sub-Agents Levels.** The supervisory agent (SRDA: Supervisory Reactive Decisional Agent) is a RDA controlling the component sub-agents, in order to achieve a goal or to solve a given problem.

This agent will manage the sequences of activation and the definition of the controlled sub-agents objectives. This management depends on:

- the actions exerted by the environment,
- the events generated by the sub-agents activities,
- the temporal constraints specific to any reactive system.

In addition, a reactive system can be summarized with a simple SRDA directly connected to the controlled process. Each sub-agent can be considered as a reactive system. Thus, its internal structure is composed by its own SRDA, communication interfaces and sub-agents. A sub-agent objectives are to carry out sequences of tasks in response to any temporal constrained action exerted on him by the higher level.

**Communication Interfaces.** The communication interfaces are of two types: decisional interface (Top/Down) and signaling interfaces (Bottom/Up).

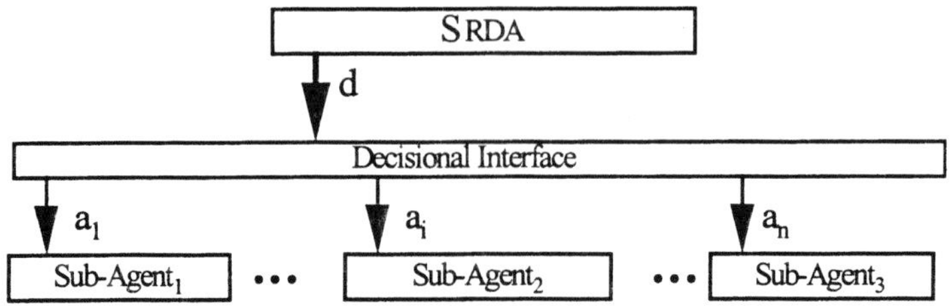


Fig. 6 Decisional interface that translates a decision ($d$) generated by the SRDA into several actions ($a_i$), each one of them is intended for a sub-agent of the lower level.

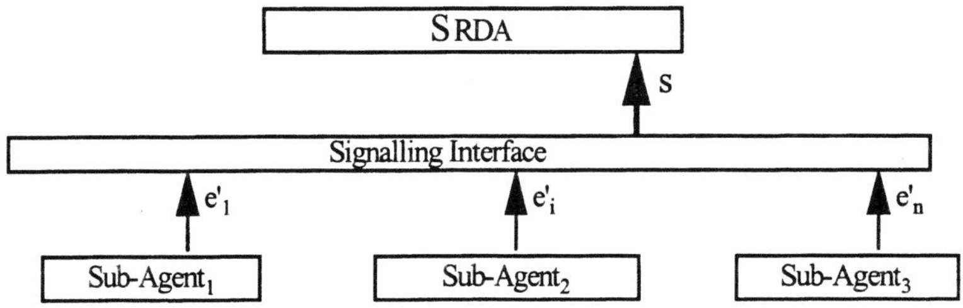


Fig. 7 Signaling interface that synchronizes the external states ($e'_i$), sent by each sub-agent, and emits one signaling ($s$) intended for the SRDA.

## 5.2 Temporal Properties of the Specified Reactive System

Through the notion of an action horizon (Ha) of a decision, the time during which the decision remains valid, the RDA-based specification of a reactive system ensures that the elements will have time periods coherent with the decision made by the agent, and coherent with the time periods of decisions made at lower levels of the hierarchy. The higher an agent is in the hierarchy, the greater the action horizon (Fig.8).

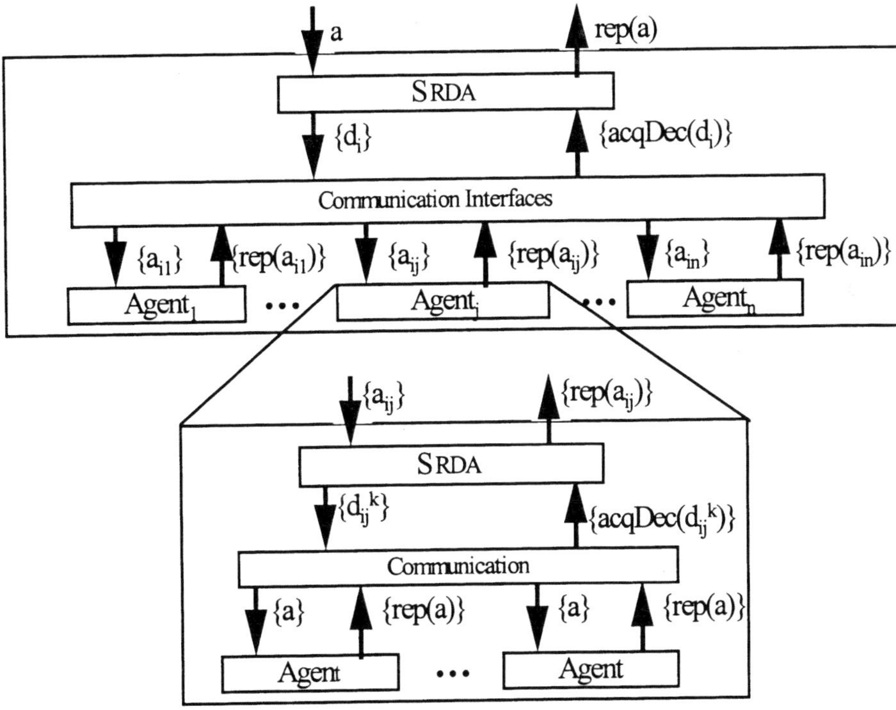


Fig. 8 Flow of information inside a SMA formed by ARDC agents.

The top-down flow consists in actions ($a$, $a_{ij}$) and their associated decisions ($d_i$, $d_{ij}^k$). The bottom-up flow consists in external states ($rep(a)$, $rep(a_{ij})$) and their associated signaling ($acqDec(d_i)$, $acqDec(d_{ij}^k)$).

The temporal constraints must be checked on each hierarchical level. The recursive character of this structure makes it possible to generalize the results obtained for only one hierarchical level. Thus, we can prove by deduction and according to notations of Fig.7:

$$d_{ij}^k \models C(d_{ij}^k) \Rightarrow a \models C(a) \qquad (10)$$

### 5.3 Protective Redundancy

**Principle.** All techniques for achieving fault tolerance rely on extra elements introduced into the system to detect and recover from faults. These components are redundant in the sense that they are not required for the system's normal mode of operation.

There are several different classifications of redundancy depending on which system components are under consideration and which terminology is being used. [17] distinguishes between static and dynamic redundancy. With static redundancy, redundant components are used inside a system to hide the effects of faults. An example of static redundancy is N Modular Redundancy (NMR). NMR consists of N identical sub-components and majority voting circuits.

Dynamic redundancy is the redundancy supplied inside a component which indicates explicitly or implicitly that the output is in error. Recovery must be provided by a protection component identical to the failed one. In this section we present how we have adapted this type of redundancy to the multi-RDA structures.

**Multi-RDA System and Protective Redundancy.** A protection agent is a duplication of a critical agent. It must be integrated to the specified system by adding 1 diferent in order to take the eventual substitution (critical agent↔protection agent) into consideration.

The return to the normal functioning mode can be made after the detection of repair external state $s_R$' emitted by the external objective.

Fig.9 shows an RDA agent composed by two principals agents (RDAC1, RDAC2). The redundant RDA (RDAC1_P) that can replace the critical agent RDCA1, after a failure detection. The failed component substitution can be achieved by changing the current external objective and after the emission of the external state $s_P$' emitted .

## 6 Example

We consider here an example borrowed from the communications field. It forms part of the Automatic Switching Protection System of the ATT&T' S [18].

### 6.1 System Description

The idea is to provide more than one line for each communication channel. If a line fails, a backup line, called the 'protection line' is used instead. A line is considered failed when the bit rate exceeds the degraded range, or whenever other hard failures have occurred, such as a complete loss of signal. The expected response to a failed signal on the working line, is to automatically switch to the protection line, if that line is in better condition.

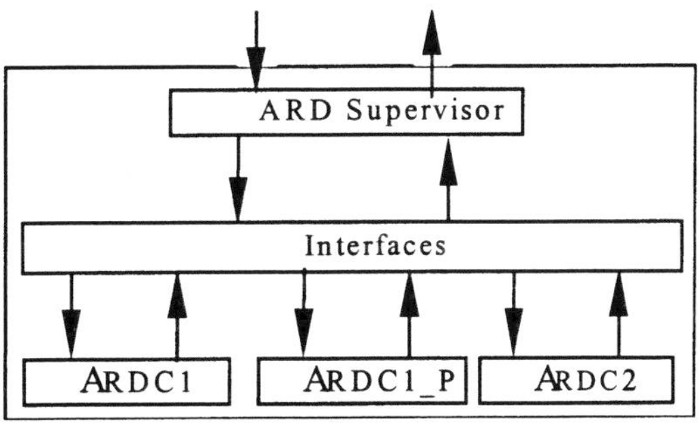


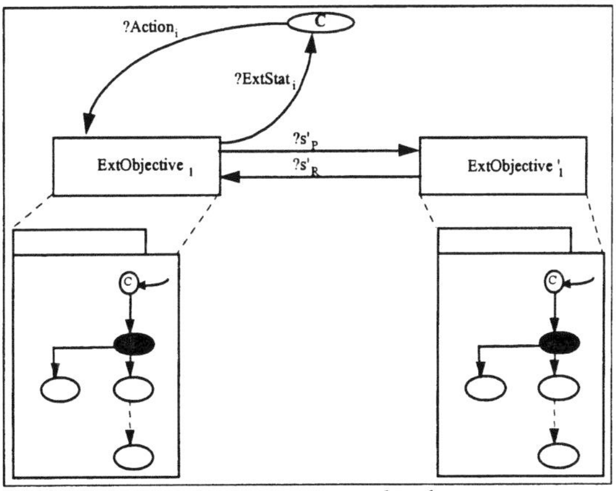


Fig. 9 Components redundancy.

The APS description consists of the specification of supervisory agent APS System, communication interfaces, and the agents Line_W and Line_P (Fig.10).

The objective X_ChangeToP consists of two SC diagrams: protection line starting and working line repair. The reception of S_WCleared implies the emission of E_APS_To_Nfunction the return to normal operation. It is showed in the external objectives manager level by the re-establishment of the initial objective (X_Install_W). The emission of an external state by an external objective SC (*?E_line_connected for example*) can be used by the external objective manager in order to change the current external objective (*!E_line_connected*).

## 6.2 APS Normal Mode Checking

The operational problem here is how to determine if a reactive system is successful. The approach adopted here is to translate the specified SC behaviors to the synchronous language ESTEREL. According to automated translation tool developed in [19], the mapping of a modelled reactive system in ESTEREL is done easily by translating the communication interfaces (ID, IS), the supervisory agent (APSS) and the sub-agents (LineW, LineP).

The ESTEREL code associated to APS module:

```
module APS:
input % APSS Actions, LineW and LineP Signalings
   A_Start_APS,A_Stop_APS,S_PCOk,S_WCOk, S_PDOk, S_WDOk,S_PReady,S_WReady;
output % APSS External States, LineW and LineP Decisions
   E_APS_Stopped,E_APS_ToStop,E_APS_NStarted,E_APS_DStarted,E_APS_ToNFunction,E
_APS_ToDFunction,D_PConnect,D_PDisconnect,D_WConnect,D_WDisconnect,D_PCheck,
D_WCheck;

signal % Interfaces Events
   A_Connect_PLine,A_Disconnect_PLine,A_Check_PLineE_PLine_Connected,E_PLine_Cleare
d,E_PLine_Disconnected,A_Connect_WLine,A_Disconnect_WLine,A_Check_WLine,E_WLine_C
onnected,E_WLine_Cleared,E_WLine_Disconnected,S_WCleared,S_PSelected,S_WSelected,S_Stop
ped,D_FSP,D_WW,D_FSW,D_Arret
 in   % Parallel ESTEREL modules
   run APSS || run ID || run IS || run Line_P || run Line_W
end signal;
```

The output of this translation is a piece of ESTEREL code which can be compiled into a finite state machine by the ESTEREL compiler and formally checked folowing temporal propreties and using ESTEREL automated verification tools.

**Sub-Agent Line Temporal Propreties.** From the property (9):

$$\forall a \in A, [\forall d \in D(act(a)), d \mid\models C(d)] \Rightarrow a \mid\models C(a)$$

we can deduce the following properties:

$$D\_Connect \mid\models C(D\_Connect) \Rightarrow A\_Connect\_Line \mid\models C(A\_Connect\_Line) \quad (11)$$

where C(D_Connect): $D\_Connect \rightarrow \lozenge_{\leq 4} S\_COk$
and C(A_Connect_Line): $A\_Connect\_Line \rightarrow \lozenge_{\leq 4} E\_Line\_Connected$

$$D\_Disconnect \mid\mid= C(D\_Disconnect) \Rightarrow A\_Disconnect\_Line \mid\mid= C(A\_Disconnect\_Line) \quad (12)$$

where C(D_Disconnect): $D\_Disconnect \rightarrow \lozenge_{\leq 3} S\_DOk$
and C(A_Disconnect_Line): $A\_Disconnect\_Line \rightarrow \lozenge_{\leq 3} E\_Line\_Connected$

$$D\_Check \mid\mid= C(D\_Check) \Rightarrow A\_Check\_Line \mid\mid= C(A\_Check\_Line) \quad (13)$$

where C(D_Check): $D\_Check \rightarrow \lozenge_{\leq 2*n} S\_Ready$
and C(A_Check _Line): $A\_Check\_Line \rightarrow \lozenge_{\leq 2*n} E\_Line\_Cleared$

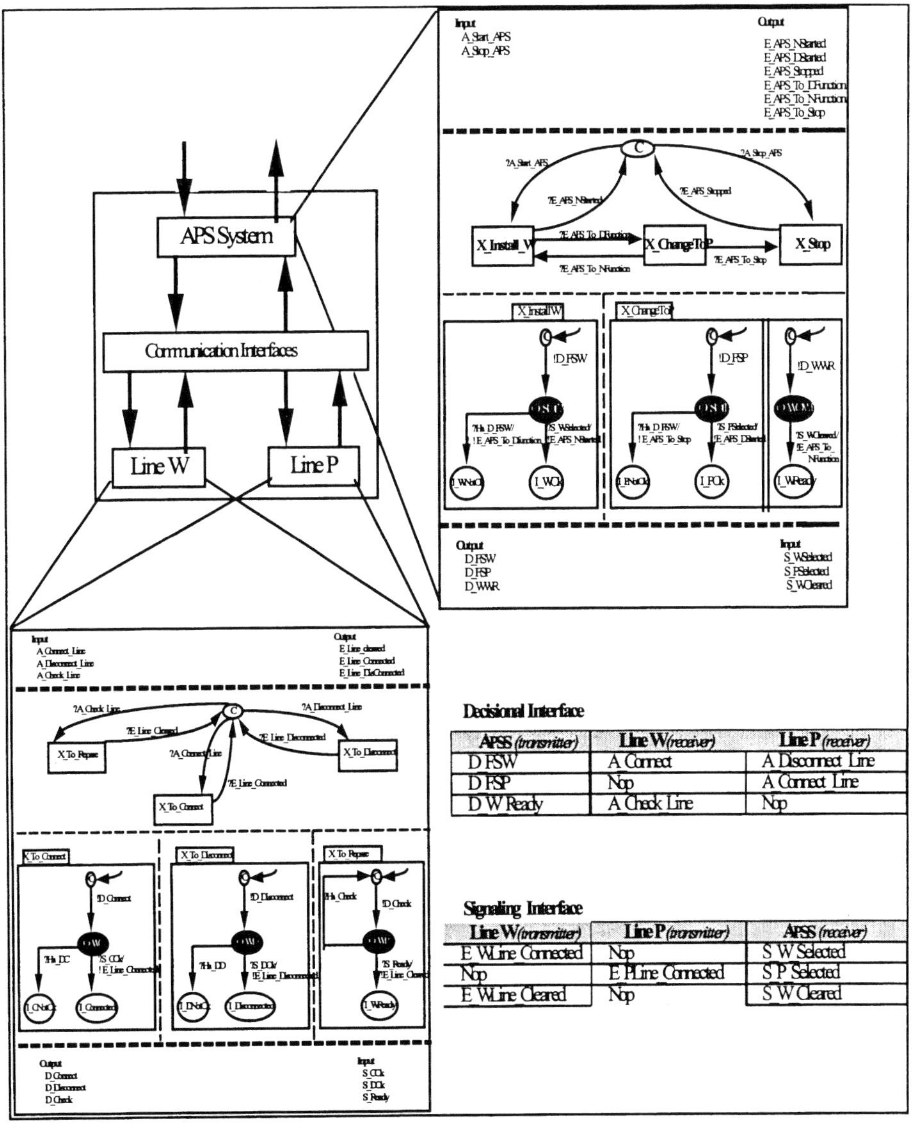


**Decisional Interface**

| APSS *(transmitter)* | Line W *(receiver)* | Line P *(receiver)* |
|---|---|---|
| D FSW | A Connect | A Disconnect Line |
| D FSP | Nop | A Connect Line |
| D W Ready | A Check Line | Nop |

**Signaling Interface**

| Line W *(transmitter)* | Line P *(transmitter)* | APSS *(receiver)* |
|---|---|---|
| E WLine Connected | Nop | S W Selected |
| Nop | E PLine Connected | S P Selected |
| E WLine Cleared | Nop | S W Cleared |

Fig. 10 APS Architecture with its SC Models and Communication Interfaces.

(11), (12), (13) can be checked by deduction(see Appendix) or by XES simulation.

*XES Simulation.* Simulator XES provides a graphical representation of the generated state machine, and helps designers to verify the different behaviors. XES Simulation of the A_Disconnect action can be summarized by Fig.11 showing the event received or emitted by the RDA Line.

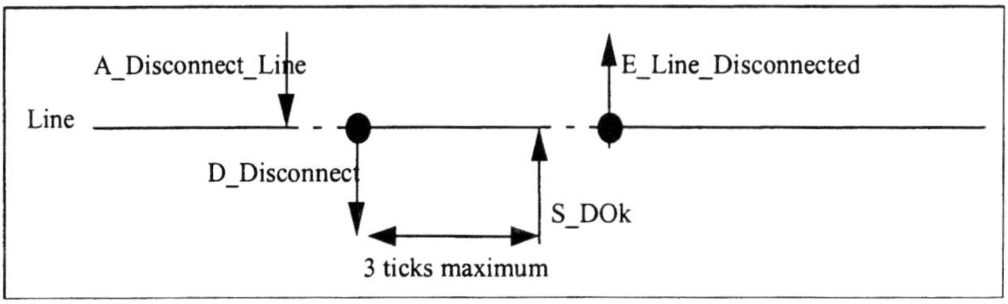


Fig.11 Simulation of the agent Line of communication. The reception of the action A_Disconnect and the emission of the decision D_Disconnect are simultaneous. The reception of S_DOk before the horizon of action (*3 ticks*) of D_Disconnect, involves the simultaneous generation of the external state E_Line_Disconnect. (12) is thus checked. The same verification can be adopted in the cases of the properties (11) and (13).

**Expression of the APS Properties.** From the property (10):

$$d_{ij}^{k} \Vdash C(d_{ij}^{k}) \Rightarrow a \mid \models C(a) \qquad (10)$$

we can deduce:

$$D\_WConnect \Vdash C(D\_WConnect) \wedge D\_PDisconnect \mid \models C(D\_PDisconnect)$$

$$\Rightarrow A\_Start\_APS \Vdash C(A\_Start\_APS) \qquad (14)$$

Where:

C(D_WConnect): D_WConnect $\rightarrow \Diamond_{\leq 4}$ S_WCOk
C(D_PDisconnect): D_PDisconnect $\rightarrow \Diamond_{\leq 3}$ S_PDOk
C(A_Start_APS): A_Start_APS $\rightarrow \Diamond_{\leq 6}$ E_APS_NStarted

*Verification.* Two types of XES simulations can be used in order to check the liveness properties of the system:

-The end-user point of view, i.e. by masking the system internal events. This simulation is carried out by the observation of the behavior of APSS (fig.12).

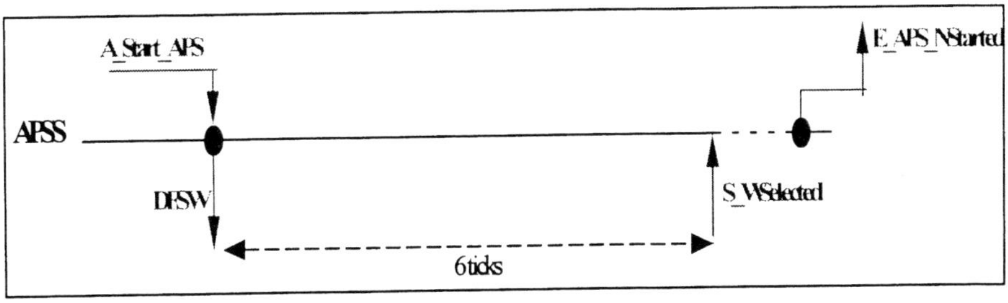


Fig.12 APS Simulation from an end-user point of view.

The reception of the action A_Start_APS and the emission of the decision DFSW are simultaneous. The reception of S_WSelected before the horizon of action (*6 ticks*) of DFSW, involves the simultaneous generation of the external state E_APS_NStarted. This checks the behavior of APSS.

- The modelled agent point of view, i.e. by showing the system internal actions as well as the entering or outgoing events of the customer. This simulation is carried out by the observation of the behavior of all the systems components (Fig.13).

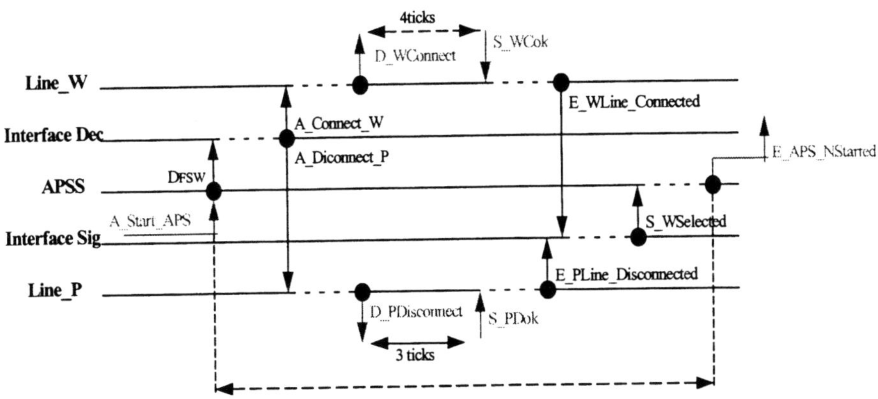


Fig. 13 APS Simulation from an agent point of view.

The reception of the action A_Start_APS implies the simultaneous of D_WConnect (*by Line_W*) and D_PDisconnect (*by Line_P*).

The Line_W reception of S_WCok before the horizon of action (*4 ticks*) of D_WConnect and The Line_P reception of S_PDok before the horizon of action (*3 ticks*) of D_PDisconnect involve the simultaneous generation of E_APS_NStarted. This is coherent with Fig.10. result.

### 6.3 APS System Graceful Degradation Modes Checking

This section, we suppose that the working line fails and then it changes its operating mode from normal functioning to degradation mode and return to normal.

**Degradation Mode Simulation.** XES simulation of graceful degradation mode can be summarized by Fig.14 and Fig.15.

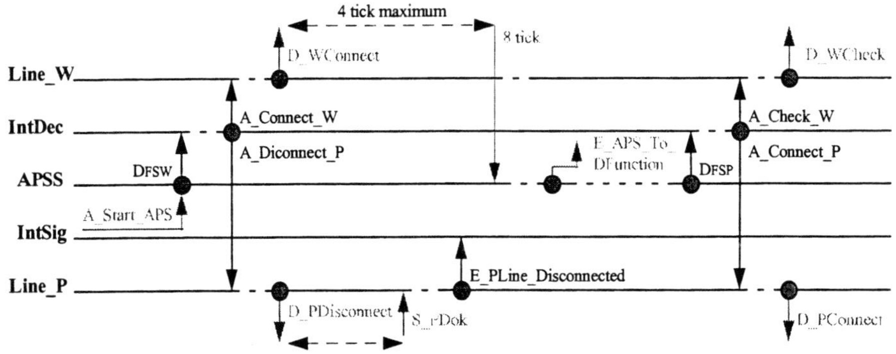


Fig. 14 APS System Internal failure detection.

The reception of the action A_START_APS implies the simultaneous generation of the decisions D_Wconnect (by LineW) and D_Pdisconnect (y Line_P). APSS detects a failure after a duration (here 8 ticks) without receiving the signalling S_Wcok and exceeding DFSW action horizon (6 ticks). APSS sends then E_APS_To_Dfunction (external state indicating Degradation mode) and actives simultaneously the new functioning mode X_ChangeToP.

The first decision generated by this external objective is DFSP, that is interpreted into two simultaneous actions A_CheckW (to LineW) and A_ConnectP (to LineP).

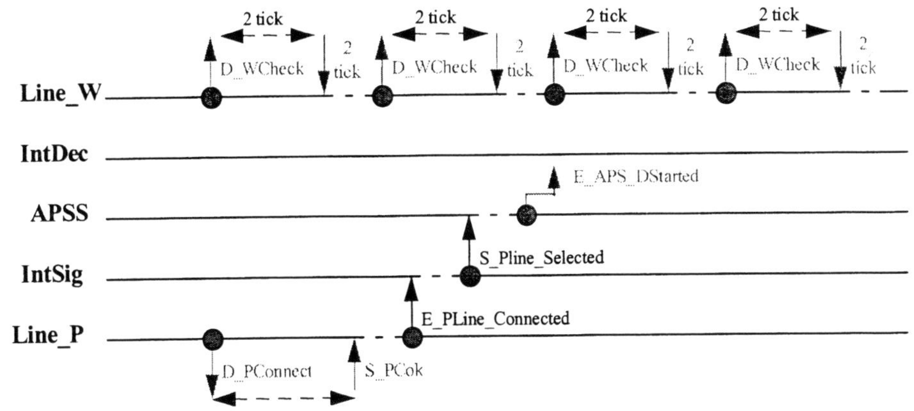


Fig. 15 APS System degradation mode.

LineW receives the action A_CheckWand sends the decision D_Wcheck each 2 ticks, waiting the signaling S_WReady that indicates that the repair of the failed line. As soon as LineP is connected (reception of S_PCOk and emission of E_Pline_Connected). This external state is translated by IntSig as a signaling acknowledgment (S_Pline_Selected) that implies the emission of E_APS_Dstarted indicating that the degradation functioning mode has started succefully.

**Simulation of the return to the normal functioning mode.** XES simulation of the return to the normal functioning mode mode can be summarized by Fig.16.

LineW sends D_Wcheck each 2 ticks, wiating S_Wready signalling that indicates working line repair. As soon S_Wready is received, LineW sends the external state E_Wline_Cleared, interpreted by APSS as a possible return to the normal functioning mode (E_APS_ToNFunction) and a possible change of external objective. Working line reconnection is simulated by the emission of external state E_APS_Nstarted.

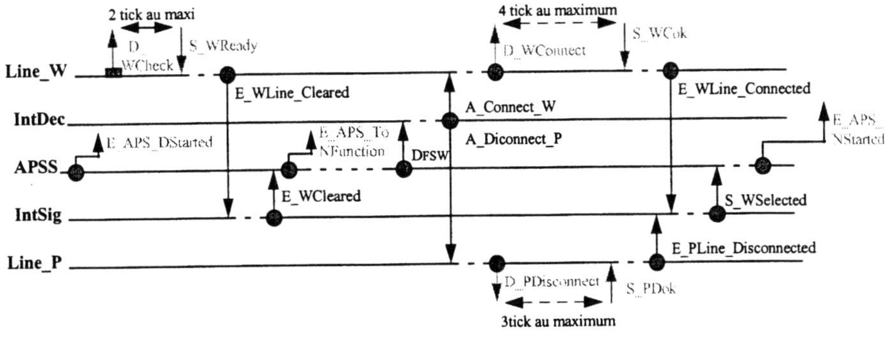


Fig. 16 Return to the normal Operating Mode Simulation.

# 7 Conclusion

The contribution of this paper is to give a new formal approach to deal with specification and verification of a reactive system operating modes, and specially failures modes. The originality is to consider each component of reactive system as a Reactive Decisional Agent. With its top-down process and its principles of decomposition, this method allows to get a model which is more easily understandable by the user. The STATECHARTS models are used here in order to describe the reactive agent behaviors. These behaviors will be checked in a qualitative way by the synchronous language ESTEREL. The mechanism of action horizon, the time during which an agent decision remains valid, is moreover useful to specify temporal performances, and then to detect abnormal functioning modes. Several fault tolerance techniques are used in the proposed approach.

The resulting model can be useful for every application in which it is necessary to include one or several reactive components, and to control operating modes changes. The specification and verification of the Automatic Switching Protection System has stressed the validity and usefulness of the approach.

# References

[1] U. FURBACH, Formal specification methods for reactive systems, *Journal of Systems Software*, No. 21, 1993, pp. 129-139.

[2] D. HAREL, Statemate: aworking environment for the development of complex systems, *IEEE Software Engineering*, Vol.16, No.4, 1987.

[3] D. HAREL, STATECHARTS: A Visual Formalism for Complex Systems. *Science of Computer Programming*, No.8, 1987, pp. 231-274.

[4] G. BERRY, *The ESTEREL V5 Language Primer. Internal Report*, CMA Ecoles des Mine, INRIA, Paris, 17 Mars 1998.

[5] F. BOUSSINOT, and R. DE SIMONE, The ESTEREL language, *Proceeding of the of the IEEE*, Vol.79, No.9, 1991, pp:1293-1304.

[6] G. BERRY, P. COURONNE, Synchronous programming of reactive systems: an introduction to ESTEREL, *IEEE Software Engineering*, Vol.16, No.4, (1987).

[7] L. LAMPORT, What Good is Temporal Logic ?, *Proceeding of IFIP, Information Processing*, 1983, pp. 657-668.

[8] A. PNUELLI, *The Temporal Semantics of Concurrent Programs*, Theoretical Computer Science, No.13, 1981, pp. 45-60.

[9] J. OSTROFF, *Temporal Logic for RealTime systems*, Advanced Software Development Series Research 1st edn, 1989.

[10] J. FERBER, *Les systèmes multiagents. Vers une intelligence collective*, IIA, InterEditions, 2th edn, 1997.

[11] H.S. NWANA, Software Agents: An overview, *Knowledge Engineering Review*, Vol.11, No.3, 1996, pp. 205-244.

[12] R. GOODWIN, Formalizing Properties of Agents, *CMU Reports*, CMUCS93159, 1993.

[13] P.A. MATAGA, P. ZAVE, Formal specification of Telephone Features, *Z User Workshop*, 1994, pp. 29-50.

[14] F. CHARPILLET, A. BOYER, Incorporating AI Techniques into Predictable Realtime Systems. *Quatorzièmes Journées Internationales d'Avignon*, 1994.

[15] J.P. BAHSSOUN, S. MERZ and C. SERVIERES, A Framework for formalizing and proving concurrent objects, *WS4ECOOP'94*, Bologna Italy, July 1994.

[16] B. BOUNABAT, *MACSOOD, Méthode d'Analyse et de Conception des Systèmes Orientée Objet Décisionnel. Application à la conception des Systèmes Automatisés de Production,* PhD Dissertation, Institut National de Télécommunications, EvryParis, 15 September (1993).

[17] T. ANDERSON, P.A. LEE , *Fault Tolerance Principles and Practice.* 2nd edn., Prentice-Hall, 1990.

[18] K.E. MARTERSTECK and A.E. SPENCER, Introduction to the 5ESS Switching System, *AT&T Technical journal*, Vol.64, No.6, 1985, pp. 305-314.

[19] B. BOUNABAT, S. LABHALLA and J.C. LAFONT, Reactive System Control using a decisional object modeling, *IFAC'97*, Campinas, Brazil 02/06 September (1997).

*Appendix:* - Verification of Formulate (11) by RTTL Deduction

A_Connect_Line → X_To_Connect (1)

X_To_Connect → D_Connect ∧ O_ Wait_Connection (2)

as D_ Connect → $\Diamond_{\leq 4}$ S_COk (4)

and X_To_Connect ∧ O_ Wait_Connection ∧ S_COk

⇒ I_Connected ∧ E_Line_Connected (3)

A_Connect_Line → $\Diamond_{\leq 4}$ E_Line_Connected (11)

The same steps of checking can be used for (12) and (33).

*Chapter 3*

# FEATURE-BASED CLASSIFICATION OF TIME-SERIES DATA*

ALEX NANOPOULOS, ROB ALCOCK AND YANNIS MANOLOPOULOS
Data Engineering Lab, Department of Informatics
Aristotle University
Thessaloniki 54006
GREECE
{alex,rob,manolopo}@delab.csd.auth.gr

*Abstract:* In this paper we propose the use of statistical features for time-series classification. The classification is performed with a multi-layer perceptron (MLP) neural network. The proposed method is examined in the context of Control Chart Pattern data, which are time series used in Statistical Process Control. Experimental results verify the efficiency of the feature-based classification method, compared to previous methods which classify time series based on the values of each time point. Moreover, the results show the robustness of the proposed method against noise and time-series length.

*Key-words:* Data mining, time series, classification, statistical features

* Research performed under the European Union's TMR Chorochronos project, contract number ERBFMRX-CT-96-0056 (DG12BDCN).

# 1 Introduction

Data mining is the process of pattern identification in large databases [1]. The main objectives of data mining are *prediction* and *description*. Data mining methods belong to several categories. *Regression* maps data to prediction values. *Generalization* produces a simple description from complex data and *association* finds dependencies among data. *Clustering* identifies a set of types with which data can be categorized, whereas *classification* maps data to a set of a predefined types. Data mining has been mainly applied to relational data. Non-relational data present important challenges to data mining due to their size and dimensionality.

Time-series data are supported by many database systems. A time series is a sequence of real numbers representing the values of a variable over time. They have found applications in temporal [2] and scientific databases, as well as in data warehouses containing a variety of data types, from stock market prices to electro-cardiograms. Mining time-series data can reveal important patterns, such as similarities [3], trends [4] or periodicity [5]. Since time-series data tend to grow rapidly over time, they present several performance issues to data mining algorithms.

Time-series classification involves the learning of a function that maps a series into a class from a set of predefined classes. Therefore, it requires the existence of a set of well-defined categories. The class definition is not always an easy task (e.g. in stock-market data) and may be obtained from a domain expert. Time-series classification finds applications in electrocardiogram (ECG) data, weather measurements, in statistical process control (SPC). More particularly, SPC uses time series for the representation of several critical parameters of a system. These time series are called control chart patterns (CCPs) and they are used for the detection of abnormalities in the system's condition.

In [6], a control chart classification approach is followed based on neural network classifiers. CCPs are synthetically generated, belonging to one of six predefined types, and are presented to a feed-forward back-propagation neural network, with every value having one input neuron. The proposed classifier achieves up to 97.1% accuracy. This approach presents the drawback of sensitivity to noise and time-series length. As will be shown in the following sections, when the amount of noise in the series is increased, the performance of classification is affected due to the implication of each distinct time point. Also, increased time-series length has an impact on both the classification performance and response times.

In this paper, we present a time-series classification method based on feature-extraction. We propose the use of several statistical, first and second order features and evaluate their benefits to classification performance. Since features carry information for the time series which is not based on individual time points, they are less sensitive to noise. Additionally, the number of features is much less compared to the length of the time series. Therefore training times are reduced drastically.

Related work in time-series data mining has mainly focused on fast similarity search. In [3], time series are represented by the first few coefficients of their Discrete Fourier Transform, which are then stored in a spatial data structure. This work was generalized by [7] for subsequence matching. In [8], two series are similar if enough of their portions can be included by the same orthogonal envelope. More recent work on similarity search include [9] and [10] where similarity is defined in terms of a set of linear transformations. In [11], normalization of time series is used to make similarity insensitive to scaling and shifting. Yi et al. [12] present algorithms for time-series similarity using time warping as a distance function. Other work related to time-series similarity include [13, 14, 15].

The rest of the paper is organized as follows: Section 2 gives a detailed description of the CCP classification problem. Previous work on CCP classification is presented in Section 3. Section 4 presents the proposed method and Section 5 contains experimental results that show the performance of all methods. Finally, Section 6 concludes the paper and gives some directions for further work.

## 2 Problem Description

There exist several examples of categorized time-series data. For instance, the *Shuttle* data[1] set consists of the output from 109 sensors from the first eight hours of Space Shuttle mission STS-067. Sensors and their output can be categorized with respect to the phenomena they measure. Other examples include electrocardiogram (ECG) data, which contain a number of human ventricular events.

In this work, we focus on a specific type of categorized time series, the CCP. Statistical Process Control procedures use such CCPs for the assessment of the status of industrial systems. In [6], CCPs are categorized into six types and the corresponding equations are provided for the synthetic generation of CCPs for each type. The types that CCPs can exhibit are: normal, cyclic, linear trends (increasing or decreasing) and shifts (upward or downward). Equations 1 - 4 describe the way to generate patterns from each type and Table 1 explains each symbol used in equations. Figure 1, illustrate examples of produced CCPs from each type.

CCP data present a context where classification can be performed effectively, since it contains well described classes. However, non stationary (in mean or variance) time series may impact the effectiveness of classification. Such series can be generated using the GARGH (Generalized Autoregressive Conditional Heteroskedasticity) model, as described in [16]. In this case, it is expected that none of the existing methods will perform effectively. In this paper we are interested in a relative comparison of time-series classification methods. Therefore, we leave the examination of the classification of these type of data as a direction of future work.

[1]Available at http://www.ics.uci.edu/ mlearn/MLRepository.html

$$
\begin{aligned}
y(t) &= \mu + r(t)\sigma \quad [Normal] && (1)\\
y(t) &= \mu + r(t)\sigma + a\sin(2\pi t/T) \quad [Cyclic] && (2)\\
y(t) &= \mu + r(t)\sigma \pm gt \quad [Linear\ \ trend] && (3)\\
y(t) &= \mu + r(t)\sigma \pm ks \quad [Shift] && (4)
\end{aligned}
$$

| | |
|---|---|
| $y(t)$ | time-series value |
| $t$ | time |
| $\mu$ | mean value (taken as 30) |
| $\sigma$ | standard deviation |
| $\alpha$ | amplitude of cyclic variations (taken in the range 5 to 15) |
| $g$ | magnitude of gradient trend (taken in the range 0.2 to 0.5) |
| $k$ | determines shift position (k is 0 before shift position, 1 after) |
| $r$ | normally distributed random number between 0 and 3 |
| $s$ | shift magnitude (taken in the range 7.5 to 20) |
| $T$ | period of cycle (taken in the range 10 to 15) |

Table 1: Parameters for synthetic generation of CCPs

There exist several types of classification methods which can be categorized into linear and non-linear. Linear classifiers include decision trees [17] and rule-induction methods. They have the advantage of simple interpretation. Due to the nature of their learning function, which is based on data attributes, they are appropriate for relational data. Time-series data lack the existence of attributes. Non-linear classification methods include neural networks, adaptive spline methods and projection pursuit regression [18].

One of the most common types of neural network classifier is the Multi-layer Perceptron (MLP) neural network. The MLP is based on the known structure of the human brain. It contains layers of neurons with weighted connections between these neurons. The output of each neuron is the sum of its inputs passed through an activation function, such as the sigmoidal function. Neurons are organized into layers: input, hidden (one or more layers) and output. The main advantages of the MLP are that it learns from examples and is able to form non-linear boundaries between classes. It finds, by adapting its weights, a relationship between input data and output types. Thus, the user does not need to have so much domain knowledge about the problem. In this work we focus on MLPs with one hidden layer. Although, several other structures may achieve improved results, we are interested on the relative comparison of the presented methods. The following two sections describe the use of the MLP neural network for CCP classification.

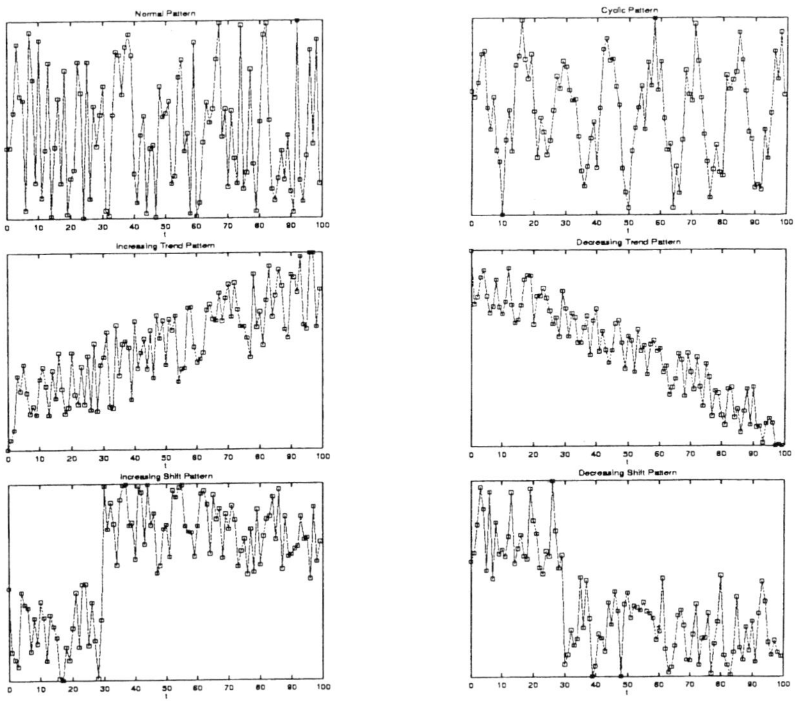


Figure 1: Examples from each type of control chart patterns.

# 3 Previous Work on Time-series Classification

Pham and Oztemel [6] worked on the classification of CCPs. They generated 83 training patterns from each of the six types, with each pattern having a length of 60 points. A MLP neural network was employed to classify the patterns. The approach employed was to have one input neuron for every value in the time series. Thus, the network had 60 inputs and 6 outputs (one for each class). For testing, 1002 unseen patterns were generated. The MLP achieved an accuracy of 96% on this test data. Next, experiments were carried out using three neural networks and combining their outputs using a decision-making module. The resulting composite system was able to classify patterns with an accuracy of 97.1%.

In later work, Pham and Oztemel [19] proposed the use of the Learning Vector Quantization (LVQ) neural network. As in the previous work, all the points in the time series were used as inputs to the network. The LVQ network gave a worse performance than the MLP network, achieving an accuracy of 92.3% on test data. A modified version of LVQ, called LVQ-X, was proposed in the paper and a higher accuracy of 97.7% was obtained.

Keogh and Pazzani [20] proposed a time-series representation based on piecewise linear segmentation [21]. This representation provides data compression and noise reduction. In the paper, a distance measure is defined which corresponds to how far two segments are from being parallel. This distance measure is insensitive to translation, linear trends and discontinuities. The classification task proposed distinguishes time series which belong to a single well-defined class from those that do not exhibit any structure. The algorithm merges all time series into a single sequence. This is done using an agglomerative clustering approach by merging each time two series belong to the same class. Due to the merging approach, this method was tested in [20] against time series belonging to a single class.

Recently, in [22], there is proposed a method for classifying CCP data. The paper discusses the use of artificial neural networks for recognition of the shape from CCP data. Synergistic, distributed and distributed synergistic neural networks are proposed and focus is given on learning efficiently non-linear characteristics and overlapping ranges of values of the data set describing CCPs.

Finally, feature selection was used in [23] for classifying speech signals. Several statistical features, along with others specifically designed for speech data, are proposed and their effectiveness is verified with experimental results. The later work motivated ours on using features for classifying CCPs with neural network classifiers.

The approach of taking the actual values of the time series as classifier inputs [6] presents the following drawbacks:

- It is sensitive to the amount of noise in the time series. Since each input contributes to the classification task, noise can affect the accuracy of the method more severely.
- It is sensitive to the length of the time series. When the time series becomes large, it is impractical to have a neural network with such a large number of inputs.
- It requires that all chart patterns are of the same length (due to the constant number of input neurons). Using features instead, patterns of different lengths could be used, as long as the same number of features is extracted.

# 4 Proposed Method

In this section, we propose the extraction of several features from time series and their use for classification. The classification is performed based on the features for each series and not on the actual values. Many different features have been employed in image processing and pattern recognition to classify objects. There are many features in image processing which can be categorized in those who describe intensity an those who describe shape. The extraction of appropriate features has been recognized as an important problem.

Evidently, the nature and the number of features needed depends on their discriminatory quality. The required characteristics for the selected features are ease of computation, insensitivity to transformations and resulting performance. For time-series data, and more particularly for CCP data, we propose the use of *statistical features*, which are commonly used in image processing.

The proposed statistical features were selected because they are simple and easy to implement. The invocation of more elaborated features, like *moments* of several orders, is expected to improve the efficiency of the method. Also, the invocation of an automated feature selection method could help to improve the results of the method. Nevertheless, statistical features are a starting point for the evaluation of the method, and the improved methods of feature selection will be addressed by future work.

Features can be divided into first and second order features. First-order features are based on the actual values of the series whereas, second-order features are based on the differences of nearby values.

The most common statistical features are the mean value $\mu$, standard deviation $\sigma$, skewness $SKEW$ and kurtosis $KURT$. Skewness and kurtosis contain information on the shape of the distribution of the time-series values. More precisely, $SKEW$ characterizes the degree of asymmetry of values around the mean value. KURT measures the relative peakness or flatness of the value distribution relative to a normal distribution. The equations for these features are:

$$\mu = \frac{\sum_{t=1}^{n} y(t)}{n} \tag{5}$$

$$\sigma = \sqrt{\frac{\sum_{t=1}^{n}(y(t)-\mu)^2}{n}} \tag{6}$$

$$SKEW = \frac{\sum_{t=1}^{n}(y(t)-\mu)^3}{n\sigma^3} \tag{7}$$

$$KURT = \frac{\sum_{t=1}^{n}(y(t)-\mu)^4}{n\sigma^4} - 3 \tag{8}$$

There exist several second-order features in image processing. The most common ones are called co-occurrence features. For this work, new second-order features are used which are more suitable for time-series classification. The features are simple to calculate and are similar to the first-order features employed. For the calculation of the second-order features used in this work, it is first necessary to calculate a transformed time series $y'(t)$ based on the original $y(t)$ and a user-specified value $D$:

$$y'(t) = y(t+D) - y(t), \quad 1 \leq t \leq n - D \tag{9}$$

D is the distance between the points in the time series being compared. From $y'(t)$, the four statistical features are calculated using equations 5 - 8. These features will be referred to as $\mu_2$, $\sigma_2$, $SKEW_2$ and $KURT_2$. $y'(t)$ contains information about the shape of the original series $y(t)$ and also acts as a noise filter. Second-order features can be employed with first-order features to give a better representation of y(t).

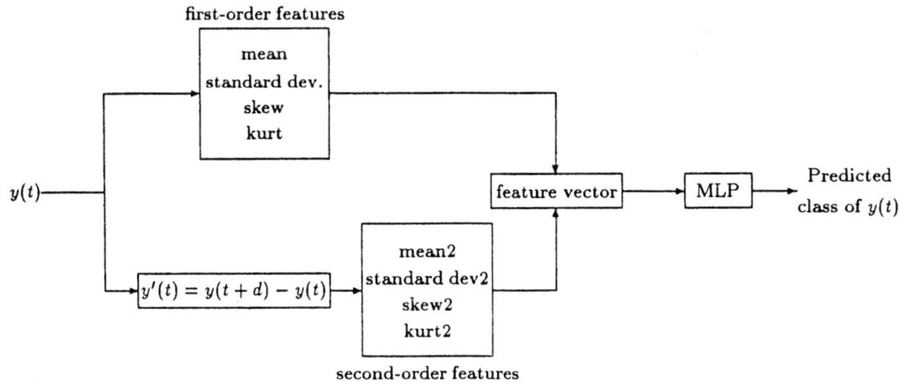


Figure 2: Proposed method

The proposed method is presented in Figure 2. First-order features are calculated from $y(t)$ using equations 5 - 8. Then, from $y'(t)$, we calculate the second-order features. First and second-order features form the feature vector. Feature vectors of each time series are presented to a MLP neural network for classification. Since the length of the feature vector is eight, the MLP has much less input neurons compared to the method described in the previous section, particularly when the time-series length increases.

# 5 Experimental Results

This section presents the results obtained from the comparison of the method proposed by [6], which will be referred to as *VB* (value based), with the proposed one, which will be referred to as *FB* (feature based). A training set was generated for both methods, consisting of 180 time series. These series were generated using equations of Section 3, where each class has the same number of instances. The neural network had three layers, one for input, one hidden and one for output.

The number of hidden neurons was equal to half the sum of the input and output neurons. The time series of the training set were presented to the neural network in a round-robin manner, i.e. one of the six types each time. The evaluation of the trained neural network was performed with 6,000 time series generated using again the equations of Section 3. Both train and test data are following the same distribution, i.e. they were generated with the same values for the corresponding parameters. The performance measure was the classification accuracy for the evaluation set. Each measure was repeated five times and the overall result was taken as the average. The averaging was performed on the results of the several experiments in order to derive more reliable results. Notice that this averaging should not be confused with the use of a structure with multiple neural networks which are combined using an average of the independent results. Of course, such neural network types are expected to improve the performance of classification, but, as explained, the objective of this paper is the relative comparison of existing methods.

First, we measured the impact of the neural network parameters *momentum* ($\alpha$) and *learning rate*($\eta$). Parameter $\eta$ represents how fast the weights at each neuron are changed with respect to the error. Parameter $\alpha$ shows how much the weights are changed compared to the change in the previous iteration. We tested three values for $\eta$: $0.001, 0.01, 0.1$, which represent a low, medium and high value, respectively. Though 0.1 may be not be considered large, for larger values of $\eta$, the neural network did not manage to be trained. For $\alpha$, we tested values $0.1, 0.5$ and 0.9, representing a low, medium and high value, respectively. Table 2 presents the results for time series generated having length 60 and standard deviation equal to 2.0. Note that the standard deviation is a measure of the noise the time series contains. The stopping criterion for the neural network training was either 10,000 iterations or an RMS value equal to 0.05.

| **VB** | $\alpha = 0.1$ | $\alpha = 0.5$ | $\alpha = 0.9$ |
|---|---|---|---|
| $\eta = 0.001$ | 0.986 | 0.981 | 0.974 |
| $\eta = 0.01$ | 0.166 | 0.166 | 0.955 |
| $\eta = 0.1$ | 0.167 | 0.167 | 0.167 |

| **FB** | $\alpha = 0.1$ | $\alpha = 0.5$ | $\alpha = 0.9$ |
|---|---|---|---|
| $\eta = 0.001$ | 0.969 | 0.967 | 0.967 |
| $\eta = 0.01$ | 0.935 | 0.964 | 0.970 |
| $\eta = 0.1$ | 0.167 | 0.167 | 0.167 |

Table 2: **a.**Accuracy of $VB$ method **b.**Accuracy of $FB$ method

Table 2 illustrates that the $VB$ method achieves high accuracy for a small $\eta$ value (0.001). The accuracy of $FB$ is also high, but slightly less than that of $VB$. For medium and high $\eta$ values, the $VM$ method did not perform well since the neural network could not been satisfactory trained. This is due to the fact that the training for the $VB$ method is based on each value of the time series. The $FB$ method performs more robustly since it achieved high accuracy for medium $\eta$ values. Parameter $\alpha$ did not have a significant impact except in the case when $\eta$ was set to 0.01 because for a high $\alpha$ value, the $VB$ method managed to produce high accuracy.

Time-series data usually contain noise. Noise can be categorized as white, i.e. Gaussian noise, which is applied to whole time series, or pulsive, which represents abrupt variations of the values of the time series at few time instances. For CCP signals, as described in Section 3, we consider noise as a function of the standard deviation $\sigma$. Since high deviation from the mean value represents a time series with a less normal shape, $\sigma$ can represent the amount of noise that the time series contains. Notice that noise is considered to corrupt the existing values of the time series and not to add new, noisy, values in the series. Figure 3a illustrates the accuracy of $VB$ and $FB$ methods versus $\sigma$. The length of the time series was set to 60, $\eta$ was 0.001 and $\alpha$ 0.5. The stopping criterion for the neural network training was either 10,000 iterations or an RMS value equal to 0.05. As shown in the figure, both methods perform well for low $\sigma$ values. As $\sigma$ increases, performance of the $VB$ method deteriorates. $FB$ outperforms the $VB$ method due to the fact that it is not based on individual values and thus it is less affected by an increase in the standard deviation.

Next, we measured the impact of time-series length on the accuracy of classification methods. Evidently, the $VB$ method is more sensitive to the time-series length because it takes as input the whole series. The length of the time series is application dependent. For instance, stock-market data tend to be very large. Figure 3b presents the accuracy of $VB$ and $FB$ methods with respect to time-series length. We tuned the parameters separately for each method. For the $VB$ method, $\eta$ was set to 0.001 and $\alpha$ to 0.8. With smaller values of $\alpha$ and larger values of $\eta$, the $VB$ method tended to reach a local minimum. For the $FB$ method, $\eta$ was set to 0.01 and $\alpha$ to 0.5. The stopping criterion for the neural network training was either 5,000 iterations or an RMS value less than 0.05. As shown in Figure 3b, the $VB$ method is sensitive to time-series length, whereas the $FB$ method is not.

Besides accuracy, time-series length has significant impact on training time. Table 3 presents the time taken for the neural network to be trained for each method. The $VB$ method requires significantly longer training times for larger time series because it involves many more computations for connections between input and hidden neurons. On the other hand, the training time for the $FB$ method is not sensitive to time-series length because it involves a small constant number of features for the training.

| | $length = 250$ | $length = 500$ | $length = 750$ | $length = 1000$ |
|---|---|---|---|---|
| $VB$ | 15 min | 45 min | 70 min | 100 min |
| $FB$ | 1.3 min | 1.25 min | 1.22 min | 1.24 min |

Table 3: Training times versus time-series length

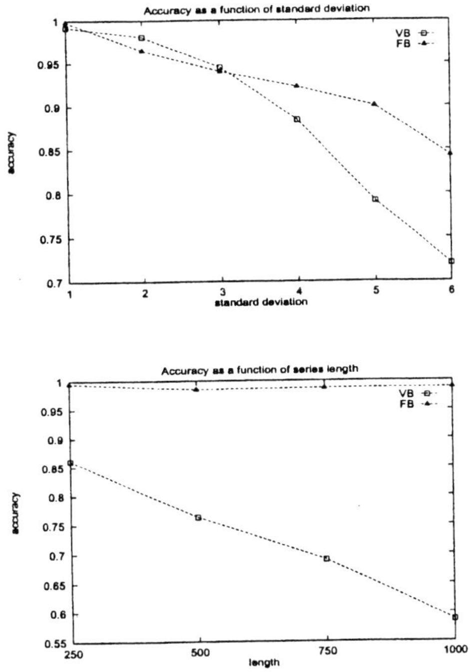


Figure 3: **a.**Accuracy versus $\sigma$ **b.**Accuracy versus series length.

# 6 Conclusions

We have proposed a feature-based classification method for time-series data. Several first and second-order statistical features have been presented. These features are based on those utilized in image processing applications. The classification task is performed using a MLP neural network. The experimental results for control chart pattern data confirm the efficiency of the proposed method compared to a previous one, which classifies time series by using the value of the series at each time point. We show that the use of features results in better classification accuracy in the presence of noise and leads to faster and better classification for large time series.

Future work may involve the examination of other features, like moments, and the implementation of a more detailed feature extraction method. Additionally, other types of time-series, like the ones produced by the GARGH model [16], and real data sets can be examined. Moreover, other classification methods (like Bayesian classifiers), instead of neural networks, can be examined.

# References

[1] Usama M. Fayyad, Gregory Piatetsky-Shapiro, Padhraic Smyth, Ramasamy Uthurusamy (eds.), *Advances in Knowledge Discovery and Data Mining*,

AAAI/MIT Press 1996.

[2] K. K. Al-Taha, R. T. Snodgrass, M. D. Soo, Bibliography on Spatiotemporal Databases, *SIGMOD Record* Vol.22, No.1, 1993, pp.59-67.

[3] R. Agrawal, C. Faloutsos, A. Swami. Efficient Similarity Search in Sequence Databases, *Proc. 4th International Conference Foundations of Data Organization and Algorithms (FODO'93)*, 1993.

[4] D. J. Berndt, J. Clifford, Finding Patterns in Time Series: A Dynamic Programming Approach, in [1].

[5] J. Han, G. Dong, Y. Yin, Efficient Mining of Partial Periodic Patterns in Time Series Databases, *Proc. of the 15th International Conference on Data Engineering*, 1999.

[6] D. T. Pham, E. Oztemel, Control Chart Pattern Recognition Using Neural Networks, *Journal of Systems Engineering*, Vol.2, 1992, pp.256-262.

[7] C. Faloutsos, M. Ranganathan, Y. Manolopoulos, Fast Subsequence Matching in Time-series Databases, *Proc. of the 1994 ACM SIGMOD International Conference on Management of Data*, 1994.

[8] R. Agrawal, K.-I. Lin, H.S. Sawhney, K. Shim, Fast Similarity Search in the Presence of Noise, Scaling, and Translation in Time-Series databases, *Proc. 21th International Conference on Very Large Data Bases (VLDB'95)*, 1995.

[9] D. Rafiei, On Similarity-Based Queries for Time Series Data, *Proc. of the 15th International Conference on Data Engineering*, 1999.

[10] D. Rafiei, A. Mendelzon, Similarity-Based Queries for Time Series Data, *Proc. ACM SIGMOD International Conference on Management of Data*, 1997.

[11] D. Q. Goldin, P.C. Kanellakis, On Similarity Queries for Time-series Data: Constraint Specification and Implementation, *Proc. First International Conference of Principles and Practice of Constraint Programming (CP'95)*, 1995.

[12] B. -K. Yi, H.V. Jagadishm, C. Faloutsos, Efficient Retrieval of Similar Time Sequences Under Time Warping, *Proc. of the Fourteenth International Conference on Data Engineering*, 1998.

[13] H. Shatkay, S. Zdonic, Approximate Queries and Representations for Large Data Sequences, *Proc. of the Twelfth International Conference on Data Engineering*, 1996.

[14] R. Agrawal, G. Psaila, E. L. Wimmers, M. Zait, Quering Shapes of Histories, *Proc. 21th International Conference on Very Large Data Bases (VLDB'95)*, 1995.

[15] P. Seshadri, M. Linvy, R. Ramakrishnan, Sequence Query Processing,*Proc. of the ACM SIGMOD International Conference on Management of Data*, 1994.

[16] P. Granses, P. Homeled, On Forecasting Exchange Rates using Neural Networks, *Applied Financial Economics*, 1998.

[17] J. R. Quinlan, *C4.5: Programs for Machine Learning*, Morgan Kaufmann, 1993.

[18] J. F. Elder, D. Pregibon, A Statistical Perspective on Knowledge Discovery in Databases, *Advances in Knowledge Discovery and Data Mining*, in [1].

[19] D. T. Pham, E. Oztemel, Control Chart Pattern Recognition Using Learning Vector Quantization Networks, *Int. J. Prod. Res*, Vol.32, 1994.

[20] E. J. Keogh, M. Pazzani, An Enhanced Representation of Time Series Which Allows Fast and Accurate Classification, Clustering and Relevance Feedback, *Proc. of the Fourth International Conference on Knowledge Discovery and Data Mining (KDD'98)*, 1998.

[21] T. Pavlidis, S. Horowitz, Segmentation of Plane Curves, *IEEE Transactions on Computers*, Vol.23, No.8, 1974.

[22] M.A. Wani, D.T. Pham, Efficient control chart pattern recognition through synergistic and distributed artificial neural networks, *Journal of Engineering Manufacture*, Vol.213, 1999, pp.157-169.

[23] F.T. Dellaert, T. Polzin, A. Waibel, Recognizing Speech, *Proc. of the 4th Intl. Conference on Spoken Language Recognition*, 1996.

*Chapter 4*

# SOFTWARE RADIO SYSTEM DESIGN FOR ACCESSING WIRELESS MULTIMEDIA SERVICES

MING-CHUNG TANG[1], R. C. CHANG[2], AND WEI-KUAN SHIH[1]

[1]Department of Computer Science
National Tsing-Hua University
101 Kuang Fu Rd, Sec.2, HsinChu 30043,
TAIWAN
mtang@cs.nthu.edu.tw, wshih@cs.nthu.edu.tw

[2]Department of Computer Information Science
National Chiao-Tung University
1001 Ta Hsueh Rd, HsinChu 30050,
TAIWAN
rc@cc.nctu.edu.tw

*Abstract:* This paper presents a software engineer's perspective for the design and implementation of a software radio (SWR) system. The key technical challenge that we want to address is the architecture design of a software radio system and the QoS control for multimedia processing in this architecture. We propose the *component-binding* based software radio architecture and the *QoS-controllable* scheduling mechanism (QSM) in this paper. The *component-binding* based software radio architecture comprises four parts: the control-flow components, the data-flow components, the reconfigurable binding interface, and the SWR management unit (SMU). The *QoS-controllable* scheduling mechanism applies *imprecise computation* techniques for SMU to ensure that time-critical tasks can meet their deadlines and multimedia services can meet their QoS requirements. QSM is coarse-and-fine adjustable. Also, we investigate the *k-tasks-look-ahead substitutable* check to further enhance the overall schedulability for the *on-line scheduler* in QSM. By taking advantage of programmability, the proposed system architecture can serve as a flexible platform for supporting the accessing and processing of wireless multimedia services.

*Key-Words:* software radio, wireless multimedia services, PCS, component-binding, QoS-controllable, imprecise computation, GSM, real-time OS

# 1 Introduction

The notion of a software radio system has been proposed for some time with specific emphasis on a tight combination of software programmability and processing hardware [12-17]. Ideally, the receiver part of a software radio system employs an analog-to-digital converter (ADC) (DAC for the transmitter part) to digitize the RF (radio frequency) at an adequate sampling rate, and then processes these samples in application software on general purpose and/or DSP processor(s) (See Fig. 1). In contrast to traditional radios that implement most of functions in dedicated analog devices, software radios implement those functions in programmable digital devices. In this way, the flexibility of designing, implementing, and testing of a radio system is increased via increased programmability.

In recent years, gradually increased attention has been focused on the realization of software radio systems, as the technology of semiconductor continues its rapid improvements and the emerging third-generation mobile telecommunication standards such as IMT-2000 are prosperously under their standardization processes [10, 11, 16]. It seems very likely that a number of third-generation radio standards (WCDMA, TD-CDMA, and cdma2000) will also co-exist while trying to keep backward compatible to current systems (2G/2.5G). Software radio systems are very promising technologies to provide excellent solutions for bridging the gap between 2G and 3G radio systems, since they can be reconfigured to enable seamless and fast changes of air interface and processing functionality between various radio systems by exploiting their programmability. Besides, the capability of over-the-air downloading has made the software radio system a flexible platform for accessing wireless multimedia content services [17].

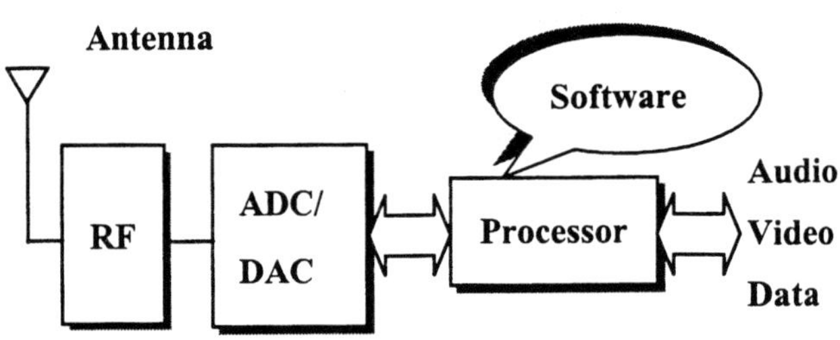


Fig. 1: An ideal software radio system.

Compared with most of existing study that focuses on hardware-related issues such as smart antennas, baseband processing, and programmable devices from electrical engineers' perspective trying to realize the system by replacing hardware with software, this paper provides a software engineer's perspective as a complement for software radio system design. Apparently, it is an irresistible trend for next generation wireless communication standards and equipment to support wireless multimedia services instead of voice services only; for example, a user may browse the web to access the real-time stock quotes while answering a phone call by a software radio-enabled notebook. In other words, a well-designed underlying software system architecture and the capability to tackle wireless multimedia processing issues are, in our viewpoint, indispensable for the design of future software radio systems, although there are still some hardware-related issues to be conquered for realizing a software radio system. Therefore, we concentrate our study on the architecture design and the mechanism to schedule and manage on-line, real-time, multimedia application tasks (e.g. Web browsing and Ftp'ing) and SWR tasks (e.g. Speech coding and Handover processing) in a software radio system.

In this paper, we propose the *component-binding* based software radio architecture that comprises four parts: the control-flow components (CFCs), the data-flow components (DFCs), the reconfigurable binding interface (RBI), and the SWR management unit (SMU). In addition, since real-time, on-line processing for data-flow components (e.g. a speech decoder) and multimedia accessing is an important issue, we also propose the *QoS-controllable* scheduling mechanism applying *imprecise computation* techniques for SMU to ensure that time-critical tasks can meet their deadlines and multimedia services can meet their QoS requirements. Furthermore, since GSM (Global System for Mobile communications) is the world's most widely deployed digital personal communications system that has gained broad acceptance and its specification is well documented by ETSI (European Telecommunications Standard Institute), we choose GSM system to illustrate and verify our software radio system design [19-21].

The remainder of this paper is organized as follows. Section 2 presents the *component-binding* based software radio architecture and the *QoS-controllable* scheduling mechanism. Section 3 illustrates the system architecture for accessing wireless multimedia services. Section 4 describes our on-going implementations for a GSM-based software radio system related issues. Section 5 discusses the related work in the area of software radio system design. And the last section concludes this paper.

# 2 Component-Binding Based Software Radio Architecture

We propose the *component-binding* based software radio architecture, as shown in Fig. 2. It includes four parts: the control-flow components (CFCs), the data-flow components (DFCs), the reconfigurable binding interface (RBI), and the software radio management unit (SMU) [1].

## 2.1 CFCs, DFCs, RBI, and SMU

The CFCs are in charge of the control aspect of a software radio architecture such as cell selection/re-selection, location registration/updating, call-setup, paging, and handover. The behaviors of CFCs are based on communicating finite state machines (FSMs). The DFCs perform the physical layer functions of a software radio such as modulation, demodulation, equalization, speech coding/decoding, interleaving/de-interleaving, channel coding/decoding, and ciphering/ deciphering. Every DFC has its own buffers and ports for input, output, and control respectively.

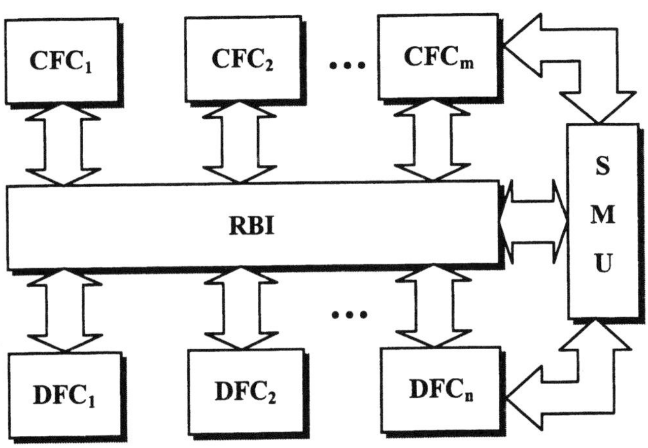


Fig. 2: The *component-binding* based software radio architecture.

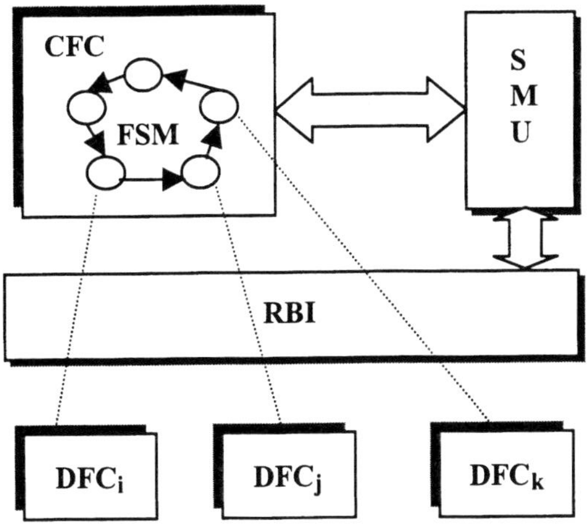


Fig. 3: Binding 1 CFC and some DFCs.

The purpose of RBI is for the binding of the CFCs and the DFCs (Refer to Fig. 3). For each state (or transition) in the CFCs, it can be associated with a group of DFCs (binding via the RBI) performing specific tasks of data processing. The binding is initialized and reconfigured by SMU. The SMU plays the most important role in this architecture, since it is the coordinator for CFCs, DFCs, resource management, performance evaluation, and QoS control. It acts somewhat like a micro controller in a cellular handset; however, in this architecture, it is realized by a software module and cooperates closely with the underlying operating system.

Since, in practice, there are lots of wireless multimedia services such as video conferences and VoD services that have strict timing constraint, it is very natural to employ a real-time operating system to appropriately support the SMU in order to deal with timeliness issues. Furthermore, most software components in this architecture also demand the support of a hard real-time operating system for processing on-line tasks which are very time-critical (for example: the speech coding/decoding, channel coding/decoding, authentication procedure, call setup, and handover process). Hence, the underlying operating system for a software radio system must be hard real-time and provides a good kernel resolution for simultaneously accessing and processing diverse wireless multimedia services. Additionally, due to the severe constraint of power consumption for most mobile and handheld equipment (PDAs, notebooks, and cellular phones, for example), the SMU should be able to efficiently manage the system power consumption.

Consequently, the SMU should provide a mechanism, which is built on a hard real-time operating system, to ensure that time-critical software components can meet their deadlines and multimedia services can meet their QoS requirements. To attain this end, we propose the *QoS-controllable* scheduling mechanism that applies *imprecise computation* model and techniques for SMU. This mechanism allows the

SMU to perform on-line scheduling and adaptation as well for QoS control via coarse and fine adjustments. It will be elaborated in next subsection.

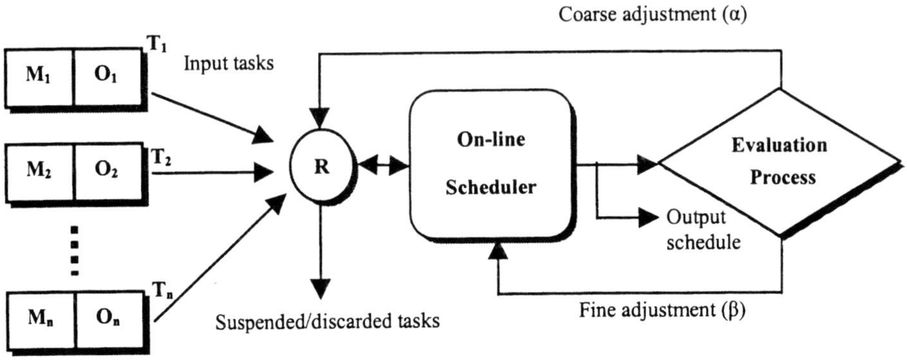


Fig. 4: A *QoS-controllable* Scheduling Mechanism for SMU.

## 2.2 QoS-Controllable Scheduling Mechanism for SMU

Fig. 4 shows the proposed *QoS-controllable* scheduling mechanism for SMU. This mechanism explicitly applies the *imprecise computation* technique. The *imprecise computation* model and related scheduling techniques have been proposed for some time [4-9] to provide more flexible real-time scheduling schemes and to support graceful degradation of a real-time system. In this model, each imprecise task is logically divided into two portions: a mandatory portion and an optional portion. The mandatory portions of imprecise tasks must be scheduled and executed to complete by their deadlines while the optional portions can be chopped in order to meet their deadlines or QoS requirements. An *error* is incurred when the optional portion of an imprecise task is chopped for a schedule. That is, *imprecise computation* can sacrifice its accuracy for meeting task deadlines or the required QoS.

Formally, for the on-line scheduling problem of *imprecise computation* model, we are given a set of on-line, preemptive, imprecise tasks $T=\{T_1, T_2, \ldots, T_n\}$ in which each task $T_i$ is characterized by the following parameters:

(1) arrival time $a_i$ at which $T_i$ arrives
(2) ready time $r_i$ at which $T_i$ becomes ready for execution
(3) deadline $d_i$ by which $T_i$ must be completed
(4) processing time $p_i$ which is the time required to execute entire $T_i$ ($p_i = m_i + o_i$)
(5) processing time $m_i$ which is the time required to execute the mandatory portion ($M_i$) of $T_i$

(6) processing time $o_i$ which is the time required to execute the optional portion ($O_i$) of $T_i$
(7) processing time $x_i$ which is the time assigned by the scheduler to execute $T_i$ ($x_i = m_i + o_i^*$)
(8) $O_i^*$ : the segment of $O_i$ that will be executed (the residual segment of $O_i$ will be chopped)
(9) processing time $o_i^*$ which is the time assigned by the scheduler to execute $O_i^*$
(10) error $e_i$ which is incurred by executing $T_i$ ($e_i = p_i - x_i$)

Note that, by definition, $x_i$ must be equal to or greater than $m_i$, and the total error incurred by executing task set T is equal to the summation of $e_i$, from $i = 1$ to $i = n$. The objective is to minimize the total error, which can be thought of as to produce the most acceptable quality of service. *Imprecise computation* model is very useful for many applications. For example, if we try to display a picture which is divided into four levels (say, A, B, C, and D), then we can, roughly speaking, obtain a 75% quality by displaying only A, B, and C. In this way, we can save some computations and power, and most importantly this may greatly increase the schedulability for on-line real-time tasks to meet their deadlines and QoS requirements. In GSM, the speech coding/decoding modules take most computations in a software radio system [31]. Every 20ms, the speech coder produces a block of 260 bits which is composed of Class $I_a$ (50 bits), Class $I_b$ (132 bits), and Class II (78 bits) [24]. Class $I_a$ and $I_b$ will be ciphered and/or convoluted for further transmission while Class II is unprotected. Thus, the tasks for speech decoding can be logically divided into mandatory portions and optional portions for *imprecise computation*. For example, when the optional portion of a task is chopped by the scheduler's decision, we can apply a fast extrapolation instead of entirely decoding the chopped portions at the price of speech quality.

It is known that optimal on-line scheduling for *imprecise computation* to minimize total error is, in general, impossible [7, 8]. However, in the paper [7], it has been proved that there are optimal on-line scheduling algorithms to minimize total error when the given task system satisfies the Feasible Mandatory Constraint (FMC). This constraint is met if at the time of arrival of every new on-line task, its mandatory portion, together with the yet-to-be-completed mandatory portions of already arrived tasks, can always be precisely scheduled to complete by their deadlines [7]. Paper [7] also proposed an algorithm, named Algorithm NORA, for scheduling on-line, imprecise task systems in which each task is ready upon arrival, and is optimal in the sense that it can minimize total error under FMC. In a subsequent paper [3], we further discovered that if $O_i^*$ is *k-tasks-look-ahead substitutable*, then we can replace it, postpone it, or scatter it for improving the overall schedulability or fairness while conserving the same optimality as the previous work under FMC. The algorithms proposed in [3] are Algorithm MOS, MOP, and MOF (execute Mandatory portion as soon as possible, and Optional portion is Substitutable/Postponable/Fair); these algorithms will not be detailed in this paper due to limited space.

| | $a_i$ | $d_i$ | $m_i$ | $o_i$ |
|---|---|---|---|---|
| $T_1$ | 2 | 12 | 1 | 2 |
| $T_2$ | 2 | 8 | 3 | 3 |
| $T_3$ | 4 | 9 | 2 | 4 |
| $T_4$ | 4 | 10 | 1 | 1 |

(a)

(assume that $a_i = r_i$)

($t_{mi}$ : the time instant that $M_i$ is completed)

($t_{bj}$ : the beginning time of j-th continuous block)

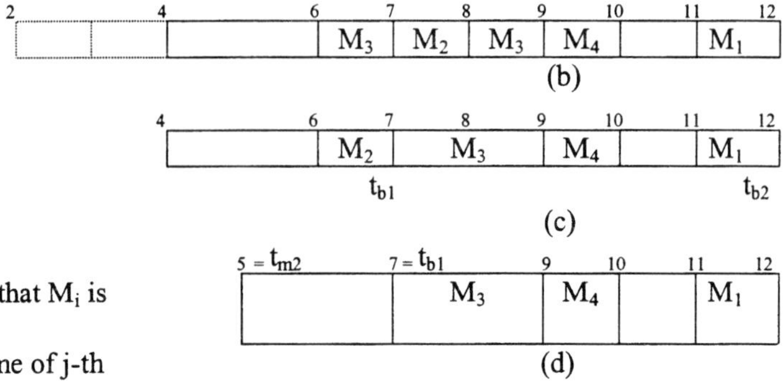


Fig. 5: An example illustrating (a) a task set T = $\{T_1, T_2, T_3, T_4\}$. (b) inserting reservations for $M_3$ and $M_4$ to the reservation list at time 4. ($d_2<d_1$ , so part of $M_2$ has executed in [2,4]. ). (c) the resulting reservation list at time 4. (d) the reservation list at time 5.

Fig. 5 illustrates an example for the *k-tasks-look-ahead substitutable* check. When new tasks arrive, we insert reserved times for executing the corresponding mandatory portions into the reservation list from their deadline toward the beginning of the list and from the task with latest deadline to the task with earliest deadline. Furthermore, we say that $O_i^*$ is *k-tasks-look-ahead substitutable*, if we move the first continuous block ahead in the reservation list from $t_{b1}$ to $t_{mi}$ , checking at most *k* tasks with the earliest deadlines in the first continuous block, and the scheduler can gain an increment of time (more than or equal to $o_i^*$ ) to schedule the optional portions of these k tasks. For example, in Fig. 5(d), at time 5, $M_2$ is completed (i.e. $t_{m2} = 5$); $o_2^* = 2$ for the time interval [5,7] and $o_3^* = 0$. If we move the first block from $t_{b1}$ to $t_{m2}$ (i.e. from time 7 to time 5), $M_3$ and $O_3$ can be scheduled in the [5,7] and [7,9] respectively. Though $O_2^*$ is chopped, we gain the increment of time for $O_3^*$ (i.e. $O_2^*$ is substituted, and $o_3^*$ is increased to 2 time units.). Hence, $O_2^*$ is *1-task-look-ahead substitutable.* In other words, $O_i^*$ is *k-tasks-look-ahead substitutable*, only when the accumulated error is not increased for chopping it at the moment of updating the reservation list. Hence, in this greedy way, the total error can keep minimized.

The proposed *QoS-controllable* scheduling mechanism (QSM) is coarse-and-fine adjustable. It performs a fine adjustment by employing various (EDF-based) algorithms such as NORA, MOS, MOP, MOF, etc. to meet different QoS requirements. Also, the parameter *k* for a *k-tasks-look-ahead substitutable* check is adjustable to further enhance the overall schedulability for the *on-line scheduler*, since, in general, the larger value of *k* means the higher probability for substituting an $O_i^*$ and hence the higher probability to make room for upcoming imprecise tasks. (This is the Mandatory-ASAP/Optional-ALAP scheduling philosophy [3].) The

*Regulator* (denoted "R" with a circle in Fig. 4) performs coarse adjustments for QSM by suspending or discarding the newly arrival tasks according to the *evaluation process*. The *Regulator* itself also monitors the arrival tasks in the *working-set window* and passes the characteristics of the *working set* to the *on-line scheduler* and the *evaluation process*. The purpose of the *Regulator* for QSM is to regulate the input tasks so that the behavior of the tasks fed to the *on-line scheduler* can fit the Mandatory Feasible Constraint as closely as possible. That is, the *on-line scheduler* can perform at its best by applying optimal algorithms (e.g. NORA, MOS, MOP, and MOF) if the *Regulator* maintains MFC for the behavior of the tasks fed to the *on-line scheduler*. The *evaluation process* evaluates the scheduling results and the characteristics of the *working set*, then passing the parameter lists, α and β, to the *Regulator* and *on-line scheduler* respectively for coarse and fine adjustments.

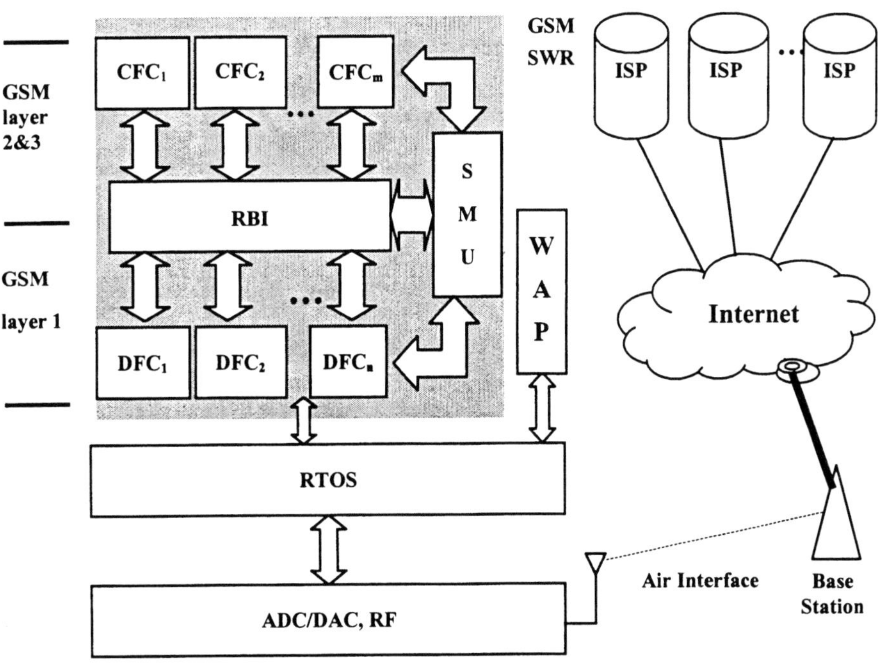


Fig. 6: A system architecture for accessing wireless multimedia services.

# 3 System Architecture for Accessing Wireless Multimedia Services

Fig. 6 illustrates a system architecture for GSM-based software radio systems to access and process wireless multimedia services. This architecture consists of four major components: the GSM SWR, the real-time operating system (RTOS), the wireless application protocol (WAP), and the remainder hardware portion. The GSM SWR (the shadowed portion in Fig. 6) plays a key role in this system architecture. It is divided into four parts (to fit the *component-binding* based architecture): the physical layer (layer 1), the data link layer (layer 2) and the application layer (layer 3), the RBI, and the SMU. The physical layer in a GSM SWR implements most functions for the baseband signal processing of a GSM transceiver such as GMSK modulation, equalization, channel coding, convolutional coding, ciphering, interleaving, and speech codec [20, 24, 25, 29, 30]. The data link layer in a GSM SWR implements functions of the LAPDm (Link Access Protocol for Dm channel) protocol providing a reliable signaling link connection through SAPs (Service Access Points) to convey information between the GSM mobile station (MS) and base station (BS) [26, 27].

The application layer in a GSM SWR is composed of 3 sublayers: connection management (CM), mobility management (MM), and radio resource management (RR). The CM sublayer is in charge of mobile originating and mobile terminating call setup/release, short message services and other supplementary services. The MM sublayer is responsible for mobility management related issues such as location management, authentication, and identification procedures. The RR sublayer, together with the data link layer and the physical layer, provides point-to-point radio connections for MM and CM to send messages such as primitives and protocol data units (PDUs) [22, 23]. The underlying RTOS supports real-time facilities, mechanisms, and APIs for the *component-binding* based SWR to deal with time-critical computations.

WAP is a 5-layered protocol for accessing WWW applications and wireless multimedia services [33]. It is prosperously deployed and promoted by handset producers and service providers. The application framework specified by this protocol will enable Internet Service Providers (ISPs) and content subscribers to work across various wireless communication systems and devices such as cellular phones, pagers, PDAs, and other wireless terminals. Thus, in the illustrative system architecture, we employ WAP as a vehicle to access multimedia services provided by ISPs.

The remainder hardware portion in this architecture contains those hardware components that do not belong to the software modules of a SWR such as antenna, ADC/DAC, linear amplifier, PLL, and other circuits that cannot be realized by software at this movement in time. Since communication technology continues its fast transition from analog to digital, more and more hardware components will be implemented in software - leading us toward an ideal SWR system. As a result of programmability, this system architecture can also serve as an excellent development platform with tremendous flexibility. We will be able to design, adjust, or replace software modules without changing underlying hardware circuits. Therefore, the testing and fine-tuning parameters of a radio system are easier than before.

# 4 Current Implementations

This section briefly introduces our on-going implementations: the layer 3 protocols for GSM system and the prototyping environment for a GSM SWR.

## 4.1 GSM Layer 3 Protocols

We use SDL (Specification and Description Language) and MSC (Message Sequence Chart) [28] to formally describe basic layer 3 functions and procedures such as cell selection, call connection setup, paging, and handover. Also, we use SDT (SDL Design Tool, from Telelogic Tau 3.4) to develop, simulate, and verify the design.

Fig. 7 illustrates part of the SDL diagram of the cell selection in RR idle mode on the MS side. Whenever the power is switched on, the MS starts the cell selection process to find a suitable cell in the PLMN (Public Land for Mobile Networks) to camp on and proceeds subsequent processes (Registration or Location Update, for example). If this selection is failed, this process will enter the 'Any Cell Selection' state and only emergency calls can be made.

Fig. 8 illustrates the SDL diagram of CC (Call Control) in CM sublayer on the MS side. This diagram contains the Mobile Terminated (MT) and Mobile Originated (MO) call-setup and release. When CC receives a MMCC_EST_IND primitive from MM, it will send a MMCC_DATA_REQ with CALL_CONF (Call Confirmation) back to MM. IF CC receives a synchronize indication (MMCC_SYNC_IND), it will send MM_DATA_REQ with ALERT as a PDU. If the subsequent CONNECT acknowledge is received, the MT call connection is setup and CC enters the dedicated mode. The MO works in a similar but inverse way. When CC receives a MMCC_DATA_IND primitive with a RELEASE message, CC will release the connection and send the release complete message. Then CC goes back to the idle mode.

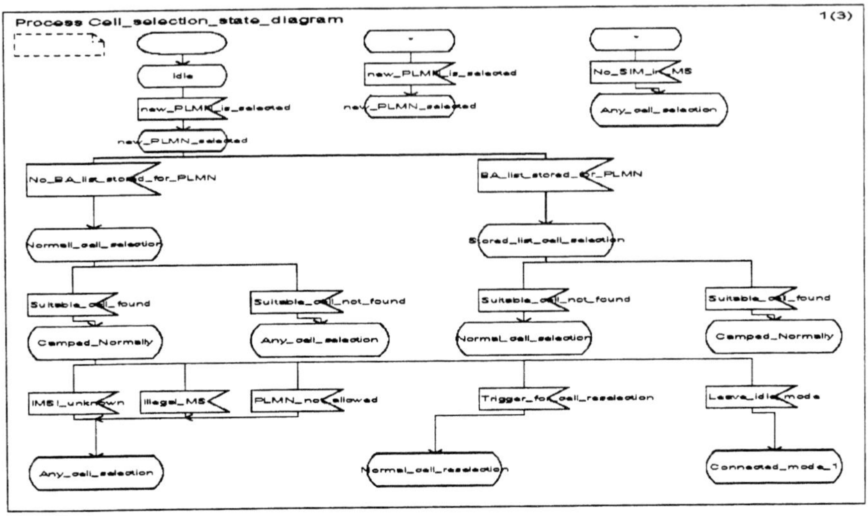


Fig. 7: Part of the SDL diagram of the cell selection in RR idle mode of the MS side.

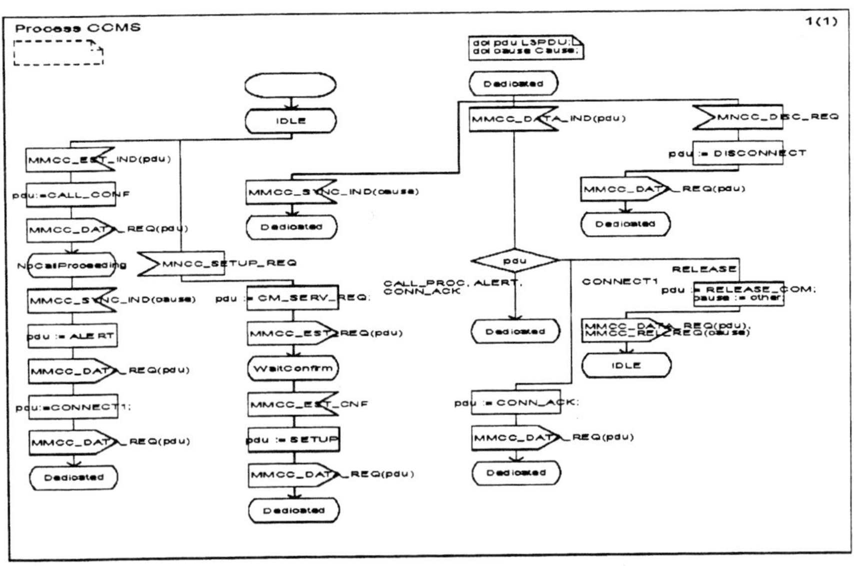


Fig. 8: The SDL diagram of CC on the MS side.

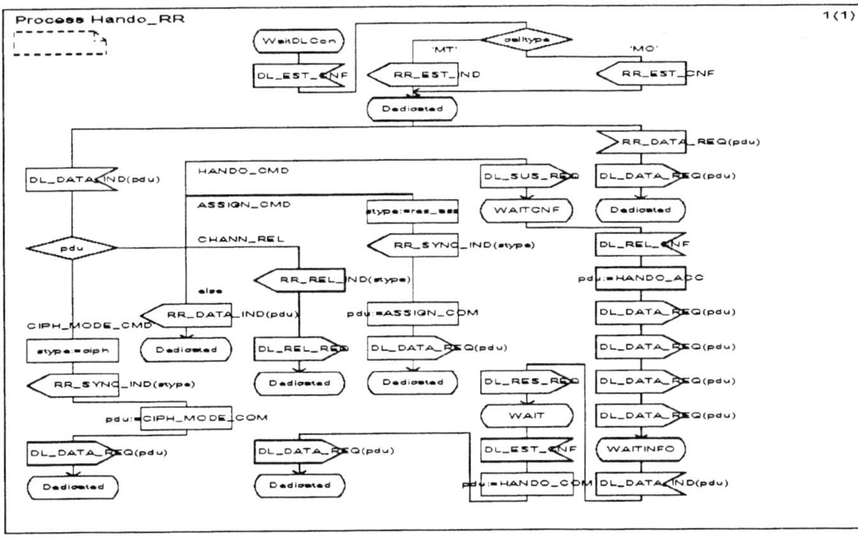


Fig. 9: SDL diagram of RR Handover process

Our implementation of the layer 3 functions and procedures has been simulated for the testing of correctness of the signaling flow by the simulator provided in Tau 3.4. The presently on-going

Fig. 9 illustrates the RR handover process. Handover can only occur in RR connected mode of a MS. When RR receives a handover command (HANDO_CMD), it first sends a suspension request (DL_SUS_REQ) to data link layer, and then waits for the confirmation. If the confirmation is received, RR will send four successive DL_DATA_REQ primitives (with PDU: Handover Access) and wait for information from physical layer. If there is an indication from DL layer (with physical layer information), RR will send a resume request (DL_RES_REQ) to DL layer and wait for confirmation. When the confirmation message is received, RR sends a DL_DATA_REQ with handover complete as the PDU and releases the old channel.

Our implementation of the layer 3 functions and procedures has been simulated for the testing of correctness of the signaling flow by the simulator provided in Tau 3.4. The presently on-going work is using ITEX (Interactive TTCN Editor and eXecutor) to run the TTCN (Tree and Tabular Combined Notation [34]) test cases specified in ETSI/GSM specifications. To pass these test cases in specifications is a formal verification process of the GSM system. There are some codes available in public domain for the physical layer modules such as speech coding and convolutional Viterbi decoder [29, 30]. However, we will focus our work on the back end (layer 2, 3, and SMU) of GSM SWR, and then utilize a RTOS and WAP for constructing a GSM SWR system.

## 4.2 The Prototyping Environment: PESRIT

We are currently designing a Prototyping Environment for Software Radios' Integration and Testing (PESRIT) [2]. It adopts RT-Linux as its development platform [18]. Besides openness and conciseness, RT-Linux is a hard real-time operating system, running real-time tasks in kernel mode and its support for SMP (Symmetric Multi-Processors) architecture can be used to improve the system performance. The RT-Linux approach to achieve a hard real-time operating system is by making the real-time module run underneath the original Linux kernel. In this way, the original Linux kernel and other non-real-time processes (applications) can be viewed as some preemptable lowest-priority processes running on RT-Linux. Hence, RT-Linux sharply separates real-time services and non-real-time services while remaining all original Linux system and applications functionally unchanged. And, most importantly, this kind of separation allows real-time tasks to dominate CPU, so RT-Linux can provide a good kernel resolution.

The PESRIT system is composed of an A-SDL editor, an SDL2RTL translator, a DFC maker, a RBI maker, and a TI maker. The A-SDL editor is used to build Annotated SDL representations for CFCs and SMU. Since SDL is very suitable for describing the system-level specification models and the control-flow components of the software radio system are basically communicating finite state machines, they can be described by SDL at the system-level for verification and conformance testing [28]. However, there are some restrictions and weakness for SDL when binding with lower level system configurations. For example, it lacks some arithmetic operations (shifting, rounding, and exponentiation for example) and ADTs (Abstract Data Types) in SDL are difficult to use. Most importantly, the timing requirements cannot be specified for a specific software or hardware system environment. Hence, the A-SDL editor is designed to attach additional data structures, parameters, functions, and timing requirements to compensate SDL for its insufficiencies.

The SDL2RTL translator is used to translate the SDL/A-SDL representations to real-time tasks in RT-Linux kernel modules. Then these tasks can utilize various facilities such as real-time schedulers, timers, fifos, semaphores, message queues, and APIs supported by RT-Linux to run in a real-time environment within certain pre-configured scheduling disciplines. The DFC maker is used to build real-time kernel modules for data-flow components. PESRIT users can configure the RBI between control-flow components and data-flow components by setting RBI maker. The TI maker can be used to setup a Testing Interface for PESRIT to cooperate with other tester (e.g. SDT/ITEX) or testing environment.

Fig. 10 illustrates a mobile-station-side Layer-3 protocol testing configuration for a GSM SWR integrated by PESRIT that cooperated with SDT/ITEX. In this configuration, SDT/ITEX can take test suites (TTCN for layer 3 from the GSM specification) as inputs, and simulate the layer 3 behavior of the base station side [19, 21, 34]. Then, we can setup a testing interface (TI) with a certain channel condition (white noise or perfect, for example) to provide a simulated link for conveying signals and PDUs between two platforms.

# 5 Related Work

The earliest survey and evaluation on software radios were proposed in [12]. The paper investigates several enabling technologies for building a software radio system, and many critical technology assessments are provided as well. Paper [15] describes an ATM-based wide-band receiver, the SpectumWare testbed, and the receiver side of a GSM base station. The ATM-based receiver consists of a RF daughter card, a FIFO queue, a PLA (Programmable Logic Array) to generate ATM cells, and the ATM network for sending data.

In paper [31], the computational requirement of a software-based GSM base station was estimated. And the performance estimation of each software module is evaluated in a % CPU metric and a metric based on SPEC benchmarks. The Speakeasy [32] is an implementation of a software radio for military. Its goal is to build a multi-band/multi-mode radio system for the integration of various military radios by using lots of DSP processors.

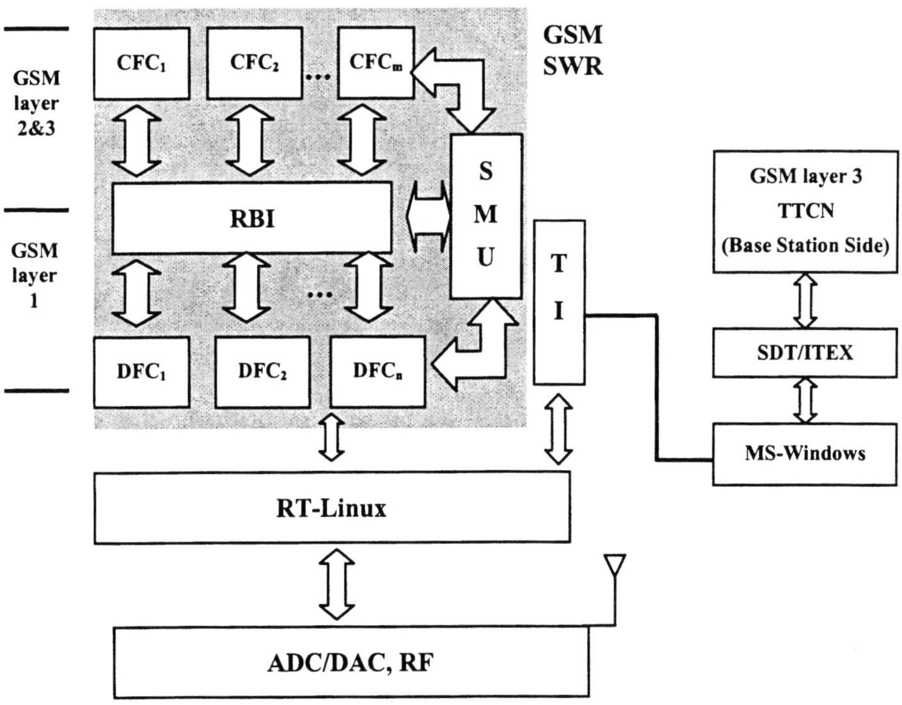


Fig. 10: A testing configuration for layer 3 protocols.

# 6 Conclusions

In this chapter, we present our recent advances for the design of a software radio system. A novel *component-binding* based architecture and the *QoS-controllable* scheduling mechanism are proposed. The proposed novel mechanism, which explicitly applies *imprecise computation* model and techniques, will provide a flexible vehicle for a software radio system to access and process multimedia services in the severe wireless environment. (i.e. real-time processing, QoS control, high latency and bit error rate, limited bandwidth, low power consumption, less storage, less computation power, and security, etc.)

Also, we briefly introduce our on-going implementations for GSM layer 3 protocols and a prototyping environment. In addition to GSM, the proposed architecture can be modified to adapt to other radio systems such as AMPS, IS-95, DECT, or other third-generation technologies for IMT-2000. Applications such as search engines, mobile agents, and E-commerce can also take advantage of this architecture to provide diverse wireless multimedia services for wireless content subscribers.

As Personal Communications System continues its widespread adoption and explosive growth, in addition to voice and short message services, people are interested in accessing diverse wireless multimedia services from Internet and WWW. We believe that a well-designed software radio system can benefit from its programmability. The architecture and mechanism presented in this work provide vehicles for deploying reliable, secure, and efficient wireless multimedia accessing technologies.

# References

[1] M. C. Tang, W. K. Shih, and R. C. Chang, "A Software Radio Based Architecture for GSM System to Access Wireless Data Services," *International Conference on Information Systems Analysis and Synthesis*, Orlando,Florida, USA, July. 1999.

[2] M. C. Tang, C. H. Tang, W. K. Shih, and R. C. Chang, "PESRIT: A Prototyping Environment for Software Radios' Integration and Testing," *IEEE Malaysia International Conference on Communication*, Malacca, Malaysia, Nov. 1999.

[3] M. C. Tang and W. K. Shih, "On-line Scheduling of Imprecise Computation Model for QoS Control," submitted to *World Multiconference on Systemics, Cybernetics and Informatics(SCI'2000).*

[4] W. K. Shih, J. W. S. Liu, and J. Y. Chung, "Fast Algorithms for Scheduling Imprecise Computations," *SIAM J. on Computing*, Vol. 20, No. 3. June 1991.

[5] J. W. S. Liu, W. K. Shih, K. J. Lin, R. Bettati and J. Y. Chung, "Imprecise Computations," *IEEE Special Issue on Real-Time Systems*, January 1994, pp. 83-94.

[6] W. K. Shih, and J. W. S. Liu, "Algorithms for Scheduling Imprecise Computations to minimize maximum error," *IEEE Transactions on Computers*, Mar. 1995, pp. 466-471.
[7] W. K. Shih, J. W. S. Liu, "On-line Algorithms for Scheduling Imprecise Computations to minimize error," *SIAM J. on Computing*, Oct. 1996, pp. 1105-1121.
[8] S. K. Baruah, M. E. Hickey, "Competitive On-line Scheduling of Imprecise Computations," *IEEE Transactions on Computers*, Sep. 1998, pp. 1027-1032.
[9] X. Chen, A. M. K. Cheng, "An imprecise algorithm for real-time compressed image and video transmission," *International Conference on Computer Communications and Networks*, 1997, pp. 390 –397.
[10] T. Ojanpera and R. Prasad, "An Overview of Air Interface Multiple Access for IMT-2000/UMTS," *IEEE Communications Magazine*, pp. 82-95, Sep. 1998.
[11] K.-J. Wee; Y.-S. Shin, "Current IMT-2000 R&D status and views in Korea," *IEEE Communications Magazine*, pp. 160 –164, Sep. 1998.
[12] J. Mitola, "Software Radios Survey, Critical Evaluation and Future Directions," *IEEE National Telesystem Conference*, Washington, DC, May 19-20, 1992.
[13] B. Brannon, "Wide-dynamic-range A/D converters pave the way for wideband digital-radio receivers," *EDN*, Vol. 41 No. 23, Nov. 7, 1996.
[14] W. Tuttlebee, "The impact of software radio," *Software Radio Workshop*, Brussels, Belgium, 1997.
[15] D. L. Tennenhouse , T. Turletti and V. G. Bose, "The SpectrumWare Testbed for ATM-based Software Radios," *IEEE International Conference on Universal Personal Communications*, Boston, MA, Sept. 29 - Oct. 2, 1996, Vol. 2, pp. 915-917.
[16] B. Kraemer, P. Chen, and D. Damerow, "Advances in Semiconductor Technology – Enabling Software Radio," *Software Radio Workshop*, Brussels, Belgium, 1997.
[17] P. Leppanen, j. Reinila, A. Nykanen, V. Tapio, M. Isohookana, J. Pyhtila, T. Kokkonen, and J.Sillanpaa, "Software Radio – An Alternative for the Future in Wireless Personal and Multimedia Communications," *IEEE International Conference on Personal Wireless Communications*, Jaipur, India, Feb.1999.
[18] M. Barabanov and V. Yodaiken, "Real-Time Linux," *Linux Journal*, Mar. 1996.
[19]. M. Redl, M. K. Weber, M. W. Oliphant, "An introduction to GSM," Artech house, ISBN: 0-89006-785-6, 1995.
[20] A. Mehrotra, "GSM system engineering," Artech House, ISBN: 0-89006-860-7, 1997.
[21] M. Mouly and M. B. Pautet, "The GSM System for Mobile Communications," ISBN: 2-9507190-0-7, 1992.
[22] ETSI/GSM Section 04.07, "European digital cellular communications (phase 2+); Mobile Radio Interface Signaling Layer 3; general aspects," Apr. 1997.
[23] ETSI/GSM Section 04.08, "European digital cellular communications (phase 2); Mobile Radio Interface Layer 3 Specification," Apr. 1997.
[24] ETSI/GSM Section 06.10, "European digital cellular communications; Full rate speech transcoding," Sep. 1994.

[25] ETSI/GSM Section 04.04, "Digital cellular telecommunications system; Layer 1; General requirements," April. 1997.

[26] ETSI/GSM Section 04.05, "Digital cellular telecommunications system; Data Link (DL) Layer ; General aspects," Apr. 1997.

[27] ETSI/GSM Section 04.06, "Digital cellular telecommunications system; Mobil Station – Base Station System (MS – BSS) interface; Data Link (DL) Layer specifications," Apr. 1997.

[28] J. Ellsberger, D. Hogrefe, A. Sarma, "SDL Formal Object-oriented Language for Communicating Systems," Prentice Hall, ISBN: 0-13-621384-7, 1997.

[29] P. Karn, "Convolutional decoder, version 2.1," URL: "http: //people.qualcomm.com/karn/ dsp.html".

[30] J. Degener, "GSM 06.10 lossy speech compression," URL: "http://kbs.cs.tu-berlin.de/~jutta/".

[31] T. Turletti and D. Tennenhouse, "Estimating the computational requirements of a software GSM base station," *IEEE International Conference on Communications*, Montreal, Jun. 1997.

[32] L. Lackey and D. Upmal, "Speakey: The Military Software Radio," *IEEE Communications Magazine*, pp. 56-61, Vol. 33, No. 5, May 1995.

[33] WAP Forum, "Wireless Application Protocol Specifications v1.1," URL: "http://www.wapforum.org/".

[34] Telelogic Inc, "Tree and Tabular Combined Notation (TTCN) Tutorial," available at the web site of URL: "http://www.webproforum.com/telelogic2/".

*Chapter 5*

# CACHING ACROSS HETEROGENEOUS INFORMATION SOURCES: AN OBJECT-BASED APPROACH*

ATHENA VAKALI YANNIS MANOLOPOULOS

Department of Informatics
Aristotle University
Thessaloniki 54006
GREECE
email: {avakali,manolopo\}@csd.auth.gr

*Abstract:* Information exchange has been increased drastically and rapidly due to the major large scale Internet expansion. The structure of information sources worldwide has been altered and both structured and semi-structured data are stored in various heterogeneous information spaces. Several tools have been developed for facilitating the rapid integration of the different information structures and accessing needs across heterogeneous sources over the Internet. This paper proposes a caching approach to extend the heterogeneous information sources integration process such that distributed objects are better accessed and retrieved. Our caching approach considers objects that are formed in response to certain queries

* A preliminary version of this work has been presented at the 9th International Database Conference (IDC'99). Work funded by the project "Modeling and management of semi-structured data for dynamic WWW applications" in the context of INTAS-RFBR program.

posed over a specified number of distinct information sources. A methodology based on the notion of genetic algorithms is studied aiming at facilitating distributed objects exchange and accessing. In the proposed model, queries refer to documents or objects identified by their information source and their location within that source. Objects remain in the cache area based on their frequency of accesses, their popularity and their server priority, whereas the cache content is regularly updated. The proposed methods are experimented and results are compared with the corresponding results of the conventional *Least Recently Used (LRU)* cache replacement algorithm. The proposed evolutionary approach based algorithm is proven to be superior than the traditional LRU algorithm with respect to both cache and byte hit ratios.

*Key-words:* heterogeneous information sources, object-based models, caching policies, distributed object caching, evolutionary and genetic algorithms.

# 1 Introduction

Current large scale information systems involve the integration of distributed objects residing over a vast number of heterogeneous information sources. This heterogeneity arises from the fact that diverse computational and information processing needs have to be facilitated and guaranteed over networks and the Internet. Semistructured information is the typical form of data available in most modern information sources over the World-Wide-Web. In a typical scenario, queries are posed by a user (identified as the client) to a target source (identified as the server). In such a case, the retrieval of requested information is performed once the related objects are identified by a number of difficult tasks or actions due to the high heterogeneity of object collections. It should be noted that semistructured data do not obey a specific schema, and thus query optimization can not be performed as in relational databases. In addition, the ongoing Internet expansion increases the access needs to diverse information sources and thus the integration of heterogeneous (and often diverse) information environments has become a major research issue.

The facilitating of efficient integration under heterogeneous information sources has been investigated in several developed prototype systems. These systems include components that extract properties from unstructured objects, translate information into a common object model, combine information from several sources, allow browsing of information and manage constraints across heterogeneous sites. Well known systems in this framework are: Tsimmis [8], Lore [1], Araneus [4], Strudel [9], W3qs [14], WebLog [15], Information Manifold [16] and WebSql [18]. Tsimmis and Lore projects are the most important efforts. Object exchange across diverse and dynamic information sources is the main aspect that has been studied and substantial progress has been shown on database integration techniques [21]. Architectures with associated algorithms for supporting the query mapping to objects have also been implemented [7, 12].

In order to improve performance of accessing heterogeneous information sources, *World-Wide Web caching* has been proposed as an effective solution to the problem of insufficient bandwidth caused by the rapid increase of web objects demands. In simple words, Web caching provides mechanisms to faster web access and improves load balancing without demanding more bandwidth. Most information servers are enhanced with appropriate tools which bring web objects closer to end users by adding specific cache consistency mechanisms and cache hierarchies. Since many web caches often fail to maintain a consistent cache, the problem of maintaining an updated cache has gained a lot of attention recently. Web caching differs from a distributed file system mainly in its access patterns since Web is orders of magnitude larger than any distributed file system [6, 11]. Furthermore, Web differs from conventional caching due to objects sizes nonhomogeneity [2]. The most critical research issues in Web caching concern cache replacement strategies as well as cache consistency and validation. Proxy cache server applications are in charge of supporting the server load balanced, as well as of facilitating the internet traffic. At the same time, a proxy cache server is responsible for the preservation of the cached object's "freshness". *Intelligent Caching* has been investigated in [28] where specific software is developed to investigate alternative Web caching techniques. In [11] a survey of contemporary cache consistency mechanisms in Internet is presented and examines recent research in Web cache consistency. The introduction of trace-driven simulation shows that a weak cache consistency protocol reduces network bandwidth and server load more than prior estimates of an objects life cycle or invalidation protocols. The need for replication is discussed in [22], where an alternative approach suggests the wide distribution of Internet load across multiple servers. The combination of caching and replication is discussed in [5], where the performance of a proxy cache server is evaluated and validated. The latter scheme has been proved beneficial with respect to both the circulation of web objects and the Web server's functionality.

*Evolutionary strategies* have been used to solve many computational problems demanding optimization and adaptation to a changing environment. The idea in all these systems was to evolve a population of candidate solutions to a given problem, using operations inspired by natural genetic variation and natural selection. Usually grouped under the term evolutionary algorithms or evolutionary computation, we find the domains of genetic algorithms, evolution strategies, and genetic programming. More specifically, genetic algorithms have been applied in the areas of scientific modeling and machine learning, but recently there has been a rapidly growing interest in their application in other fields [10, 19, 20, 23]. A web-based evolutionary model has been presented in [25] where cache content is updated by evolving over a number of successive cache objects populations and it is shown by trace-driven simulation that cache content is improved. A genetic algorithm model is presented in [26] for Web objects replication and caching. Cache replacement is performed by the evolution of Web objects cache population accompanied by replication policies employed to the most recently accessed objects.

The present work addresses the problem of improving the process of accessing diverse distributed objects in order to respond to queries posed across heterogeneous information sources. The presented model extends the model of [24] so that the cache content is optimized due to both the cache being formed by objects with high access frequencies and the cache replacement scheme which is further applied. Our goal is to provide a model for facilitating the response and service of the querying process between clients and heterogeneous servers located across the Internet. The introduction of caching algorithms which could be adopted by developed heterogeneous sources integrating tools, since is shown to be quite effective towards objects availability and locality. More specifically, in this paper we focus on the retrieval of objects identified by their information source and their specific location within their source (server). A model based on the evolutionary idea (such as the genetic algorithm), is simulated in order to develop a cache with a "population" of objects at the client side. The population of objects evolves over the simulated time under two operations and the proposed model is compared to a conventional cache scheme based on the LRU approach. The cached objects population is formed with respect to their popularity, frequency of access and their server priority. The model is experimented under artificial queries workload and the proposed approach has been proven to be quite effective.

The remainder of the paper is organized as follows. The next section describes the structure of heterogeneous information sources, with emphasis on query processing. Section 3 analyzes the considered object-based caching model whereas the proposed caching approach is fully described and explained in Section 4. Sections 5 and 6 present the simulation model structure and the experimentation results, respectively. Finally, Section 7 points some conclusions and discusses potential future work.

## 2 Heterogeneous Information Spaces

A common problem found on various organizations and systems is that of multiple diverse information sources such as databases, electronic mail systems, digital libraries, knowledge bases and information retrieval systems. Most often the required information resides on various sources and is not always available due to the difficulties of accessing different systems as well as due to the network traffic. Therefore, the development of tools to access multiple heterogeneous sources in an integrated manner became quite crucial. Some data integration projects have been developed (e.g. Lore, Tsimmis), which are based on specific functions and different components to implement the query processing into a common object model. In the sequel, the project Tsimmis is further described as a representative case of modern heterogeneous information sources integration tool.

Figure 1 shows the most basic structural parts of the Tsimmis architecture. This architecture consists of a number of different heterogeneous information sources referred by the queries posed by a client machine. Above each source is the translator that logically converts the underlying data objects to a common information model. On one hand, the translator converts queries over information in the common model into requests that the source can execute, and, on the other hand, it converts the data returned by the source into the common model. The Object Exchange Model (OEM) serves as a simple tagged object model [8]. Above the translators lie the mediators, which refine in some way information from one or more sources. A mediator embeds the knowledge that is necessary for processing a specific type of information. End users can access information either by writing applications that request OEM objects or by using generic browsing tools. The latter process involves a user writing a query on an interactive Web page, whereas the answer is received as a hypertext document. Constraint management is performed by additional managers dedicated to this task. Finally, Tsimmis system provides

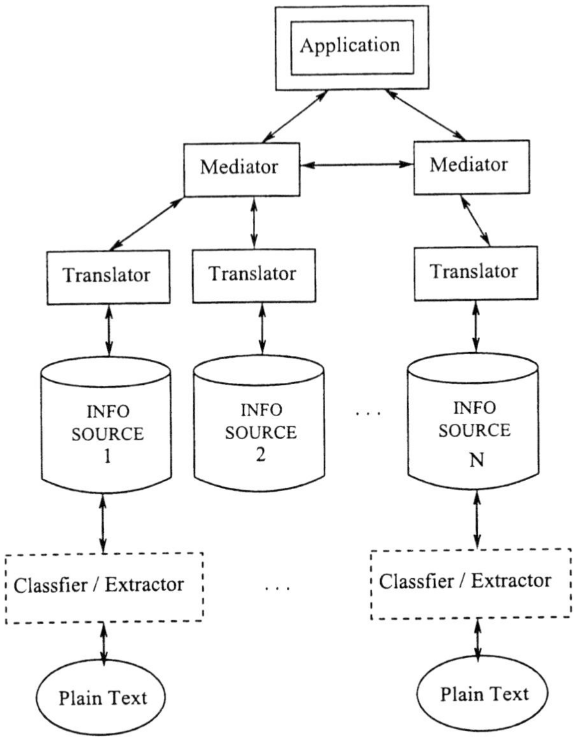


Figure 1: The main parts of the Tsimmis Project Architecture.

a mechanism for exploring heterogeneous information sources that is easy to interact with and that is based on commonly used Web interfaces.

Generally, there are three main issues with respect to the tools for heterogeneous information integration [21]:

*information exchange*, since the information systems need to exchange data objects residing on various sources. Therefore, there is a need for specifying the way the objects will be requested, represented and transferred over a network infrastructure.

*information discovery and browsing*, because users demand the exploration and browsing of objects residing among heterogeneous and probably distant servers.

*mediators*, which are programs that collect information from multiple sources in order to process, combine and export the resulting information to the user.

In this paper we focus on the information discovery problem by proposing schemes to improve object availability, since this is a major problem in the overall information demand process. We introduce evolutionary caching policies to strengthen the consistency, the discovery and the availability of objects to the requesting client.

As discussed in [8, 21] an object-based information model needs to be identified in order to formulate the information exchange and the query processing. OEM is the typical model proposed in order to define the objects located across several diverse heterogeneous information sources. The most common definition and specification of each object in OEM follows.

**Definition 1:** Each object is a tuple the following structure:

*[ Label, Type, Value, Object-ID ]*

where *Label* is a string describing the object representation, *Type* is the object data type, *Value* is the variable length value of the object and *Object-ID* is the object identifier.

The above object definition guides the query processing since several querying languages have been proposed based on this definition. A client is considered to issue a query in a language similar to SQL-like languages in the form of typical SELECT expressions:

```
SELECT Fetch_expression
FROM Object
WHERE Condition
```

The result to the above query is an object itself as given in Definition 1 with the particular *Label* = *answer*. Here, we consider queries which result in certain objects and we focus on appropriate actions in order to cache the most often requested objects at locations closer to the client(s). Our model focuses on the query responses and considers the objects that result while answering specific queries posed over a number of distinct heterogeneous information sources.

# 3 The Object-based Caching Model

Caching was initially introduced to provide an intermediate storage space between main memory and processor. Thus, the locality of reference is enhanced since the most recently accessed data have higher probability to be accessed again in the near future. The caching principle was extended to Web servers by considering them as another level in the memory hierarchy.

Cache area is a finite local area in which data could be stored. As mentioned in the previous, in our model the objects are the results to specific queries posed to a variety of information sources. Each object could be placed in the cache area so that it will be further available in a future request for the same object. The cache has a limited space, so that the cache content has to be updated regularly in order to be beneficial. Clients request information that might be located on an object residing at some source across a network (e.g. Internet). If the client poses another request for the same object, cache will use its own copy instead of requesting the original source again for the same object. The two main caching advantages are the reduction in both latency (e.g. requests are satisfied by the cache which is closer to the client) and network traffic (e.g. each object is retrieved from the server once, thus reducing the bandwidth used by a client). A question arising in relation to all caching actions is the object's freshness. Formally, an object is considered *stale* when the original server must be contacted to validate the existence of the cache copy. Object staleness results from the lack of awareness on server cache about the changes of original object. In practice, almost each proxy cache server implementation is reinforced with specific staleness confrontation. The goal of caching across heterogeneous information sources could be stated by the answers to the following questions:

- *when* to cache object(s) from heterogeneous information sources ?
- *which* objects(s) to cache from heterogeneous information sources ?
- *which* objects(s) to be replaced when the cache space becomes full?

The answers to the above questions and the criteria to perform the proposed caching policy are given in the next section.

Our model proposed a caching scheme in order to facilitate the following actions:

1. A client demands objects from various information sources.
2. Appropriate client caching policies are applied such that the access to objects from heterogeneous spaces is performed at improved rates.
3. An update caching scheme is supported to eliminate cached objects staleness.

Figure 2 depicts the process of the query servicing with the introduction of a cache area between the client and the disperse information sources. Our model proposes an evolutionary approach in order to confront with the following key caching issues:

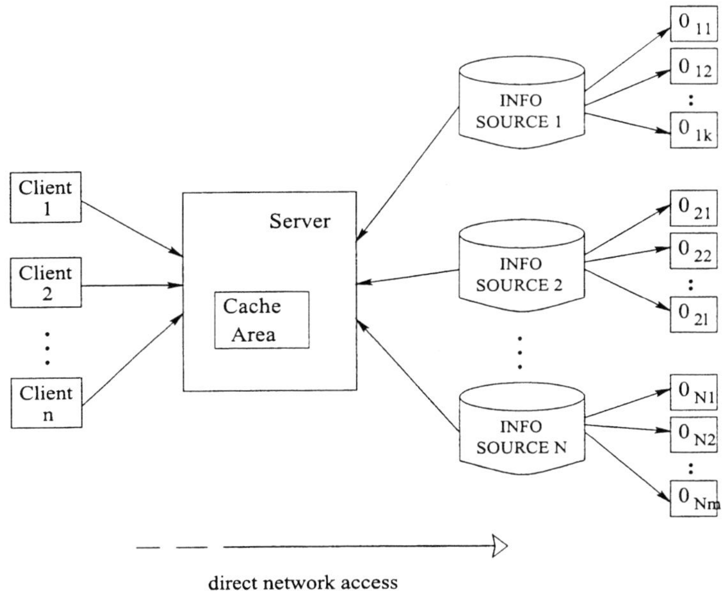


Figure 2: The object-based caching model.

- The *identification* of *Objects* to be cached in the considered reserved cache area. The objects chosen form a "population" of objects to be copied to the reserved area in a considered local server. The choice of objects will be made under certain criteria such as frequency of access, popularity and retrieval cost.
- The *replacement* and *update* of the cache area will be performed at regular intervals in order to meet the criteria of reliability and accessibility. The time intervals to apply a caching algorithm are identified by certain access frequency information.
- The *information discovery* of objects residing at different information sources with variation in access and retrieval costs.

For each requested object the file system has to determine the location of the requested data blocks in order to perform the request servicing. The present paper supports this process by having the cache being searched first, prior to accessing the original information source. Information discovery is a challenging issue due to the large number of information sources. In the proposed model, a priority scheme is proposed for the considered sources/servers, to support the distinct information sources (dedicated to advances services and applications) which need to be prioritized. To better manage the information objects residing at the most crucial sources, we assign a number in the range $[1 \ldots N]$ to each of the considered information sources in decreasing order of priority, i.e. the smallest priority number the larger priority of the considered information sources. The following metric is introduced in order to manage the sources priority scheme.

**Definition 2:** The information source *priority coefficient*, $pc$, for an information source $s$ which has been assigned priority number $pn_s$ $(1 \leq pn_s \leq N)$ is defined by:

$$pc_s = \frac{1}{pn_s}$$

Therefore, it is true that the higher the values of $pc_s$, the most important the considered server $s$ is.

Furthermore, the cached objects should be also been prioritized in order to favor the most popular and frequently accessed objects. Here objects popularity is defined as follows.

**Definition 3:** The *popularity* of an object $i$ is defined by:

$$pop_i = \frac{hits_i}{hits_{tot}}$$

where $hits_i$ refer to the number of hits for the cached object $i$ out of the total number of hits $hits_{tot}$ on the considered cached objects.

# 4 The Evolutionary Caching Approach

## 4.1 The Caching Criteria

The selection of the objects to be cached should be done based on a priority decision scheme which should favor the choice of objects which are accessed most frequently at a desirable retrieval rate. Some criteria are needed in order to better formulate the problem statement. The following definitions are needed for the criteria which will identify the selection of objects to be cached.

**Definition 4:** The *dynamic frequency* of object $i$ is defined by:

$$df_i = \frac{pop_i}{a_i}$$

where $a_i$ is the metric to identify the number of accesses to other objects since object $i$ was last referenced (see Table 1). Therefore, it is true that

| parameter | description |
|---|---|
| $N$ | total number of information sources |
| $S$ | number of objects considered for caching |
| $pn_s$ | priority number assigned to source $s$, $1 \leq s \leq N$ |
| $pc_s$ | priority coefficient for source $s$, $1 \leq s \leq N$ |
| $s_i$ | size (in KBytes) of object $i$, $1 \leq i \leq S$ |
| $pop_i$ | popularity of object $i$, $1 \leq i \leq S$ |
| $df_i$ | dynamic frequency of object $i$, $1 \leq i \leq S$ |
| $a_i$ | number of accesses since the last time object $i$ was accessed |

Table 1: The most useful attributes of each cached object $i$.

the higher the values of $df_i$, the most popular and recently the object $i$ was accessed.

At each selection step the algorithm considers whether an object should be cached or not. Therefore, there are two actions related to caching process, either the object will be chosen for caching or not. A function is needed to identify the action that should be taken for each considered object.

**Definition 5:** The *action function* for object $i$ is defined by:

$$act_i = \begin{cases} 1 & \text{if object } i \text{ is chosen for caching} \\ 0 & \text{otherwise} \end{cases}$$

**Problem Statement:** Suppose that $S$ is the number of requested objects which could be considered for caching and $AREA$ is the total capacity of the area reserved for caching. The caching area content optimization problem is defined as follows:

$$\text{Maximize} \quad \textstyle\sum_{i=1}^{S} act_i \times df_i \times pc_s[i] \tag{1}$$

$$\text{subject to} \quad \textstyle\sum_{i=1}^{S} act_i \times s_i \leq \text{AREA}$$

where $s_i$ is the size of object $i$ and $pc_s(i)$ refers to the priority coefficient of server $s$ where the object $i$ resides (see Table 1). In the optimization formula the quantity $df_i \times pc_s[i]$ is used as a "weight" factor associated with each object, since it is related to the objects popularity, access frequency and its source priority. The basic aim of the proposed caching approach is to support and enforce the caching of the most popular, frequently accessed objects, which are retrieved by the most important information sources.

## 4.2 Identifying Objects to be Cached

The genetic algorithm (GA) approach is considered for the selection of the objects to be cached due to the following two main reasons:

- First, the basic idea of the genetic algorithms is based on the evolution of populations by the criterion "survival of the fittest" and the objects to be cached should be the "fittest" (i.e. the most popular and frequently accessed at best retrieval rates) objects.

- Second, the GAs are applied to problems demanding optimization out of spaces which are too large to be exhaustively searched and all information sources have a huge amount of objects, impossible to be searched exhaustively in a realistic amount of time.

As depicted in Figure 3 a GA is an iterative procedure on a constant-size population of individual objects encoding a possible solution in a given problem space. In the present paper, the objects considered for caching are modeled as the individuals considered for evolution. Mapping the solution to the genetic space is an important task for the GA. The proposed algorithm starts with a specified number of objects $S$, which have been requested at the last evolutionary cycle. Each object is uniquely identified by its id, which is kept as a pointer to the relevant object record. Furthermore, an array $A$ is used to keep record of the objects caching status, i.e. $A[i]$ is 1 if the object $i$ is cached and 0 otherwise. Therefore, the optimization process uses an one-dimensional matrix suitable for the bit-string representations in the GA. Each GA cycle results in a bit-based representation string, which identifies the objects to be cached. Thus, each element at the genetic space can be decoded to a feasible element in the solution space.

The individual objects are assessed according to predefined quality criterion, called *objective or fitness function.* Two genetically-inspired operations, known as *crossover* and *mutation* are applied to selected cached objects (considered to be the population individuals) to successively create stronger "generations" of considered objects. The proposed GA model follows the simple GA proposed in [10].

### Encoding and Operators

Each object individual must be identified according to a predetermined

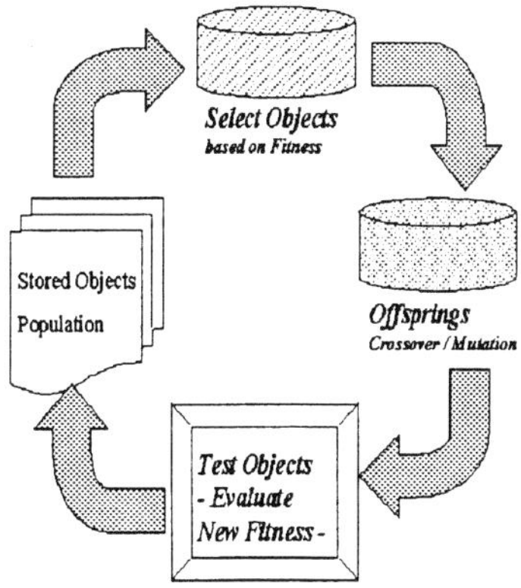


Figure 3: The Genetic Algorithm Cycle.

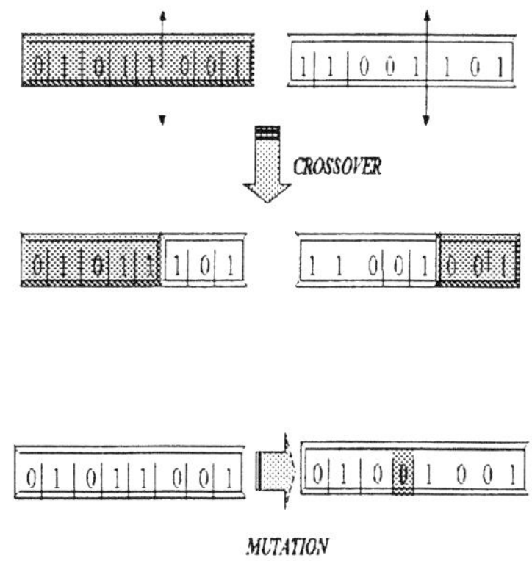


Figure 4: GA operators: crossover and mutation.

encoded string. The encoding scheme is chosen such that the potential solution to our problem may be represented as a set of parameters. These parameters are joined together to form the encoded string. In order to consider the identification of each object individual, the objects identifications are mapped to the integer values $1, 2, \ldots, S$, where $S$ is the total number of objects considered for caching. According to the problem statement (as defined in Formula 1) the parameters $act_i$, $df_i$, $pc_s$ and $s_i$ are the ones to guide the optimization problem, therefore they are included in the proposed encoded string. Each parameter is assigned a value and the presence of that parameter is signaled by the presence of that value in the ordered encoded string. The standard GA manipulations, namely the crossover and mutation, mix and recombine "genes" of an initial objects population to form the new objects to be cached for the next generation.

*Crossover* is performed between two object individuals ("parents") with some probability, in order to identify two new individuals resulting by exchanging parts of the parent strings. These exchangings are performed by cutting each individual at a specific position and produce two head and two tail segments. The tail segments are then swapped over to produce two new full length individual strings. Figure 4 presents the crossover operation on an example of an 8-bit binary encoded string, partitioned after its 5th bit, in order to result into two new 8-bit individuals.

*Mutation* is introduced in order to prevent premature convergence to local optima by randomly sampling new points in the search space. Mutation is applied to each "child" individually after crossover. It randomly alters each individual with a (usually) small probability (e.g. 0.001). Figure 4 depicts the mutation operation in an binary 8-bit string where the 4th bit is mutated to result in a new individual.

The objects population will evolve over successive generations such that the fitness of the best and the average object individual in each generation is improved towards the global optimum.

### The Objective Function

An objective (or fitness) function must be devised based on the need to have a figure of merit proportional to the utility or ability of the encoded object individual. The following formula defines the fitness function, $F(x)$, that considers both access frequency and retrieval rate for an object population $x$:

$$F(x) = \sum_{i=1}^{S} act_i \times df_i \times pc_s[i] \qquad (2)$$

The above fitness function has been introduced in the present research effort in order to consider the effect of access frequency and retrieval cost in the overall caching process.

### The GA Caching Algorithm

The proposed GA-based caching algorithm generates an initial population of objects located at various information sources. To make the search efficient, the initial population consists of objects characterized of being as frequently accessed and faster retrieved as possible. Thus, each population is formed by the most promising and strong objects of all considered information spaces. Then, the standard operators defined above mix and recombine the encoded strings of the initial population to form offspring of the next generation. In this evolution process, the fitter object individuals will create a larger number of offspring, and thus have a higher chance of "surviving" to subsequent generations. The GA-based caching evolves under a termination criterion, which is identified by the number of generations i.e. the number of successive GA cycle runs. A pseudo-code version of the GA-based caching algorithm follows.

```
// Algorithm cache_form(CACHE, population_C)

        old_pop <- population_C // current objects population
        generation <- 1
        while (generation <= maxgen)  do
            par1 <- selection(popsize, fitness, old_pop)
```

```
        par2 <- selection(popsize, fitness, old_pop)
        crossover(par1,par2,old_pop,new_pop,p_cross)
        mutation(new_pop, p_mutate)
        evaluate_fitness(new_pop)
        statistical_report(new_pop)
        old_pop <- new_pop
        generation <- generation + 1
```

In the above algorithm the cache content is formed by using the variable *maxgen*, which corresponds to the maximum number of successive generation runs, whereas *popsize* is the objects population size and *fitness* is the objects update metric as described above by function $F(x)$ in Expression (2). Variables *par*1 and *par*2 define the parents chosen for the reform of each generation, *p_cross*, *p_mutate* are the probabilities for the crossover and mutation operators, respectively. The *old_pop* refers to the initial population in every GA cycle, whereas the *new_pop* is the resulting population of each GA run. The above algorithm is appropriately structured such that it provides a solution to the problem statement as defined by Expression 1.

Furthermore, we do consider the cache replacement process in order to maintain the most often requested non-stale objects. We employ several "runs" in order to question the cache content "staleness" and our proposed approach is summarized by the following main algorithm:

```
    evaluate(frequencies, Objects)
    t  <- 0
    while (t <= TIME)  do
        request_arrival()
        if ( frequencies < RATE ) then
            population_C <- most_frequent_objects
            cache_form(CACHE, population_C)

        request servicing()
        evaluate(frequencies, Objects)
        t <- t + 1
```

In the above algorithm (considered to run for a time period determined by the variable $TIME$), the population to be cached is determined by the *cache_form* routine. It is important to note that the caching control process is performed at regular time intervals according to the access frequencies evaluated by the *evaluate* routine. The objects remain cached until the next running cycle. A parameter ($RATE$) defines the upper bound for performing the cache replacement, i.e. when frequencies are under the specified $RATE$ the current cached objects do not match with the requests access patterns and thus, reconsidering of the cache content has to be performed. The $CACHE$ and *population_C* are the input parameters for routine $cache\_form$ in order to appropriately place the chosen objects population on the reserved cache area.

# 5 The Simulation Approach

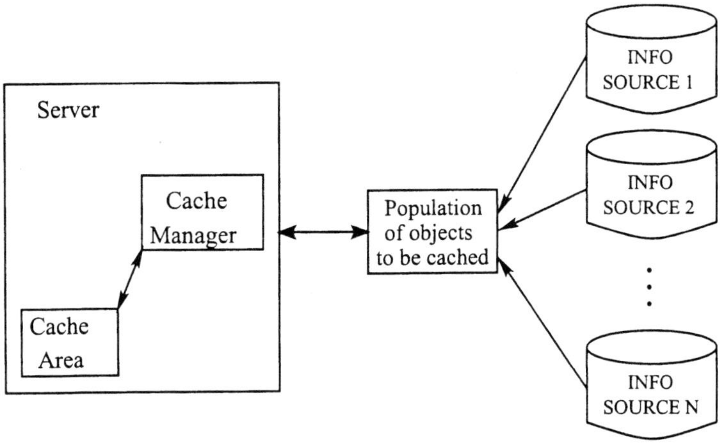


Figure 5: The modules of the Caching simulation model.

The following distinct structural modules are supported in our model in order to better formulate the simulation model (see Figure 5).

**The Information Sources.** A finite number of information sources (IS), namely $IS_1$, $IS_2$, ..., $IS_n$, is supported. Each $IS_i$ contains a number of distinct objects that might be the response to a query posed by a client.

**The Objects.** Each object within an IS is identified by a distinct number as given by the Object-ID (see Definition 1). Therefore, objects $O_{11}, O_{12}, ..., O_{1k}$ are the objects located in $IS_1$, objects $O_{21}, O_{22}, ..., O_{2l}$ are the objects located in $IS_2$ and so on.

**The Queries.** Each query posed by a client includes the pair of the identification of the IS, where the object is located, and the identification number of the object within this specific IS. Therefore, the general query format includes the pair: $< IS_i, O_{ij} >$.

The proposed simulation model is composed of distinct components for the workload, the cache and the information sources. Figure 6 represents the different components or modules of the analytic model and their interaction in relation to request servicing. The model supports a workload of requests posed by the clients to a central storage server which guides the request servicing. Aspects of resource management are simplified for both cache and information sources, in order to support timing and synchronization on request servicing. Each information source has a corresponding manager/controller that guides the requests servicing. The cache area is questioned and request servicing is performed when the cached objects match the requested data. The Cache manager takes a formalized workload as input, transforms this workload to an appropriate format adapted to the objects structure, the request servicing is performed and the performance metrics can be evaluated.

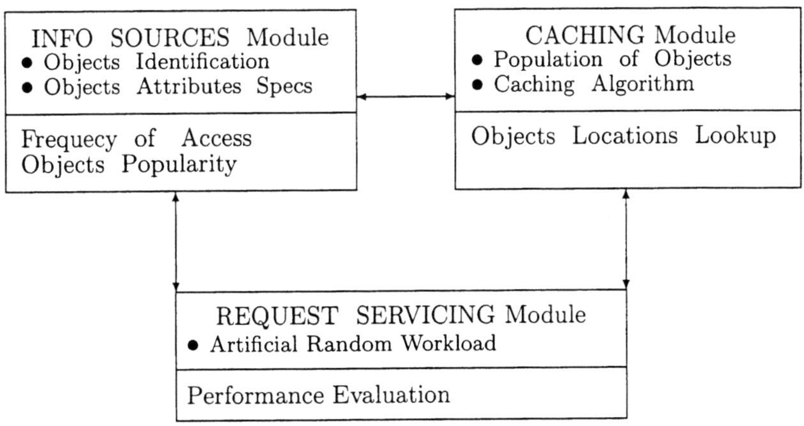


Figure 6: Simulation Model Components and their interaction.

**The Workload and the Request Servicing**

A typical request consists of the attributes for:

- *Information Source*, i.e. the id of the information source to serve the request,
- *Objects Id* , i.e. the identification number assigned to objects within the information sources,
- *Operation*, in the present model only reads are considered in order to study the request servicing,

- *Size* , i.e. the amount of data blocks to be read, and the
- *Arrival Time* , i.e. the time when the request arrived at the controller.

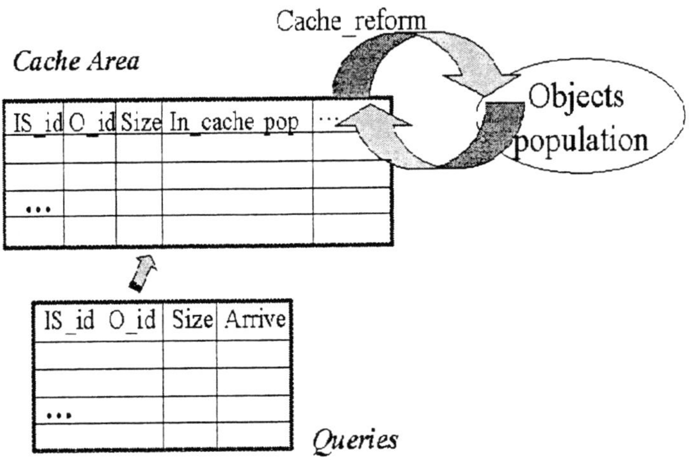


Figure 7: The Workload and Request servicing.

According to a conventional controller, the above request pattern will be directed to the appropriate information source in order to be served. In the presented approach the request is modified by the *Cache Manager*, which checks the caching area before requesting the objects from its original storage location as identified by its request pattern. It should be noted that the present model concerns reading requests since this is the typical operation involved in information sources objects exchange. Requests arrive to the system randomly by various independent processes. Some requests arrive while others are being serviced. Requests arrival rate could be either constant or independent and exponentially distributed or bursty. Here, both random and correlated requests are considered. The correlated requests arrivals refer to higher priority sources, so the $pc_s$ for an information source $s$ (Definition 2) is involved in the requests arrival pattern.

Workload is characterized by the number of queries that will have to be serviced. Therefore, the simulator needs to be experimented under different query sets. The Query servicing routine guides the queries to the cache area in order to identify whether the requested objects are cached or not. Figure 7 depicts the most important parameters of both query workload and cache area structures. The pair of *IS_id* and *O_id* are the IS and Object identifications respectively (noted as $< IS_i, O_{ij} >$ above). As shown in Figure 7 this pair is the actual index for identifying the objects residing in the cache area. *Size* is the requested object's size and the *Arrive* is the time of this specific query arrival. Arrival times are produced randomly by a workload generator routine such that the request patterns follow the priority values as assigned to the information sources.

**The Caching Component**

The Caching Component consists of a *timing module* to model the timing devoted to caching such that synchronize and coordinate the request servicing. The cache manager serves requests in an FCFS basis and appropriate indexing is used to identify the requested object. The cache size is determined in the model and the cache area can be occupied by a certain number of data objects. The cache manager module is appropriately configured such that the performance metrics can be estimated. The cache area has a specific cache retrieval rate (in MB/sec) which estimates the consuming rate of the requested objects which belkong in the cache.

**The Heterogeneous Information Sources**

All information sources could be contacted by clients as in the developed prototype systems (see Section 2). Here, we model the distinct information sources by identifying them uniquely and by considering them to have appropriate storage units to host the data objects. Their own storage units are defined to have similar configuration and metrics.

The performance metrics used in the presented simulation model focus on the cached objects cache-hit ratio and byte-hit ratio, defined as follows:

*Cache hit ratio* represents the percentage of all requests being serviced by a cache copy of the requested object, instead of contacting the original object's information source.

*Byte hit ratio* represents the percentage of all data transferred from cache, i.e. corresponds to ratio of the size of objects retrieved from the cache server. Byte hit ratio provides an indication of the network bandwidth use.

The above metrics are considered to be the most typical ones which capture and analyze the cache replacement policies (e.g. [2, 3]) and the results for these metrics are presented in the next experimentation section.

**Convergence of the Genetic Algorithm**

A GA is a randomized parallel search method modeled on natural selection. Since natural selection uses diversity in a population to produce adaptation, the GA converges when most of the population is identical, i.e. when the diversity is minimized. There is no mathematical proof of convergence or any guarantee that the GAs find the global minimum [13]. There have been some efforts in specifying bounds or prediction for times and speed of convergence for GAs. For example, in [17] average hamming distance is introduced as a measure for population diversity and bounds for time to minimal diversity are derived.

As a stochastic search method successful GAs must maintain a balance between the exploration of a wide area of the solution space and there must be an exploitation of beneficial aspects of existing solutions. In the considered maximization problem, the GA continues for a specified simulation time and the *cache_form* algorithm is repeated for a certain number of iterations as identified by a maximum number of GA generations (Section 4.2). As estimated by the *statistical_report* routine, the same cached objects tend to appear for a number of iterations. As pointed in [27] convergence and homogeneity are not typical problems in simulations that last for a number of generations up to 100, whereas these issues become critical in simulations which last hundreds or thousands of generations. Therefore, in the proposed simulation model the *cache_form* routine is repeated for a maximum number of 100 generations as an indicative parameter that will guarantee that the proposed GA converges at a beneficial solution within a specified number of repetitions.

## 6 Experimentation - Results

We have adopted two different cache management policies to manage the objects exchange across heterogeneous information sources. The LRU caching is a scheme that has been applied widely in many cache servers. Cache is usually implemented as a hash table with a fixed number of locations that could host objects. In our model, the LRU caching was implemented to serve as a typical basis for comparisons with the proposed genetic algorithm cache scheme (called *GA Caching*). We have considered two different types of request workloads: random and bursty. The bursty request arrivals favor the most important information sources since the priority coefficient $pc_s$ for sources $s$ determines the request arrival pattern.

### LRU Caching on the Client

The LRU algorithm is a typical page replacement algorithm which is used in modern operating systems and database systems. The same method has been followed by many modern cache servers. It has been proven that applying the LRU policy helps in maintaining a consistent cache content, as well as in improving the overall performance of many Web servers.

The idea of the LRU schemes applied to caching is that objects should be removed from the cache at the same rate they are added, since objects have to be removed when the used cache space reaches its upper capacity. Each object in the cache is associated with the time it was last used. This way, when a new object has to be fetched in the cache area, LRU chooses to replace the object that has not been used for the longest time period, i.e. objects with large LRU values are removed before objects with small LRU values.

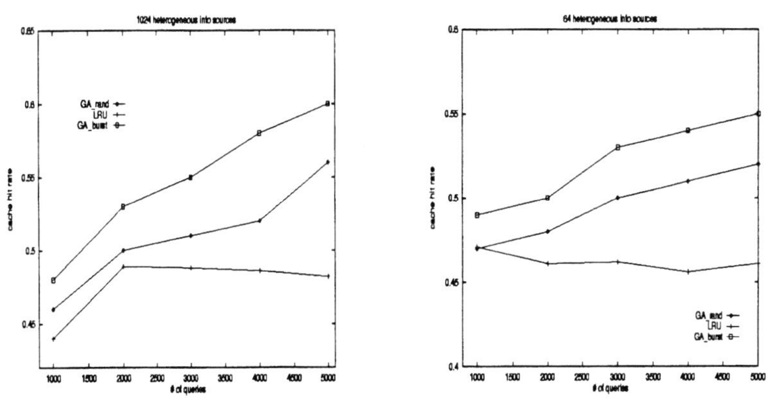


Figure 8: Cache hit rates (1024 IS and 64 IS).

### The Results

The simulator was tested and experimented under artificial query workloads defined by a varying number of information spaces and by several queries requesting distributed objects. Figure 8 depicts the results for the query processing of a cache population formed of objects among 1024 and 64 heterogeneous information sources (left and right part respectively).

The cache effectiveness is measured by the percentage of cache "hits" for a varying number of queries. More specifically, Figure 8 presents the LRU and GA caching hit rates for a cache population reproduced for 1000, 2000, ..., 5000 queries. Therefore, the simulator has been experimented under various workloads of various query sets. Crossover probability is 0.6, whereas mutation probability is 0.033, since these values have been suggested as a representative trial set for most GA optimizations. The importance of GA and LRU caching is obvious on the considered model with more information spaces (see Figure 8). It is interesting to note that the GA performs better when we have bursty request arrivals, which was expected due to the introduction of the sources priority coefficients in the GA fitness evaluation. It should be also noted that the GA outperforms the conventional LRU caching in all cases the improvement due to GA caching reaches high rates. For example, there is an almost 25% improvement due to the GA under bursty request arrivals, in the case of 1024 heterogeneous sources and 5000 queries.

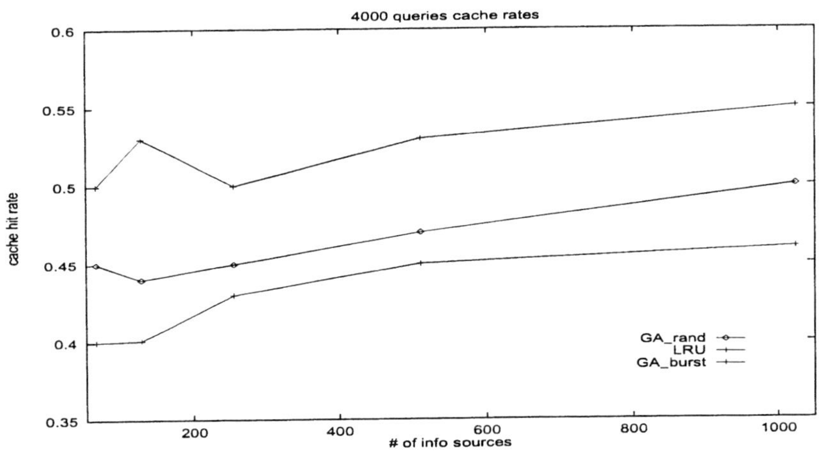


Figure 9: Cache hit rates (4000 queries).

Similarly, Figure 9 presents the LRU and GA caching hit rates for a cache population reproduced over 64, 128, ..., 1024 distinct information sources under a typical data trial set of 4000 queries. GA caching proves to be more effective as the number of heterogeneous information sources increases. This is a positive remark for the adoption of such a scheme in the integration of responding over heterogeneous sources. More specifically, both GA and LRU caching seem to be unstable for less than 200 information sources and the GA under bursty arrivals has resulted

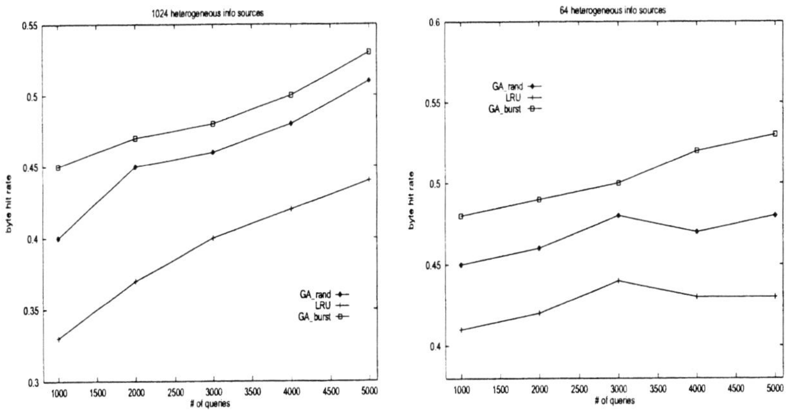


Figure 10: Byte hit rates (1024 IS and 64 IS).

in better hit rates in all cases. The benefits of GA are emphasized for an increased number of information sources since it shows an improved cache hit rate, as opposed to the slight decreasing of LRU (under the same number of information sources).

Figure 10 depicts the results for the byte hit rates by a cache of objects collected across several heterogeneous information sources. The cache effectiveness is measured by the percentage of byte hits for a varying number of queries. In this figure the LRU and GA caching hit rates are presented for a cache population reproduced for 1000, 2000, ..., 5000 queries, under 1024 and 64 information sources (left and right parts of Figure 10, respectively). It should be noted that the byte hit rates show similar curves as the cache hit rates (see Figure 8). The byte hits are not as high as the cache hits but the behavior of LRU and GA caching algorithms is similar to that when cache hits are considered. Again, in Figure 11 the LRU and GA byte hit rates are presented, for a cache population reproduced over 64, 128, ..., 1024 distinct information sources under a typical data trial set of 4000 queries. GA caching proves to be more effective as the number of heterogeneous information sources increases and still the GA under bursty arrivals is considered to be the best choice as compared to the typical LRU and the GA under random request arrivals.

Figure 12 depicts the results for the average and maximum access frequency of the cached objects under GA caching, over 1024 and 64 heterogeneous information sources (left and right parts of Figure 12, respectively). This figure refers to runs for a cache population reproduced

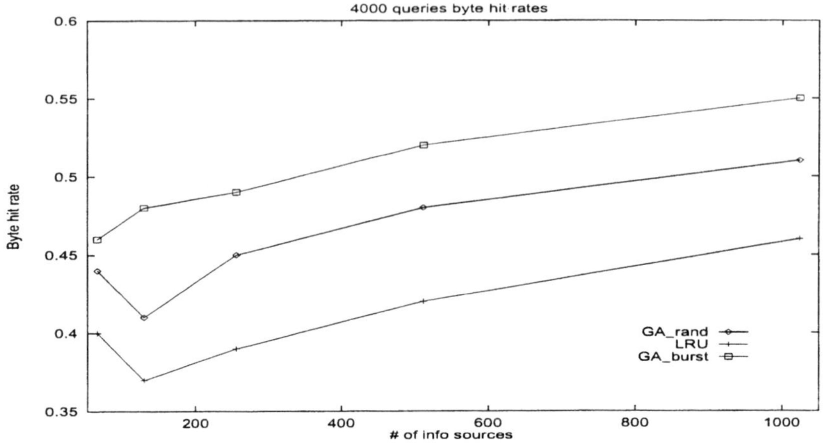


Figure 11: Byte hit rates (4000 queries).

for 1000, 2000, ..., 5000 queries under random request arrivals. Note, also, that the cache access frequency is the actual fitness measure needed for the GA process. In case of 1024 information sources (see left part of Figure 12) both average and maximum fitness have a linear-like slope, with the average access frequency being beneficial as the number of queries increases. The values of maximum and average access frequency converge when the system supports fewer information sources (see right part of Figure 12). This fact was expected since the system with more information sources has a broader collection of objects which might not be accessed as frequently as the objects within a system with fewer information sources. As depicted in this figure, the population fitness stabilizes as the number of information sources is high (e.g. 1024 ISs) and the number of queries increases.

Figure 13 presents the average and maximum GA caching fitness for a cache population reproduced over 64, 128, ..., 1024 distinct information sources under a typical data set of 4000 queries. Both average and maximum fitness values are unstable for fewer information sources. The values of these metrics seem to stabilize for more than 500 information sources which is depicted in Figure 8 as well.

Overall the GA caching scheme has shown the best cache and byte hit rates and access frequency. GA scheme has resulted in better performance metrics than the corresponding LRU caching scheme. As presented in the above figures applying caching on objects from a large number of different information sources is quite significant since almost half of the

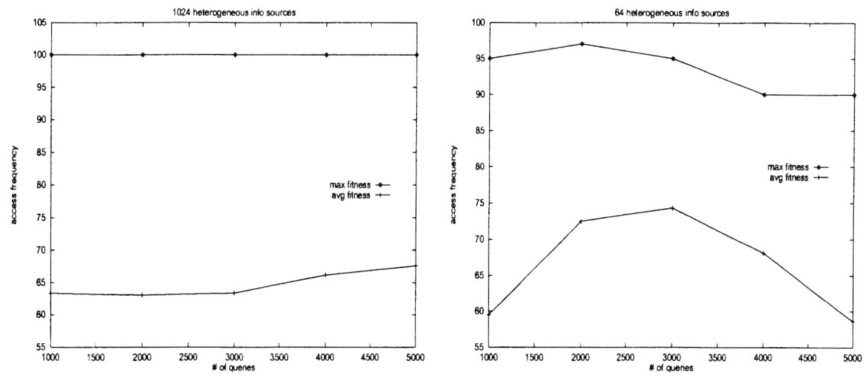


Figure 12: Cache fitness (1024 IS and 64 IS).

objects are found locally with no need to overload the client system with network search and transfer costs.

# 7 Conclusions - Further Research

Caching has been introduced towards an effective object circulation across heterogeneous information sources. The adoption of an object-based caching according to a genetic algorithm scheme, has been proposed to enhance the performance of such complex diverse systems. The proposed caching scheme, included a cache replacement policy employed at regular intervals in order to optimize the cache content. A simulation model has been experimented under both random and bursty artificial query workloads of a varying number of information sources and certain conclusions were discussed about the proposed GA scheme. The GA scheme has been proven quite beneficial in comparison to the typical LRU caching since cache population evolved over the simulation time for an increasing number of queries.

Further research should examine the above scheme in conjunction with a developed heterogeneous information source tool by mapping query results to the objects identified as in the presented work. The proposed scheme could be experimented under real traces and query types and over different fitness selection policies, which might include rates of object file types or bytes length. Other evolving computation schemes, such as simulated annealing and threshold acceptance, could be adopted in objects caching in order to study their effect on object refreshment policy

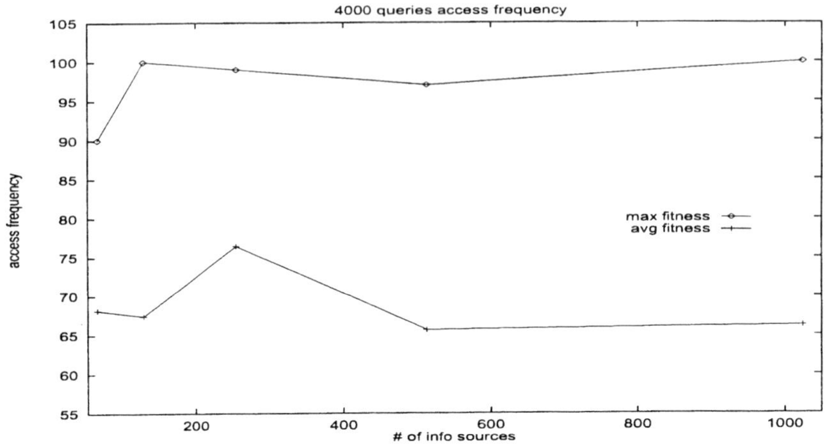


Figure 13: Cache hit rates (4000 queries).

towards a better cache content. Replication is another subject which can be applied to GA caching since the crossover operation replicates individuals between generations. The basic idea here is to keep replicated individuals over successive generations to various servers in order to test the caching and replication of heterogeneous objects.

# References


[1] S. Abiteboul, D. Quass, J. McHugh, J. Widom and J. Wiener: The Lorel Query Language for Semistructured Data, *International Journal on Digital Libraries*, Vol.1, No.1, pp.68-88, 1997.

[2] C. Aggarwal, J. Wolf and P.S. Yu: Caching on the World Wide Web, *IEEE Transactions on Knowledge and Data Engineering*, Vol.11, No.1, pp.94-107, 1999.

[3] M. Arlitt, R. Friedrich and T. Jin: Performance Evaluation of Web Proxy Cache Replacement Policies, Hewlett-Packard Technical Report HPL 98-97, to appear in *Performance Evaluation Journal*.

[4] P. Atzeni, G. Mecca and P. Merialdo: To Weave the Web, *Proceedings 23nd VLDB Conference*, pp.206-215, Athens, Greece, 1997.

[5] M. Baentsch et al.: Enhancing the Web's Infrastructure: from Caching to Replication, *IEEE Internet Computing*, Vol.1, No.2, pp.18-27, 1997.

[6] M.A. Blaze: Caching in Large-Scale Distributed File Systems, Ph.D. dissertation, Princeton University, 1993.

[7] K.C.C. Chang, H. Garcia-Molina and A. Paepcke: Boolean Query Mapping Across Heterogeneous Information Sources, *IEEE Transactions on Knowledge and Data Engineering*, Vol.8, No.4, pp.515-521, 1996.

[8] S. Chawathe, H. Garcia-Molina, J. Hammer, K. Ireland, Y. Papakonstantinou, J. Ullman and J. Widom: The Tsimmis Project - Integration of Heterogeneous Information Sources, *Proceedings 10th Anniversary Meeting of the Information Processing Society of Japan*, Tokyo, Japan, 1994.

[9] M. Fernandez, D. Florescu, J. Kang, A. Levy and D. Suciu: STRUDEL - a Web Site Management System, *Proceedings ACM SIGMOD'97 Conference*, pp.549-552, Tucson, AZ, 1997.

[10] D. Goldberg: *Genetic Algorithms in Search, Optimization, and Machine Learning*, Addison-Wesley, 1989.

[11] J. Gwertzman and M. Seltzer: World Wide Web Cache Consistency, *Proceedings USENIX 1996 Annual Technical Conference*, pp.141-151, San Diego, CA, 1996.

[12] J. Hammer, H. Garcia-Molina, J. Cho, R. Aranha and A. Crespo: Extracting Semistructured Information from the Web, *Proceedings Workshop on Management of Semistructured Data*, Tuscon, AZ, 1997.

[13] R. L. Haupt and S.E. Haupt: *Practical Genetic Algorithms*, John Wiley, 1998.

[14] D. Konopnicki and O. Shmueli: W3QS - a Query System for the World Wide Web, *Proceedings 21st VLDB Conference*, pp.54-65, Zurich, Switzerland, 1995.

[15] L.V.S. Lakshman, F. Sadri and I.N. Subramanian: A Declarative Language for Querying and restructuring the World-Wide-Web, *Proceedings IEEE RIDE Workshop*, pp.12-21, New Orleans, LO, 1996.

[16] A.Y. Levy, A. Rajaraman and J.J. Ordille: Querying Heterogeneous Information Sources using Source Descriptions, *Proceedings 22nd VLDB Conference*, pp.251-262, Bombay, India, 1996.

[17] S.J. Louis: Genetic Algorithms as a Viable Computational Tool for Design, Ph.D. dissertation, Computer Science Department, Indiana University, 1993.

[18] A. Mendelzon, G. Mihaila and T. Milo: Querying the World Wide Web, *Proceedings 4th PDIS Conference*, pp.80-91, Miami, FL, 1996.

[19] Z. Michalewicz: *Genetic Algorithms + Data Structures = Evolutionary Programs*, Springer Verlag, New York, 1992.

[20] M. Mitchell: *An Introduction to Genetic Algorithms*, The MIT Press, Cambridge, London, 1998.

[21] Y. Papakonstantinou, H. Garcia-Molina and J. Widom: Object Exchange Across Heterogeneous Information Sources, *Proceedings 11th ICDE Conference*, pp.251-260, Taipei, Taiwan, 1995.

[22] D. Povey and J. Harrison: A Distributed Internet Object Cache, *Proceedings 20th Australasian Computer Science Conference*, Sydney, Australia, 1997.

[23] T. Starkweather, D. Whitley and K. Mathias: *Optimization Using Distributed Genetic Algorithms - Parallel Problem Solving*, Springer Verlag, 1991.

[24] A. Vakali and Y. Manolopoulos: Caching Objects from Heterogeneous Information Sources, *Proceedings 9th International Database Conference (IDC'99)*, pp.377-389, Hong Kong, China, 1999.

[25] A. Vakali: A Web-based Evolutionary Model for Internet Data Caching, *Proceedings 2nd International Workshop on Network-Based Information Systems (NBIS'99)*, pp.650-654, Florence, Italy, 1999.

[26] A. Vakali: A Genetic Algorithm scheme for Web Replication and Caching, *Proceedings 3rd IMACS/IEEE International Conference on Circuits, Systems, Communications and Computers, (CSCC'99)*, Athens, Greece, 1999.

[27] M.G. Cooper and V. Vemuri: Genetic Algorithms, Chapter in *CRC Handbook on Industrial Electronics*, CRC Press, 1997.

[28] D. Wessels: Intelligent Caching World-Wide Web Objects, *Proceedings INET'95 Conference*, 1995.

*Chapter 6*

# A LANGUAGE FOR IMPLEMENTING PARALLEL AND DISTRIBUTED SYSTEMS USING ASYNCHRONOUS POINT-TO-POINT COMMUNICATION

A. S. BAVAN E. ILLINGWORTH[1]

School of Computing Science
Hendon Campus
Middlesex University
The Burroughs
London NW4 4BT
e-mail: s.bavan@mdx.ac.uk

[1]School of Computing and Mathematics
London Guildhall University
100 Minories
London EC3 1JY
UNITED KINGDOM
Illing@lgu.ac.uk

*Abstract:-* LIPS (Language for Implementing Parallel Systems) is a parallel/distributed message passing language that promotes the separation of communication from the necessary computation by using a technique based on a modified form of the calculus of communicating systems by Milner [20,21]. The approach adopted here is to define a network of dedicated communication channels for data exchange in LIPS-compliant programs, thus promoting portability between different computing platforms. This has also permitted the use of a modified

SCCS[10,19] notation to formulate a design pattern based on a framework of four system design rules to guarantee reliable point-to-point intercommunication between LIPS nodes. The results achieved using this design pattern allow the development of programs that eliminate the likelihood of deadlock conditions with the minimum of software support tools. The LIPS nodes that make up a program are reusable and allow the dynamic creation of interconnected programs for performing distributed computation using a plug and play approach to achieve an optimum network performance.

*Keywords*:- parallel, distributed, platform independence, reusability, asynchronous, point-to-point, intercommunication.

# 1 Introduction

The term *distributed processing system* has been used to describe many forms of networked hardware/software systems and is commonly associated with 'Client Server' based systems. Client Server intercommunication patterns have become more and more the focus of distributed systems design because of the lack of a reliable development environment for point-to-point intercommunication based systems. However, they restrict the development of point-to-point distributed algorithms hence falling short of delivering truly distributed computing systems. In this work a distributed computing environment is viewed as a computing system consisting of multiple autonomous processors that do not share primary memory, but co-operate by exchanging messages over a communications network [4,5,7].

The problem of creating a formal method for concurrent systems has been addressed in the work reported in Communicating Sequential Processes (CSP) [8,12,22] and in Calculus of Communicating Systems (CCS) [20,21]. Despite the considerable successes, the complexity issues in establishing reliable intercommunication patterns and the user resistance to adopting mathematical notations, validation proofs and tools based on CSP and CCS have prevented the use of these approaches in mainstream computing.

The LIPS distributed processing paradigm introduces a versatile and expressive approach for designing complex intercommunication patterns. This is because it formally stipulates the permissible operations and the states that underpin the design of a valid LIPS network definition. These design patterns set out four rules that control the design of intercommunication patterns and lead to the reliable operation of LIPS programs.

Section 2 of this paper includes a discussion on the background and the philosophy behind the distributed/parallel processing and the strengths and weaknesses of some of the currently available languages. LIPS language is described in section 3 followed by an example in section 4. Section 5 addresses the concurrency issues that underpin the LIPS design and goes on to present four design rules that form the design pattern that guarantees reliable intercommunication. Finally, the conclusion is presented in section 6.

# 2 Background and Design Philosophy

A popular approach to achieve distributed processing is to extend an existing sequential language with a set of library routines. Although this approach is easy to implement it has a number of disadvantages; one of them is that the application's programmer has to take responsibility for arranging the computational parts and communication tasks in such a way as to reduce the possibility of a deadlock. Another approach is to rely on an intelligent compiler to generate code for distributed processing from sequential source code. This significantly reduces the burden on the programmer although producing such compilers is very difficult and the results are often unsatisfactory. The other major issue that concerns distributed processing is *portability*. A good distributed language should be portable across a number of platforms with minimum software support.

Let us consider the characteristics that are deemed essential for a language to support distributed applications effectively and efficiently. A natural choice of a model is one that facilitates the running of a number of sequential processes in parallel and the exchange of data through message passing. This type of model reflects the characteristics of the basic distributed architecture and its style of communication (message passing). Examples of languages that use this type of model include CSP [12] and OCCAM [17]. CSP in its original form is a formal specification language created in the late seventies using synchronous message passing for the communication between concurrent sequential processes. Later, because of the popularity of CSP, tools were built to make it executable. One of its most famous offsprings was OCCAM that was specifically designed to run on the TRANSPUTER [14].

There have been some efforts to port OCCAM to other platforms including networks of SUNs and PCs. On the other hand, the SR language [1,2,3] includes a plethora of communication techniques such as asynchronous message passing and it supports the creation of dynamic processes. Languages like OCCAM, which use synchronous message passing, block on the sender to allow the receiver to get the message. Clearly, the synchronisation of send and receive message operations can introduce a significant overhead that restricts the overall efficiency of a parallel system [13,15].

Other well-known systems that should be considered when designing a parallel/distributed language include PVM[9] and MPI[11,13]. These two approaches add communication primitives to existing sequential languages. One of the drawbacks of MPI/PVM networks is that the performance throughput can degrade significantly even with a limited number of users. The main problem is the insufficient support for preventing the occurrence of conditions such as deadlock or livelock. The very nature of the LIPS language helps to alleviate the chances of deadlock or livelock occurring.

The MPI model allows point-to-point communication between processes as well as collective operations like broadcasting of messages.

The need for a portable language that is simple, expressive, secure, and efficient gave rise to the design and implementation of the LIPS language. With these objectives in mind and given the need to design a distributed language that will lend itself to future modifications, we have designed and implemented a language that satisfies the goals set out above. Thus, LIPS is a message passing language with data flow properties built into it to facilitate programming. LIPS uses a simple computational model which is easy to map on hardware that supports MIMD computing and it can lend itself to implementations using a shared memory model. LIPS assumes half-duplex asynchronous channels for the communications subsystem to promote efficient communication between processes. The dataflow characteristics of LIPS encourage a pipelining effect to occur across the parallel system.

# 3 LIPS: A Language for Implementing Parallel Systems

A LIPS program consists of interconnected nodes, where a node refers to an instantiation of a node definition. A LIPS program is specified in three parts:

**a)** a network definition part that describes the topology of the network of nodes
**b)** a node definition part that defines the computational steps in a node
**c)** a host definition part that defines the computation and control exercised by the host node.

The host node controls the network and facilitates user interactions by providing the necessary interfaces. A program written in LIPS has the following syntactic structure (see figure 1).

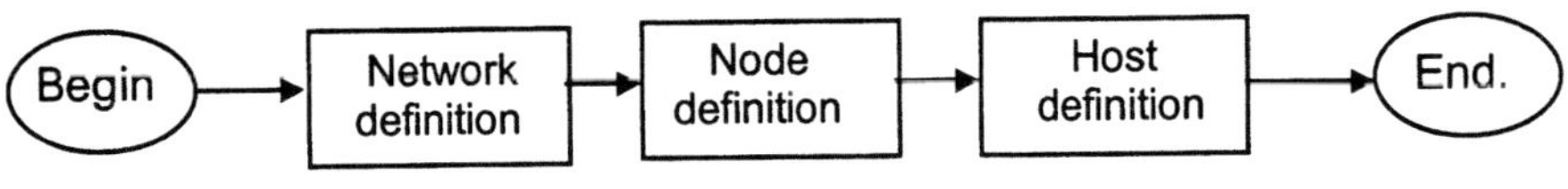


Fig.1 LIPS syntactic structure

## 3.1 Network Definition

The network definition describes the topology of the program by naming each node and its relationships (in terms of input and output data) to other nodes in the system. There are two types of link statements, namely *connect* and *rep* which are available for specifying the connectivity of a node in a program. These statement types can be described as follows:

**connect** statement - this specifies input and output (I/O) channels to a node and the name of the process to be executed in that node. It does not specify how such I/O channels may be linked to the rest of the system but only the I/O interface to a particular node. The reasons behind this will become clear in section 5 which deals with formal aspects of the language. The syntax of the connect statement is as follows:

*node_label*:**connect** *process_name*(*input channels*) **->** (*output channels*)

An example of a connect statement that links two input channels, *a* and *b,* to a node that executes a process *P* with a node label *7* and produces an output on channel *c* is as follows (see figure 2):

[7]: connect P([a, b]) -> ([c])

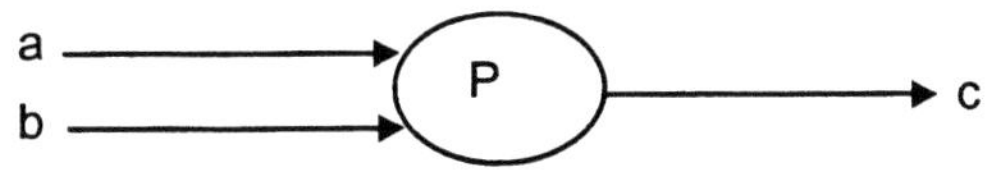


Fig.2 The *connect* process

The square brackets are used to group data belonging to a particular data type or category.

**rep** statement- This is more powerful than the connect statement and it is used to replicate a node and its connections either serially or in parallel. There are two forms of **rep** statements; the first form generates a network of a process serially as shown below.

[5]: seqrep[3] P(x[i], y[i]) -> (x[i+1], y[i+1])

The above statement is equivalent to the following three connect statements.

[5]: connect P([x[0]],[y[0]]) -> ([x[1]],[y[1]])
[6]: connect P([x[1]],[y[1]]) -> ([x[2]],[y[2]])
[7]: connect P([x[2]],[y[2]]) -> ([x[3]],[y[3]])

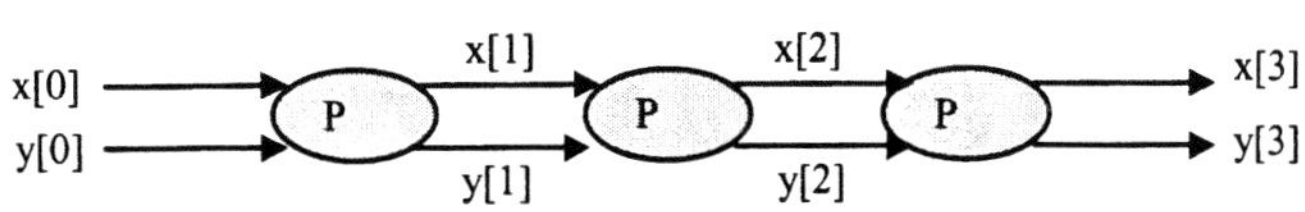


Fig.3 Sequential replication

The second form of replication allows the user to replicate a process and its connections in parallel and has the following form:

[8]: parrep[3] P([x[i], y[i]) -> (z[i])

In this case process P is replicated three times and input and output links are generated using the number of replications (3) and the index (i). The above statement is equivalent to the following three connect statements.

[8]: connect P([x[0]],[y[0]]) -> ([z[0]])
[9]: connect P([x[1]],[y[1]]) -> ([z[1]])
[10]: connect P([x[2]],[y[2]]) -> ([z[2]])

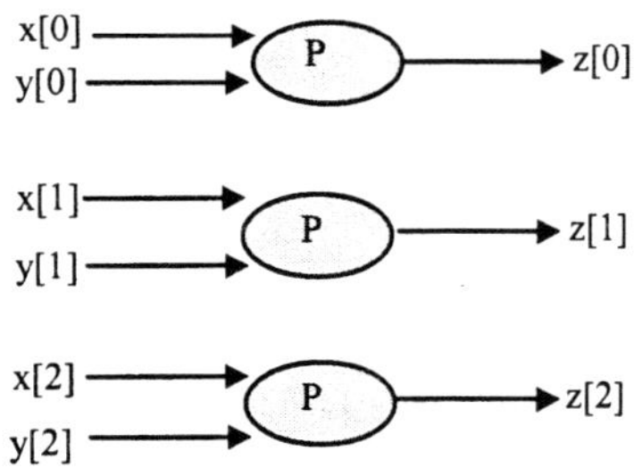


Fig.4 Parallel replication

Using the **connect** and **rep** statements one can build networks of any complexity. The link statements allow the user to fan in and fan out messages as shown in figure 5 using the connect statements below.

[1]: connect u([h]) -> ([i])
[2]: connect r([i]) -> ([j])
[3]: connect s([i]) -> ([k])
[4]: connect t([i]) -> ([l])
[5]: connect v([j,k,l]) -> ([m])

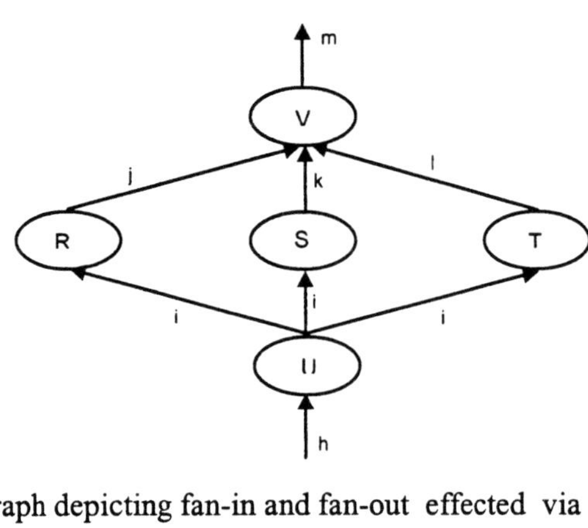


Fig.5 Data flow graph depicting fan-in and fan-out effected via *connect*

For a given problem, the link statements can be used to build a dataflow graph to represent the solution without the need for a specification of the computation at network level. This promotes good design practice by motivating the programmer to produce the target solution model at a higher level of abstraction using communication as the framework; thus divorcing computation from it. This is in line with the original design philosophy of this language. A feedback loop can be implemented with a single statement as shown below.

[6]: connect p([x],[z]) -> ([y],[z])

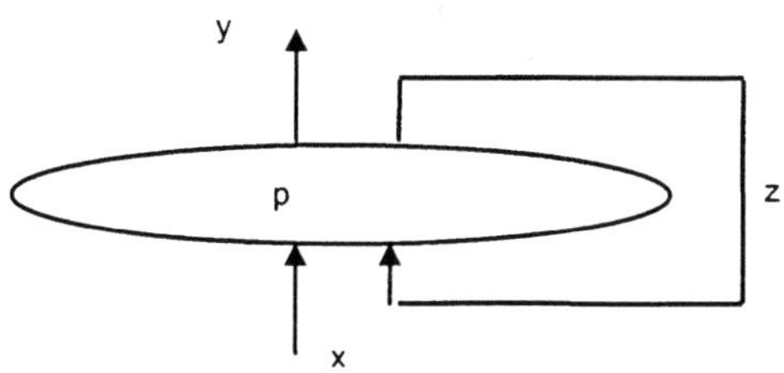


Fig.6 Feedback Loop

## 3.2 Node Definition

The definition of a node in this model is based on the notion of the *guarded process* which we shall define shortly. A node in the LIPS language consists of one or more guarded processes and is specified as a function with the following syntax.

**node** *name*(*input_vectors*) **->**(*output_vectors*)
{ *declaration;*

*guarded_process_1*
:
*guarded_process_n*
}

The elements of the I/O vectors represent a set of *virtual input/output channels* through which the data messages are sent and received by the nodes. The length of each I/O vector is determined by the information given in the associated connect statement during instantiation of a node. These virtual channels provide us with a point-to-point connection with other related processes independent of their location; they can be on the same machine or on a remote machine. The implementation details are left to the implementers to decide depending on the hardware platforms and the networking systems used. For example, if LIPS is to be implemented on a network of workstations that uses client server approach to communicate, then the data transfer between two workstations may use it at the intermediate level provided the programmer is not involved in the actual communication process.

The declaration used within a given function is local to that function. A guarded process consists of a guard and its associated body. The guard is a list of channels waiting for data to activate it (all the channels in a guard must receive new data before activation occurs). The body uses data defined in the guards and processes them according to its specification. **In the case of two or more guarded processes being eligible for execution, only one is selected**. The input channels in different guards are mutually exclusive. This reduces the ambiguity in selecting a process for execution. A typical guarded process has the following syntax.

[*input_condition*] => {*statements*}

For example, the following guarded process evaluates *y* **only** when all the input channels, *x1*, *x2*, and *x3* contain *new* and *unused* data.

[x1, x2, x3] = { y = 2*x1 + 3*x2 - x4; }

Complex input conditions can be constructed using logical ("," to represent 'and' ) operators and a *range operator* (denoted by ".."). For example, *[a,b]* implies that new data appearing on channels *'a' and 'b'* will satisfy the condition for executing the associated process. The range operator ("..") can be used to specify ranges and sub-ranges of an array of channel variables. A process is defined by using C language statements [16].

Transfer of data via channels is achieved by simple assignment of values to variables that represent virtual channels. This divorces the communication from computation and removes the burden of dealing with deadlock from the programmer. For instance, if a node which is known to be part of a network happens to be actually disconnected from it then the communication support system of the language can detect its isolated state. This assignment approach to communication eliminates the need for complex communication primitives which require source and destination data; thus causing complex communication patterns that can increase the likelihood of deadlock conditions.

### 3.3 Host Definition

The host specification part consists of a control process which acts as a master that controls the network of nodes and an interface between the user and the network of nodes. Again, this process is described by C language statements as in the case of guarded processes mentioned above.

A host process has the same syntax as the *main( )* function in C language statements and has the following structure:

**host()** { declarations; statement_list; }

The *statement_list* includes some special statements for loading, running and controlling the network. These include:

- stopping and starting the network;
- saving and re-loading an incomplete network.

# 4 An Example

In this section we present an example program written in LIPS that calculates the area under the curve $4/(1+X^2)$ ($\pi$) using Simpson's rule within an interval of [0-1]. The network consists of two types of nodes, ***area*** which calculates the area of a slice using its width(*ww*) and its height calculated using the segment number(*k[]*) and ***sum*** which adds all the areas of the segments(10) to produce the total area. The topology of the system is as shown in figure 7.

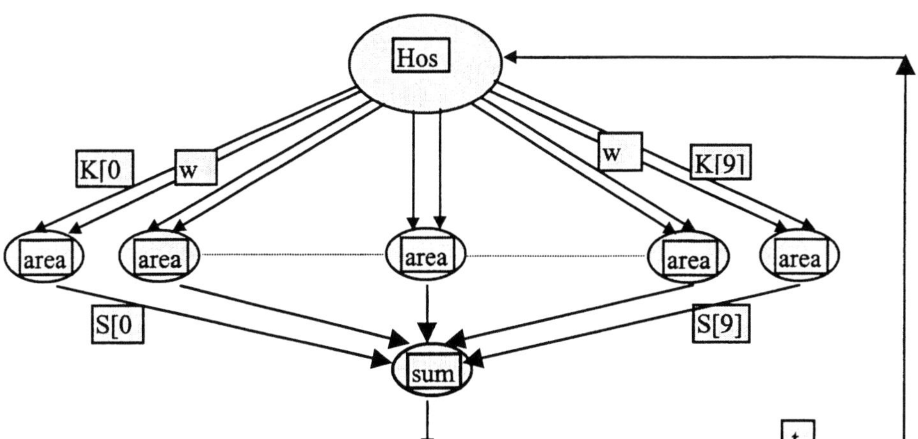


Fig.7 Topology of the system

```
program simpson;
begin
/* This program calculates pi using simpson rule */
[2]: connect area([k[0]], [ww]) -> ([s[0]])
[3]: connect area([k[1]], [ww]) -> ([s[1]])
[4]: connect area([k[2]], [ww]) -> ([s[2]])
```

```
[5]: connect area([k[3]], [ww]) -> ([s[3]])
[6]: connect area([k[4]], [ww]) -> ([s[4]])
[7]: connect area([k[5]], [ww]) -> ([s[5]])
[8]: connect area([k[6]], [ww]) -> ([s[6]])
[9]: connect area([k[7]], [ww]) -> ([s[7]])
[10]: connect area([k[8]], [ww]) -> ([s[8]])
[11]: connect area([k[9]], [ww]) -> ([s[9]])
[12]: connect sum([s[0..9]]) -> ([t])
/* node area calculates the area of each slice under the
curve 4/(1+x*x)
      and sends the result to sum node  */
node area(int kk, float w) -> (float s)
{ float x, y, garea;
     [kk, w] => {     x = w * (2.0 * kk + 1.0)/2.0;
                    y = 4.0 / (1.0 + (x * x));  garea = w *
y;
                    s = garea;          /* outputs to channel
s */
                  }
}
/* sum node sums all the input channel value and sends it
to the host */
node sum(float sarea[n]) -> (float tarea)
{  int i; float s;
   [sarea[0..n]] => {   s = 0.0;
                           for(i=0; i<10; ++i) s = s +
sarea[i];
                        tarea = s;
                     }
}
host()
{   int i,x[10];
    float pi, width;

    width = 1.0 / 10.0;        /*calculate width size */
    for(i=0; i<10; ++i)
    {
     x[i]=i;             /* load the input channels of the
nodes 0-9*/
     k[i] = x[i];/*put interval num. on chanels k[i]*/
    }
    ww = width; /*put width on chanel ww */
    runnet;          /* trigger the net */
    pi = t;       /* get the output from channel t*/
    printf("\nEstimate of PI[0-1]=%f",pi);
```

```
    stop;
}
end.
```

# 5 Issues of Concurrency

Formal Methods can be used to derive various properties about a particular design. These include detecting and avoiding deadlock and livelock. The Synchronous Calculus of Communicating Systems (SCCS) [19] is an example of such a formal method but it requires software tools such as the Concurrency Work Bench (CWB) [6] to deal with even small models. Unfortunately, the CWB cannot cope with large scale models due to the large increase in state space [18].

Utilising the major LIPS feature i.e. the separation of communication primitives from computational code, four formal design rules are proposed that should reduce/eliminate deadlock when applied to the SCCS design process. CCS can be used to model the change of states (Agents) by the invocation of events (Actions). In this paper SCCS style of notation is used [10]. Consider the traditional concurrency problem, Producer-Consumer, which might be expressed as

PRODUCER = 1 : PRO_BDY //where PRODUCER is an agent representing the process definition. The '1' is an idle operator. The ':' represents a sequential 'AND' //

PRO_BDY = ∂y! : PRODUCER //PRO_BDY is a body of code whose execution is conditional upon the arrival of data on all the channels preceding, ∂y! is an output channel port determined by the '!' operator. All the output tasks proceed after the termination of the body. //

CONSUMER = ∂y? : CON_BDY
CON_BDY = 1 : CONSUMER

This can be analysed as

SYSTEM = PRODUCER x CONSUMER //SYSTEM consists of two concurrent processes, PRODUCER and CONSUMER , where 'x' represents a concurrency operator//

= 1 : PRO_BDY x ∂y? : CON_BDY //'?' represents an input operator. The processes body awaits the arrival of data before it starts executing. //

= 1 : PRO_BDY x ( 1: ∂y? + y?) : CON_BDY
= 1 : (∂y! : PRODUCER x ∂y? : CON_BDY )
= 1 : ( ( 1: ∂y! + y! ) : PRODUCER x ( 1: ∂y? + y? ) : CON_BDY )

= 1: 1y : ( 1 : PRO_BDY x 1 : CONSUMER )

In this example the PRODUCER generates data that are passed to the CONSUMER for disposal. Two issues are raised by this PRODUCER/CONSUMER example and need further explanation. The first issue is that SCCS uses a synchronous approach to message passing operations. Namely, the send and receive pairs have to synchronise when they exchange a message. This version of the PRODUCER/CONSUMER problem effectively transfers the data in lockstep because of the synchronous message passing intercommunication. The second issue is a synchronous notation used to create an asynchronous model. The idler ( 1 ) is introducing delays into the system so that the send/receive pairs can synchronise.

One delay ($\partial$) proposition is defined as follows

$\partial E = 1 : \partial E + E$

This leads to the first design rule.

**Rule 1**

*Every Process agent in a concurrent system operates in an iterative fashion and obeys the LIPS – SCCS – TEMPLATE.*

Rule 1 effectively states that a concurrent system is made up of autonomous processes that inter communicate using message passing. The following template should clarify rule 1.

**The LIPS – SCCS - TEMPLATE**

Process_agent_1 = input_ch1[ [ . | : | +] input_chx ] : Process_agent_1_Bdy_1 +

[ input_chx [ [ . | : | +]input_chy] : Process_agent_1_Bdy_z]

Process_agent_1_Bdy_1 = output_ch1 [ [ . | : | + ]output_chx ] : [ @ | Process_agent_1 ]

[Process_agent_1_Bdy_z = output_chx [[ . | : | + ]output_chy] : [ @ | Process_agent_1]}

. = &
: = seq &
| = 'or' within the context of the definition
+ = 'or' SCCS operator
[..] = optional

The LIPS-SCCS-TEMPLATE will be explained using an example. Process_agent_1 is the template's representation of a software process in a LIPS node. The input ch represents one instance of the many possible input channels within a software node. A body of code transforms input data into output data. The output data is then sent to other nodes in the system via output channels. In the LIPS language terminology a body of code is guarded by input channels implying that data must arrive at every channel in the guard before the body of code executes.

Consider the following example:

A = x? . y? : A_BDY_1 + a? : b? : A_BDY_2 + (m? + n?) : A_BDY_3
A_BDY_1 = v! . w! : A
A_BDY_2 = c! : d! : A
A_BDY_3 = (o! + p!) : A

x? , y? ,a? ,b?, m? and n? are the input channels of process agent A
v! , w!, c!, d!, o! and p! are the output channels of process agent A

x? and y? must synchronise simultaneously with x! and y! (not shown) because they are separated by the '.' operator. a? and b? must synchronise sequentially with a! and b! (not shown) because they are separated by the ':' operator. Either m? or n? must synchronise with m! or n! (not shown) because they are separated by the '+' operator. Once all the input channels guarding a body of code have synchronised (i.e. received data) then the body of code executes. Each of the input channels of a specific guard can be separated by SIMULTANEOUS AND '.', SEQUENTIAL AND ':' or the OR '+' operators. The output channels can also be combined using the same operators. The idler operator can replace either input or output channels implying that internal processing is occurring at this point. One can think of the idler operator as a boolean TRUE event. According to the SCCS terminology the agent's A_BDY_1 , A_BDY_2 and A_BDY_3 represent three different bodies of code within Node A. Consider the following scenario:

Node A is ready to receive data.
The x and y channels of Node A synchronise simultaneously.
The body of code A_BDY_1 transforms the input data into output data.
This output data is transferred to other nodes in the system via the v and w channels.
Node A is ready to receive data again.

Node A is ready to receive data.
The m channel of Node A synchronises.
The body of code A_BDY_3 transforms the input data into output data.
The output data are transferred to other nodes in the system via the p channel.
Node A is ready to receive data again.

Any process defined using LIPS-SCCS notation may be terminated by the inaction agent (@). This is illustrated by the following example.

B = s? : B_BDY_1
B_BDY_1 = 1 : @

In this example when data arrives via the s input channel the body of code B_BDY_1 processes it and then the node B terminates. A system consists of several interacting process agents.

**Rule 2**

*A channel must only have one input port and one output port.*

Design rule 2 specifies a point to point communication. This naturally effects fan-in and fan-out that have to be expressed explicitly.

**Fan-in**

Consider the following example.

A = ∂y1? . ∂y2? : A_BDY_1
A_BDY_1 = 1 : A
B = 1 : B_BDY_1
B_BDY_1 = ∂y1! : B

C = 1 : C_BDY_1
C_BDY_1 = ∂y2! : C

Which can be analysed as

SYSTEM = A x B x C
= ∂y1? . ∂y2?: A_BDY_1 x 1 : B_BDY_1 x 1 : C_BDY_1
= (1: ∂∂y1? + y1?).(1: ∂y2? + y2?): A_BDY_1 x 1: B_BDY_1 x 1 : C_BDY_1
= 1: (∂y1? . ∂y2? : A_BDY_1 x ∂y1! : B x ∂y2! : C)
= 1 : ( (1: ∂y1? + y1?).(1: ∂y2? + y2?) : A_BDY_1 x (1: ∂y1! + y1!):B x (1: ∂y2! + y2!) : C )
= 1 : 1y1 . 1y2: ( 1: A x 1: B_BDY_1 x 1: C_BDY_1)

Note that true concurrency is in operation in the above example. The channels y1 and y2 are synchronising simultaneously and not sequentially.

**Fan-out**

Consider the example below

A = 1 : A_BDY
A_BDY = ∂y1! . ∂y2! : A

B = ∂y1?: B_BDY
B_BDY = 1 : B

C = ∂y2? : C_BDY
C_BDY = 1 : C

Which can be analysed as

SYSTEM = A x B x C

$$= 1 : A\_BDY \times \partial y1?: B\_BDY \times \partial y2? : C\_BDY$$
$$= 1 : A\_BDY \times ( 1: \partial y1? + y1?) : B\_BDY \times ( 1: \partial y2? + y2?) : C\_BDY$$
$$= 1 (\partial y1! . \partial y2! : A \times \partial y1? : B\_BDY \times \partial y2? : C\_BDY)$$
$$= 1 ( ( 1 : \partial y1! + y1!) . ( 1: \partial y2! + y2! ) : A \times (1: \partial y1? + y1?) : B\_BDY \times (1: \partial y2? + y2? ) : C\_BDY)$$
$$= 1 : 1y1 . 1y2 : ( 1 : A\_BDY \times 1 : B \times 1 : C)$$

Again, true concurrency is in operation in the above example. The examples on Fan-in and Fan-out raise an important issue about the use of SCCS to model asynchronous behaviour. When two channels are grouped together should they synchronise simultaneously or sequentially? This is really a design issue and it is up to the designer. However, it should be noted that even if each of the above examples were coded to synchronise in sequence the fan-in and fan-out examples would still work (i.e. they would not deadlock). The delay operator $\partial$ would effectively introduce delays into the system to allow channel synchronisation.

Rule 2 also affects the choice of input channel names. If the same name is used more than once within a process definition then mutual exclusion does not apply resulting in an operational/implementation paradox.

The following example

$$A = \partial y? : A\_BDY\_1 + \partial y? : A\_BDY\_2$$

is invalid in our modified use of SCCS notation.

**Rule 3**

*A channel input/output port pair may not be used within the same process.*

This is because the output port may be prevented from synchronising with the input port on account of the process being made up of sequential code e.g.

$$A = y? : A\_BDY\_1$$
$$A\_BDY\_1 = y! : A$$

In this case, deadlock will take place. It does not matter which side of the channel waits forever.

**Rule 4**

*A self-contained system must include at least one idler operator in an input channel position.*

A self-contained system is one with no channels crossing the application domain. The implication would be that a non self-contained system would have one or more channels with just one port. All of the examples in this paper are self contained systems. The examples of LIPS – SCCS – TEMPLATE design show how difficult it is to prove that they will not deadlock. Even using software tools such as CWB does not solve the problem because the CWB can not process large-scale examples.

**Validating LIPS-SCCS-TEMPLATE based designs using Set Theory**

In this work, it has been shown that deadlock can be detected with a LIPS-SCCS-TEMPLATE model using set theory. Currently, the process is being automated so that a system design based on LIPS-SCCS-TEMPLATE and the four design rules can be verified for presence or absence of deadlock. In the meantime, it can be demonstrated empirically by a set theoretic validation approach. The assumptions made in the proof are as follows:

If no data is passed across system boundaries then it is a self-contained system.
An idler operator will have to start the system. The idler will trigger the execution of a body of code which will result in data being passed by output channels into the system.
Since channels can only occur in input/output port pairs the data will flow around the system providing every input port has a corresponding output port and vice versa.

Consider the dining philosophers' problem. There are typically 5 philosophers seated around a table with one fork separating each philosopher from the other. In order to eat, each philosopher needs to be simultaneously in possession of both forks beside him. This means that only some of the philosophers can eat at the same time. Let us suppose that each philosopher picks up the fork on his left at the same time as his companions and refuses to put it down before he can pick up the fork on his right side as well. Clearly, deadlock will occur and all the philosophers will starve. The decentralised version of the dining philosophers' problem requires one waiter assigned to each fork. The waiters have to communicate with each other in order to reach a consensus to grant possession of two forks to a philosopher thus allowing him to eat. The centralised solution requires each philosopher to seek permission to pick up both forks at the same time from an omnipotent authority called the FORKSERVER. The FORKSERVER records the state of all the forks on the table and grants permission for a philosopher to eat when possible. Following is the specification of the centralised solution.

```
//Only one out of five philosophers is modelled by P1 for brevity.
//Note that a philosopher cannot make a request to eat until its ∂start?
//synchronises with the host ∂start! The response to a
//request to eat using req_forks! will either be req_granted? or
req_not_granted?.
//The actions ∂Lock1a and ∂Lock1b prevent race conditions occurring
//within a philosopher

P1 = (∂start1? + ∂Lock1a? + ∂∂Lock1b?): P1_BDY_1 +
                    ∂req_granted1and2? : P1_EAT_BDY_2 +
                    ∂req_not_granted1and2? : P1_BDY_3
P1_BDY_1 = ∂req_forks1and2!: P1
```

```
P1_EAT_BDY2 = ∂rel_forks1and2!. ∂Lock1aa! : P1
P1_BDY_3 = ∂Lock1bb! : P1

//The fork server allocates forks to philosophers by either granting a request or not
//granting a request. Note that the fork server will always respond to a request for
//forks. Note that when this design is coded various global variables like fork-free
//flags will only be changed within the atomic code FS_BDY_x. It is
//important to realise that each body of code in the LIPS paradigm is atomic

FS = ∂req_forks1and2? : FS_BDY_1 + ∂rel_forks1and2? : FS_BDY_6
FS_BDY_1 = (∂ req_granted1and2! + ∂req_not_granted1and2! ) : FS
FS_BDY_6 = 1: FS
//A Lock Server provides a buffer interface. See Rule 3.
LS = ∂Lock1aa? : LS_BDY_1 + ∂Lock1bb? : LS_BDY_2
LS_BDY_1 = ∂Lock1a! : LS
LS_BDY_2 = ∂Lock1b! : LS
//the host starts the model

HOST = 1 : HOST_BDY
HOST_BDY = ∂start1! : @
```

Note that @ is an inaction agent i.e. nothing happens after @

In order to verify that this example will not deadlock using simple set theory one must collect all the input channels for each process into a set and do likewise with all the output channels. These input and output sets should be pre-processed to find idler actions ( '1' ). If any process is found to contain an idler action, then that part of the model should be checked for algorithmic error. Note that a self-contained system (one that does not have any channels crossing its boundaries i.e. no channels with only one port) must have at least one idler action. If all the idler actions are now removed, all the input channel sets are combined to form a system.inch set and all the output channel sets are combined to form a system.outch set, then the system can be validated for presence or absence of deadlock.

If SYSTEM.inch \ SYSTEM.outch ∪ SYSTEM.outch \ SYSTEM.inch = 0 then every channel consists of one input port and one output port pairing and the system is unlikely to deadlock and is self contained.

**Proving the Set Theoretic verification technique**

If a system obeys the four LIPS-SCCS design rules and follows the LIPS-SCCS-TEMPLATE style for the design of distributed systems then it should not deadlock. This section will attempt to prove this.

An example of a distributed system that uses the LIPS-SCCS paradigm will have an input set (I) containing all the input channels and an output set (O) containing all the output channels. There will also be a separate input set for every node in the system, SYS_IN(j), and a separate output set for every node in the system, SYS_OUT(j) for every node j in the system. Consider the following statement:

Data must flow through a LIPS-SCCS based design if it is to function correctly. In order for this to happen channels in every input set (SYS_IN(j)) have a matching channel in the output set (O) and every channel in the corresponding output set (SYS_OUT(j)) has a matching channel in the input set (I).

This can be represented as:

$\forall j$ { $x \in$ SYS_IN(j) $y \in$ SYS_OUT(j) | $((x \in O) \wedge (y \in I)) \vee ((x \notin O) \vee (y \notin I))$

The logic above links the data arriving into a node and its transformation into output data. The input channels (x) of each input set (SYS_IN(j)) are linked with the output channels (y) of each matching output set (SYS_OUT(j)). The contents of SYS_IN(j) = I(j) and the contents of SYS_OUT(j) = O(j) for all j.

The union of all I(j) is equal to the union of all O(j). This means that there exists a one-to-one and onto relationship between I and O.

Therefore x=y and thus

$$(((x \in I) \wedge (x \in O)) \wedge ((x \in O) \wedge (x \in I))) \vee (((x \in I) \wedge (x \notin O)) \vee ((x \in O) \wedge (x \notin I)))$$

let P(x) represent $x \in I$ and Q(x) represent $x \in O$

and

$$((P(x) \wedge Q(x)) \wedge ((Q(x) \wedge P(x)) \vee ((P(x) \wedge \neg Q(x)) \vee ((Q(x) \wedge \neg P(x))$$

using the Commutative law $A \wedge B = B \wedge A$, gives

$$((P(x) \wedge Q(x)) \vee (((P(x) \wedge \neg Q(x)) \vee ((Q(x) \wedge \neg P(x))) \quad (1)$$

This translates to

$$(I \cap O) \vee ((I \setminus O) \cup (O \setminus I))$$

where $(I \cap O)$ and $((I \setminus O) \cup (O \setminus I))$ are mutually exclusive i.e. the system is either SELF CONTAINED (where every input channel has a matching output channel) or is CLUSTER BASED( where unmatched input channels or output channels exist). This is because a cluster based system will have channels crossing the system boundaries.

Using sentential logic we are able to prove that $(P(x) \wedge Q(x))$ and $((P(x) \wedge \neg Q(x)) \vee (Q(x) \wedge \neg P(x)))$ from (1) are mutually exclusive. That is, if X represents the first expression and Y represents the second then we should have the following situations:

Given $X \vee Y$ and if X is true then $\neg Y$
and given $X \vee Y$ and if Y is true then $\neg X$
it can be proved using truth tables

Table 1

| | | | **Premises** | **Conclusion** |
|---|---|---|---|---|
| **P** | **Q** | **$(P \wedge Q)$** | **$(P \wedge Q) \vee ((P \wedge \neg Q) \vee (Q \wedge \neg P))$** | **$\neg ((P \wedge \neg Q) \vee (Q \wedge \neg P))$** |
| F | F | F | F | T |
| F | T | F | T | F |
| T | F | F | T | F |
| T | T | T | T | T |

Note that the only row where the premises are both true is row 4 and that the conclusion is also true in row 4.

Table 2

| | | | **Premises** | **Conclusion** |
|---|---|---|---|---|
| **P** | **Q** | **$((P \wedge \neg Q) \vee (Q \wedge \neg P))$** | **$(P \wedge Q) \vee ((P \wedge \neg Q) \vee (Q \wedge \neg P))$** | **$\neg (P \wedge Q)$** |
| F | F | F | F | T |
| F | T | T | T | T |
| T | F | T | T | T |
| T | T | F | T | F |

In the above case the premises are both true in row 2 and 3 and the conclusions are also true in both cases. Therefore $(P \wedge Q)$ AND $((P \wedge \neg Q) \vee (Q \wedge \neg P))$ are mutually exclusive and the resulting system is either self contained or cluster based.

# 6 Conclusion

This paper attempted to describe the formalisms supporting LIPS, a language for implementing parallel systems with examples to illustrate the features of a LIPS-compliant environment for successful *point-to-point* inter-communication in distributed systems. An outline of the four key elements of a design patterns framework for LIPS-compliant programming has been proposed. The four rules of the LIPS-SCCS-TEMPLATE method support successful concurrent system design. In order to develop reliable distributed applications, we envisage a LIPS-SCCS-TEMPLATE based CASE TOOL.

This work makes a clear distinction between distributed systems and client server based systems. Client/server based systems use send/receive intercommunication patterns and they respond to requests for system services. However, in the case of truly distributed software communication directly contributes to computation by feeding-in the data required. That is, communication takes place as a result of computation and computational needs rather than to provide systems services. The server-centric architecture is particularly suited to application domains whose dominant requirement is system services; such as I/O services. On the other hand, processing that involves mathematical and engineering types of problems relies mainly on communication for sending and receiving relatively small quantities of data. Client server systems can be differentiated from truly distributed processing systems by the programming requirements of the latter where the communication patterns are *point-to-point*. If one were to attempt anything more adventurous than simple 'client server' communication patterns using traditional point-to-point systems then this would most likely lead to deadlock conditions.

## References

[1] Andrews, G. R. and Olssen R A., Evolution of the SR Language, *Journal of Distributed Computing,* Vol.1, No.3, 1986, pp. 133-149.

[2] Andrews, G. R., Olssen, R. A., Coffin, M., Elshoff, I., Neilsen, K., Purdin, T. and Townsend, G., An overview of the SR Language and Implementation, *ACM Transactions on Parallel Languages & Systems*, Vol.10, No.1, 1988, pp.51-86.

[3] Andrews, G. R., and Olssen, R. A., *The SR Programming Language; Concurrency in Practice*, Benjamin-Cummings, 1993

[4] Bal, H. E., and Kaashoek, M. F., ORCA: A Language for Parallel Programming of Distributed Systems, *IEEE Transactions on Software Engineering*, Vol.18, No.3, 1992, pp.190-205.

[5] Bavan, A. S., Flora, G. S., and Mianger, Y., An Integrated Environment for Coding and Testing Parallel Software, *EuroSTAR '93*, London, October 25-28, 1993.

[6] Cleaveland. R., Parow. J. and Stefin B., The Concurrency WorkBench: A Semantics Based Verification Tool for the Verification of Concurrent Systems, *Proc. Workshop on Automated Verification Methods for finite state systems,* Lecture Notes in Computer Science 407, Springer-Verlag, 1989

[7] Dijkstra, E. W., Cooperating Sequential Processes, *Programming Languages*, Edited by F. Genuys, pp.43-112, Academic Press, New York, 1968

[8] Fencott, C., *Formal Methods for Concurrency*, Thompson, 1996

[9] Geist, A., Beguelin, A., Dongarra, J., Jiang, W., Manchek, R., and Sunderam, V., *PVM Parallel Virtual Machine - A User's Guide and Tutorial for Networked Parallel Computing*, MIT Press, 1994

[10] Gray, D., *Introduction to the Formal Design of Real-Time Systems,* Springer Verlag, 1999
[11] Gropp, W., Lusk, E., and Skjellum, A., *Using MPI Portable Parallel Programming with Message Passing Interface*, Pub MIT Press, 1994
[12] Hoare, C. A. R., *Communicating Sequential Processes,* Prentice-Hall, 1985
[13] http://www-unix.mcs.anl.gov/mpi, 1999
[14] *Transputer Data Book*, INMOS Ltd, 3rd Edition, 1992
[15] Illingworth, E., Bavan, A. S., and Flora, G. S., An asynchronous harness for a network of Transputers, *NTUG'95 - Nordic Transputer Conference, Parallel Computing and Transputers*, Sweden, 1995
[16] Kernighan, B. W. and Ritchie, D. M., *The C Programming Language*, Prentice HalL, 1988
[17] Kerridge, J., *OCCAM programming: A Practical Approach*, Blackwell Scientific Publication, 1987
[18] Lichtenecker, R., Gotthardt. K., Zalewski. J., Automated Verification of Communication Protocols using CCS and BDD's, *Parallel and Distributed Processing*, Lecture Notes in Computer Science, 1998
[19] Milner, R., Calculi for Synchrony and Asynchrony, *Theoretic. Comp. Sci.* Vol.25, 1983, pp.267-310.
[20] Milner, R., *Communication and Concurrency*, Prentice Hall, 1989
[21] Milner, R., Calculus of Communicating Systems, *Proceedings of the LNCS*, Springer Verlag, 1992
[22] Roscoe, A. W., *Theory and Practice of Concurrency* , Prentice Hall, 1998.

*Chapter 7*

# FAULT TOLERANT SUPERCOMPUTING: A SOFTWARE APPROACH

E. VERENTZIOTIS[1], T. VARVARIGOU[1], D. VERGADOS[1], G. DECONINCK[2]

[1]Dept. of Elect. & Comp. Eng.
National Technical University of Athens
Iroon Politechniou 9, 15733 Zographou,
GREECE
*{verentz,dora,vergados}@telecom.ntua.gr* *http://www.telecom.ntua.gr*

[2]Dept. Elektrotechniek (ESAT)
K.U.Leuven
Kard. Mercierlaan 94, 3001 Heverlee
BELGIUM
*Geert.Deconinck@esat.kuleuven.ac.be* *http://www.esat.kuleuven.ac.be/acca/*

*Abstract:* Adding fault tolerance to embedded supercomputing applications is becoming an issue of great significance, especially as these applications support critical parts of our everyday life in the modern "Information Society". To this end, a software middleware framework is presented that features a collection of flexible and reusable fault tolerance modules acting at different levels and coping with common fault tolerance requirements. The burden of ad hoc fault tolerance programming is removed from the application developer, while at the same time average fault tolerance support taken at operating system level is avoided. A high-level description helps the developer specify the fault tolerance strategies of the application as a sort of second application layer; this separates functional from fault tolerance aspects of an application, shortening the development cycle and improving maintainability. Integration of this functionality in real embedded applications validates this approach.

*Key-Words:* Software fault tolerance, high performance computing, embedded parallel and distributed systems, fault-tolerant communication, user-specified recovery strategies, maintainability, separation of design concerns.

# 1 Introduction

As we move into the "Information Age", embedded supercomputing becomes indispensable, since it is an enabling technology for many complex and, often, critical applications (like signal processing, pattern recognition etc). In such applications, however, system failures are associated with high costs, or even human and environmental safety risks. The consequent demand for more dependable systems brings *fault tolerance* into play and makes it a key issue in the design of a system. Fault tolerance attributes have traditionally been incorporated at two different system levels:

- At the hardware/operating system (OS) level (hardware redundancy, OS-level error detection mechanisms etc.). In this approach fault tolerance is transparent to the application and fault tolerance mechanisms are maintained and upgraded by the platform providers. However, a very general solution cannot respond to special application requirements.
- At the application level. In this approach fault tolerance solutions are tailored to the needs of the application, resulting in better performance and better predictability. This approach, however, increases the code size and complexity (which often leads to additional faults, or software bugs), increases the development costs and makes the code difficult to maintain, document and upgrade. Furthermore, the fault tolerance components are not reusable; the wheel is often reinvented for each application.

Industrial embedded applications (like, for instance, mail-sorters [1] and controllers of high-voltage substations [2]) clearly illustrate the lack of a standard approach towards fault tolerance and thc inappropriateness of non-reusable ad hoc solutions. In this paper an alternative approach is presented, the EFTOS[1] approach, that provides efficient, reusable and cost-effective solutions to fault tolerance. It is a middleware layer positioned between the two above-mentioned levels, so that the advantages of both can be combined.

The EFTOS approach consists of a framework of software fault tolerance solutions, organized into different layers, that can be integrated according to the needs of an application [3]. This framework is implemented as middleware (i.e., as a layer between the application and the target platform). Hence, application developers can choose from a variety of fault tolerance tools the most appropriate ones and combine them to obtain the level of dependability required for their system. This integrated

[1] EFTOS is the acronym of the European ESPRIT project 21012, Embedded Fault-Tolerant Supercomputing.

approach, as well as the possibility to express recovery strategies through a specific high-level language, are the key-points of the EFTOS framework approach.

In the recent years, several research initiatives have investigated fault tolerance in a distributed environment. *Delta-4* [4, 5] proposes an open, fault-tolerant, distributed system architecture, based on multiplication of modules, which relies on fail-silent hardware and on an atomic multicast protocol. *MARS* (Maintainable Real-Time System) [6] is a predictably dependable computing system, consisting of a number of processors that are interconnected via a proprietary bus and using active replication. Several hardware fault tolerance measures have also been adopted to meet hard real-time constraints. *FTMPS* (Fault Tolerance in off-the-shelf Massively Parallel Systems) [7] provides long-running number crunching applications with fault tolerance measures. Its solutions are purely software solutions, mainly based on checkpointing and reconfiguration or remapping techniques. Another approach comes with meta-level architectures for the development of adaptively dependable systems [8]. In addition, other research (e.g., [9, 10, 11]) shows the suitability and advantages of software-based fault tolerance solutions to improve the dependability of distributed applications. In most of these cases, however, very specific custom hardware architectures or complex software layers are required to fulfil the proposed goals. Also, several systems encompass only some specific aspects of fault tolerance, for example, error detection, without explicitly dealing with certain equally important others, like error recovery. This choice is certainly good for their goals, though it means that these solutions have limited portability.

The remaining of this paper is structured as follows. Section 2 gives an overview of the different elements that constitute the EFTOS framework. Section 3 focuses on the configurability of the framework. Section 4 discusses the imposed overhead and the dependability improvement of an application that uses EFTOS framework. Finally, the main points of the paper are summarized in section 5. It should be emphasized that this paper is not meant to present a complete analysis of the EFTOS middleware package. It rather presents qualitatively the functionality of the framework, referring the reader to other cited sources for a more formal and complete analysis.

# 2 Overview of the EFTOS framework

## 2.1 Framework Architecture

With extendibility and maintainability in mind, the EFTOS framework is built as a distributed and reusable fault tolerance framework that can be flexibly and easily integrated into the target applications, according to a layered software architecture where the framework is a mid-layer between the application and the target platform. For portability issues the framework is built as a core block with a well-defined interface and some adaptation layers. This architecture is depicted in Fig. 1.

The layered architecture is maintained throughout the framework core, as well. We distinguish five layers in the framework:

- The **adaptation layer** (base layer) to the underlying OS that supports additional services to upper layers (e.g., remote thread creation, recollection of information messages). Clearly, its configuration depends on the services provided by the OS.
- The **detection/isolation/recovery layer** that gathers all basic fault tolerance tools for error detection, isolation and recovery. These tools do not interact and can be either coordinated by the upper layer (the DIR net), or tied straightforward to the application. These tools are discussed in section 2.2.
- The **control layer** that hosts the Detection-Isolation-Recovery network (or DIR net, in short). The DIR net is the backbone of the EFTOS framework that coordinates all the fault tolerance actions among the involved nodes and applies consistent recovery strategies. Its structure and functionality are discussed in section 2.3.
- The **application layer** that combines user code with high-level fault tolerance mechanisms (e.g., Stable Memory, Fault Tolerant Communication). These mechanisms depend on the application structure and on lower level tools and mechanisms and are therefore best positioned at this level. An overview of these mechanisms is provided in section 2.4.
- The **presentation layer** (top layer) that provides system monitoring and fault injection services, for testing and evaluation purposes. The role of the presentation layer in the framework is further discussed in section 2.5.

## 2.2 The Detection/Isolation/Recovery Layer

This layer includes the basic fault tolerance tools, i.e. tools that have a low-level functionality in the framework. These elementary tools may be used on their own (standalone tools), or as cooperating entities attached to the framework backbone. They are software implementations of well-known fault tolerance techniques, grouped in a library of adaptable functions.

The framework includes a set of ready-to-use tools as examples:

- The *watchdog timer* that employs user-driven time-stamps to detect processing errors on local or remote nodes.
- The *trap handler* to perform exception handling in a fully user transparent way under usage of the DIR net.
- The a*tomic action tool* that provides atomicity for distributed actions.
- *Assertions* that additionally inform the backbone.
- The distributed *voting mechanism* [12] featuring majority, median, plurality, weighted average and consensus voting.

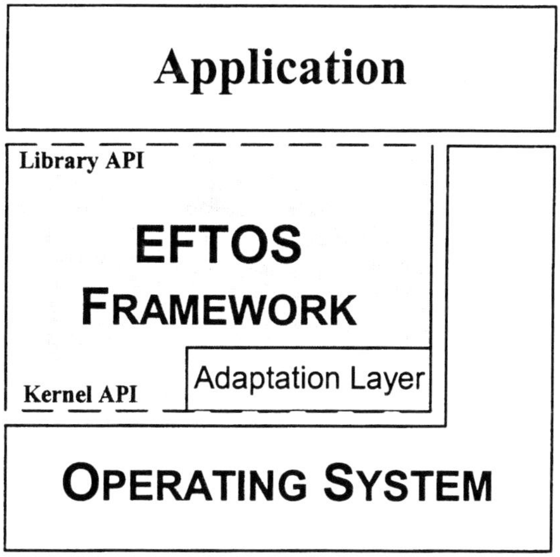


Fig. 1: Positioning the EFTOS framework in a layered architecture.

Users, however, are free to design and develop their own customized tools, expressing specific application needs. To this end, users are supported by a detailed documentation (analyzing each tool's functionality, API description, interrelationships with other framework elements, dependencies and limitations) and several functions to integrate these user-defined tools with the framework.

## 2.3 The Control Layer

The control layer includes the **D**etection-**I**solation-**R**ecovery network, *DIR net* in short, which is the backbone of the EFTOS framework [13]. It is structured as a hierarchical network that gathers information on the topology and status of the application elements and allows taking distributed coordinated actions to provide resilience against faults, preventing these from resulting in failures. It consists of three control modules that are distributed over the nodes of the user-allocated partition, as shown in Fig. 2: the *Normal Agent,* the *Backup Agent* and the *Manager.*

- *The Normal Agent* is connected to the Manager and all Backup Agents. It keeps a node-local view of the application and interacts with the local basic fault tolerance tools that are hooked on it. Normal Agents assist the DIR net Manager, one Agent on each node.

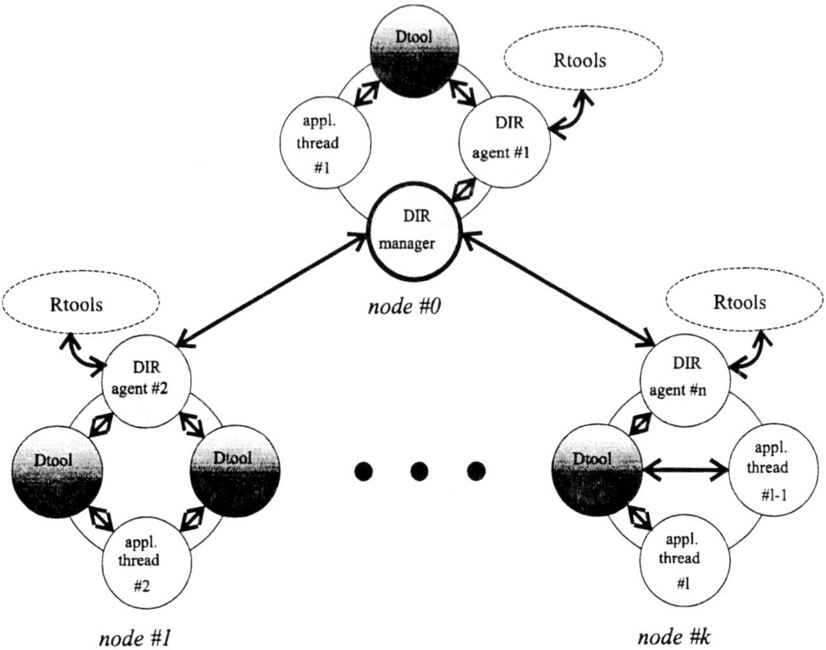


Fig. 2: An architectural view of the DIR net.

- *The Backup Agent* keeps a global view of the system. It is connected to all Normal Agents, all Backup Agents and the Manager. It uses buffered communication and receives all information the Normal Agents gather. Every Backup Agent keeps an updated copy of a system database, which contains information about application topology, integration of fault tolerance tools and mechanisms, error history, and application status. This database is actively used only by the Manager when performing recovery actions. This way, upon Manager failure detection, a Backup Agent can immediately take over.
- *The Manager*, with a global view of the system, is the main module in the DIR net. It is functionally a Backup Agent that has however been elected to become the Manager. It is the administrator and supervisor of all Agents and allows for global recovery actions to be executed. The ability to do global recovery is an advantage over several other systems. The Manager can also connect to an Operator module, establishing this way a bi-directional interface between the Operator and the DIR net to perform user-driven recovery actions and to visualize the behavior of the fault-tolerant application.

The basic fault tolerance tools, which can be started by the application or autonomously, connect to a DIR net control module (i.e. a Normal Agent, a Backup Agent, or even the Manager) via a standard interface. When one of them detects an error, it passes the necessary information (type of error, location and identification) to the local DIR net Agent. The DIR net Agent, in turn, warns the Manager and the Backup Agents. The diagnosis engine of the DIR net analyzes incoming error messages to derive affected components and the nature of the fault (permanent or transient). This allows isolating affected entities by disabling inter-process communication involved. Recovery actions can then be initiated by the DIR net to bring the application back into a consistent state. These recovery actions are described using a high level language (RL), as further explained in section 3.

The DIR net has several built-in mechanisms to provide self-fault tolerance. Provisions are taken to safeguard the backbone's database, to guarantee communications of the Backup Agents and the Manager and to detect complete node, Agent or Manager failures. The latter is based on the *"I'm alive"* module, which is present on each node. The user has no control over the position of the Manager. Instead, the Backup Agents will decide which of them will become a Manager via a safe protocol. Also, the DIR net is built in such a way that DIR net components will reintegrate themselves upon restarting or rebooting of a specific node.

## 2.4 The Application Layer

The application layer includes high-level integrated fault tolerance mechanisms, which combine several basic tools into more elaborated fault tolerance techniques. The three ready-to-use examples are the *fault-tolerant communication*, the *distributed memory mechanism* and the *stable memory module*. These are described in the next subsections.

### *2.4.1 Fault-tolerant Communication*

Two versions of fault-tolerant communication have been implemented: one uses channels for synchronous blocking communication and the other mailboxes for asynchronous non-blocking communication [14].

In a **synchronous blocking system**, problems arise when links (i.e., communication channels) or communicating threads are in an erroneous state (broken links, threads in infinite loops etc.) and hence threads remain blocked. Under these circumstances, no communication can be initiated or completed. Such deadlocks are avoided with the *Message Delivery Time-out mechanism.* This mechanism detects if a message is delivered before a certain deadline by utilizing a simple acknowledgment protocol. For each communicating thread, it creates a *Channel Control Thread* (CCT) thread to handle time-outs and to trigger isolation and recovery actions. Complementary, the CCT passes information or control to the DIR net.

The protocol implemented works as follows: each time an application thread wants to communicate (send or receive data) with its partner, it sends a relevant signal to its associated CCT. At the same time, a timeout mechanism is initiated at the specific CCT. This timeout value is related to the average time waited for the other partner to be available for communication. The two CCTs are synchronized by a control signal, which is sent by the sending side to the receiving side within the timeout period. After synchronization is complete, the CCTs send a signal to the application threads to inform them that they are ready to exchange data. This avoids the problem of blocking one thread because its partner is not responding. If the partner is not ready to communicate within the timeout period, the synchronization between the CCTs fails and an error message is sent to the DIR agent at the side of the application thread that requested the communication. If after the recovery phase initiated by the DIR net the communication still cannot be achieved, an error signal is returned by the CCT to the application thread that requested the communication. After the exchange of data between the application threads, a second synchronization takes place between the sender and receiver CCTs in the same way as before, but with another value of timeout. This timeout is related to the maximum time needed for data transmission on the link. If this synchronization fails and if the recovery tried by the DIR net also fails, an error signal is sent to both application threads to inform them that the transmission was not achieved.

This protocol is transparent to the user. This means that the application thread makes a simple call to the appropriate function of the library, and the fault tolerant transaction of the communication requested is completely taken care of by the CCT threads. In case of error, the CCT threads inform the DIR net, which, in turn, assumes control of the faulty situation by taking isolation and recovery actions (e.g. restart/kill faulty threads, inactivate links etc.). The result of these actions is communicated to the CCT threads, which either return normally (on successful error handling) or return a time-out error to the application threads they connect to (to inform them that the communication requested failed).

**Asynchronous non-blocking communication** is based on the mailbox concept: the sending thread does not block while sending a message. Instead, the message is stored in a buffer or mailbox, from where it is retrieved by the receiving thread. The Message Delivery Time-out mechanism in this case detects when the delivery to the receiver's mailbox cannot be completed within a time-out period (specified by the application) or when the receiver does not retrieve the message from the mailbox within a time-out period. If this occurs, the backbone is informed.

Possible recovery actions associated with the fault-tolerant asynchronous communication are:

i. Leaving the mail in the mailbox (no recovery).
ii. Deleting the mail when the mailbox is full.
iii. Resetting the receiver via an interrupt signal.
iv. Resetting both the sender and the receiver.
v. Performing an application-dependent recovery action.

In case 3 and 4, the entire mailbox is cleared. The recovery strategy, specified in RL, determines which action is executed and which additional actions need to be taken.

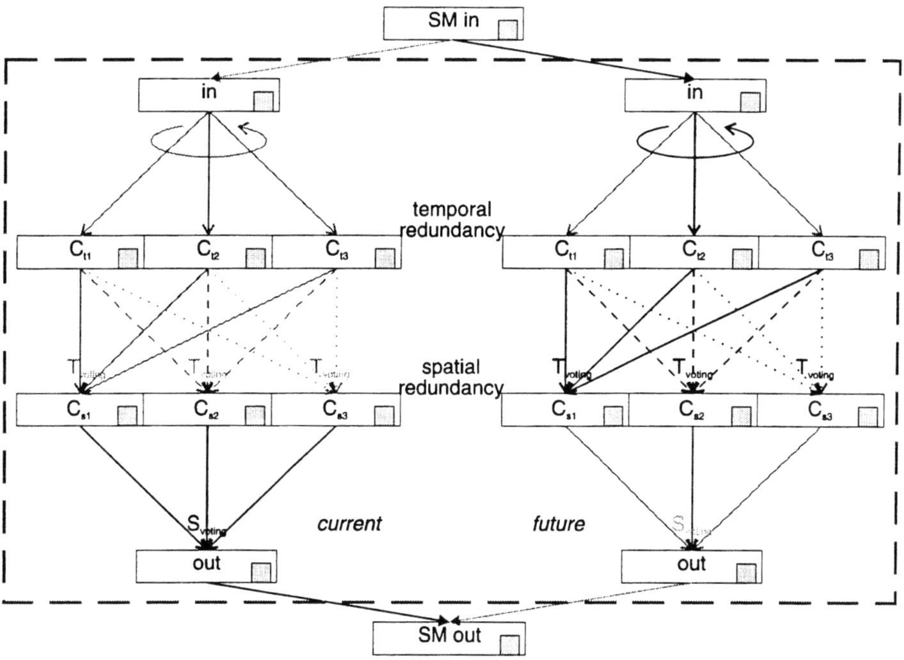


Fig. 3: An architectural view of the Stable memory module.

### *2.4.2 Distributed Memory Mechanism*

Typical for many embedded, distributed systems is a cyclic behavior, where in each cycle data is read from the status variables and stored at the end of the cycle, to be used in the next cycle. This data may for instance describe the actual state of the system, for which the integrity is required to guarantee the correct deterministic behavior of a finite state machine. The *distributed memory mechanism* allows for protection of this data via replication in the memory of remote nodes at the write statements (scattering). In this context, a read statement implies gathering the contents of the involved memory cells and executing a voting among all replicas. The distributed memory mechanism, which is located at the application layer, manages these tasks for the user and allows masking transient or permanent faults in memory.

All technicalities concerning the set up and the internal communication of the mechanism have been masked to the user module. This lets the user see only the local memory handler, and all interactions are hidden to him. Communication is hidden in terms of function calls. The whole memory module can be seen as a handler that is object of commands or requests as they are used in an object oriented approach.

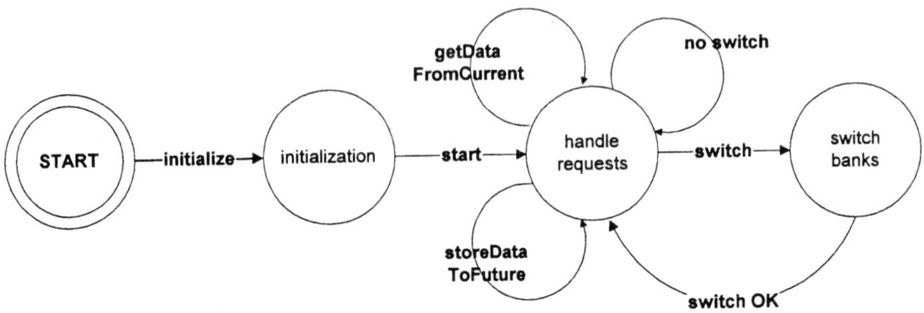


Fig. 4: State transition diagram of the central part of the stable memory module.

*2.4.3 Stable Memory Module*

The stable memory module executes a strategy based on time redundancy in order to stabilize input and status data for a finite state machine. It hereby complements and incorporates the spatial redundancy of the distributed memory mechanism.

Assume a cyclic application, e.g., describing a finite state machine, which calculates its new state based on the previous state and input data. To ensure that the results are correct, also in spite of transient faults affecting the input samples or corrupt computations, the application executes the calculations repeatedly. At the beginning of each cycle, the system's state is reset to a known, correct starting point; hence, eliminating the effects of possible transient faults during the previous cycle. The consecutive results are compared, and if they have been stabilized (i.e., repeated a predefined number of times), the application switches to the new state.

The stable memory module implements this stabilization of the user data and it provides the application with the stable (i.e., previously stabilized) data. In view of that, the stable memory module uses two memory 'banks': one ('*future*') to stabilize the data and another ('*current*') to provide stable data (see Fig. 3). The latter is possible by using the distributed memory mechanism within the stable memory module. If the data has been stabilized, both banks change their function. The bank switch is done in a transparent to the application way. It is obvious that this internal state of the stable memory module also has to be recalculated in the beginning of each cycle, and that the same level of protection has to be applied to it. Fig. 4 shows the state transition diagram of the central part of the stable memory module.

The prototypal use of this stable memory module in a case study of electric substation automation allows tolerating permanent faults in memory and transient faults affecting computation, input and memory devices. Transient faults lead to extra cycles before data is stabilized; permanent faults can be masked or lead to reconfiguration [2].

## 2.5 The Presentation Layer

The presentation layer visualizes information from the backbone via a monitor. During the execution of an application on top of the EFTOS framework, the DIR net produces large volumes of text messages on the system console. These messages are meant to keep the user informed of diagnosed faults, warnings and fault tolerance activity going on altogether in the safeguarded application. This stream of information can, however, be of limited practical use, mainly due to its fragmented and unstructured nature. The *EFTOS Monitor,* by turning this "raw" information into meaningful representations, provides the user with a hierarchical, dynamic, macroscopic and quasi real-time view of the structure and behavior of the system, including its **current shape** (on which node which components are running, and their topology), the **current state** of its components (for instance, whether they are regarded to be correct, faulty, or are being recovered) and each component's **running history**.

In order to quickly deliver human-comprehensible information from the gigantic stream of data produced by an EFTOS application, the EFTOS Monitor was developed to satisfy the following requirements:

- **Hierarchical representation of data**. All data have to be organized and made browsable at levels:

  *at the highest level*, only the logical structure of the application should be displayed: the nodes that are used, the DIR net roles played by each node, the EFTOS components active on each node, and their overall status,
  *at a medium level*, a concise description of the events pertaining each particular node should be available,
  *at the lowest level*, a deeper description of each particular event may also be supplied on user-demand.

- **Use of multimedia**, since the use of colors, sounds etc. traditionally associated to meanings (e.g., traffic lights colors) can further speed up the delivery of information to the user.

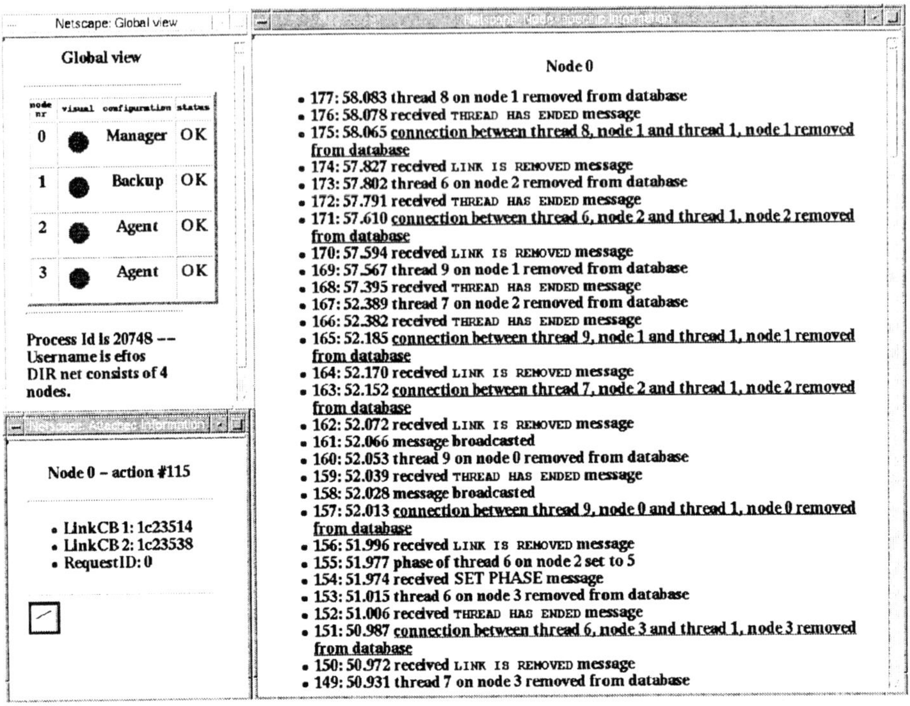

Fig. 5: A snapshot of the EFTOS Monitor.

A snapshot of the EFTOS Monitor that depicts the aforementioned features is shown in Fig. 5. This monitor can also be used during development or operation to evaluate the fault-tolerant strategies, as it allows injecting of software faults into the system [15].

# 3 Configuring the Fault Tolerance Framework

A distinctive feature of the EFTOS framework is its efficient configuration scheme. According to it, the application developer can not only adapt the structure of the FT framework set-up, but also change the way the system will react upon detection of an error. This is accomplished with only minor changes to the original user application, while the bulk of the framework configuration is shifted to a virtual machine interpreting a separately defined, user provided *recovery script* [16]. This is written in a high-level language, the so-called "*Recovery Language*" (RL). The human-readable script, by means of this virtual machine, is translated into a compact code that is interpreted and executed at run-time by the backbone.

The RL language serves two purposes: to enhance the configurability of an application (with roles configuration and default action setting) and to express the user's recovery strategy, i.e. which fault tolerance actions have to be executed when specific errors are detected. Examples include stopping a certain thread, restarting it, starting an alternative task, resetting a specific node, etc. This recovery language implements a sort of *meta*-level representation of the fault tolerance aspects of a user application. Within the language, it is possible:

- to work with logical groups of threads (e.g. application tasks, which are logically dependent, can be warned or reset with a single action);
- to indicate generalities (all tasks on a node, a faulty task, the non-faulty tasks, etc.);
- to specify default actions (if no other rules apply), etc.

The recovery strategy may be made dependent on the actual state or progress of the application (as it is possible for the application to inform the backbone of its current state). Therefore, following the EFTOS approach, a user application is made fault-tolerant in two steps:

- Integration of the library functions within the application. Some functions can be transparently added (e.g., informing the backbone when a new task is started), others require a function call to the basic tools and mechanisms (e.g., to set the parameters for a watchdog timer).
- Specification of the fault tolerance strategy to be followed.

This two-step tailoring of the framework for an application minimizes overhead. Only required parts of the framework are integrated into the application, while unneeded parts are not incorporated. As such, the application developer is able to trade off the resulting enhanced application dependability against performance or resource consumption.

# 4 Overhead and Dependability Improvement

The EFTOS framework has been evaluated in three different application environments and platforms:

- A Parsytec CC system [17] with an EPX/nK environment on top of a PowerPC-based parallel system for an image processing application, part of a postal automation system.
- A Parsytec CCi system [18] with an EPX/WinNT environment on top of a Pentium Pro multiprocessor for a surface inspection application in steel industry.

- An ENEL proprietary system with the TXT TEX environment [19] on top of a DEC-Alpha based distributed system for a sequence controller from energy transport.

Above and below the common core functions, an adaptation layer was required to link the application and computing platforms to the EFTOS APIs. Measurements on the different platforms allowed to obtain time and resource overheads. These concern the different elements of the framework in standalone configuration, integrated framework measurements and application measurements. For the tested industrial target applications, time overhead is typically 5% in the fault-free case. Recovery times are determined by the time required to reset/reboot the system, the reintegration of the fresh resources and the application recovery. The size of the entire library ranges from 100 KB to 500 KB for the given development platforms.

The increased dependability (viz., availability, integrity or maintainability) is dependent on the application itself and on the environment (type and frequency of faults). Table 1 summarizes the coverage of several of the EFTOS framework elements.

| Mechanism | Detection | Recovery |
|---|---|---|
| DIR net | Permanent omissions (crash failures of nodes) | Allows reintegration upon reboot, and via RL |
| | Backbone failures | |
| Watchdog | Timing failures | Via RL |
| Stable memory | Value failures | Fault masking, and via RL |
| Fault-tolerant communication | Communication failures (temporary/permanent omission) | From mild to drastic reset (Sect. 2.4.1), and via RL |
| Assertions | Value failures | Via RL |

Table 1: Coverage of several EFTOS framework elements: which errors can be detected, and how recovery is possible.

# 5 Conclusions

The EFTOS framework approach, comprising basic fault tolerance tools and mechanisms, a backbone and a high-level language for specifying recovery strategies, allows for flexible integration of fault tolerance into embedded applications on parallel and distributed platforms. The application developer integrates only those parts of the framework that are really required; those elements can be adapted, and be used in a stand-alone configuration or coupled to the backbone. In the latter case, the existence of a sort of second application layer, viz. RL, devoted to specifying recovery strategies, allows for the separation of design concerns. The flexibility is further ensured by the modularity and openness of the framework, such that additional detection, isolation or recovery mechanisms can be added and that portability to other environments is facilitated.

The future research concentrates on support for validation and verification of the dependability requirements of the application, during the life cycle of an application – from design, through development and implementation, to operation. In addition, the focus is on the integration with hard real-time applications and interoperability with emerging technologies, standards and products (e.g., Java, POSIX, CORBA).

## References


[1] G. Deconinck, R. Lauwereins, N. vom Schemm, Fault Tolerance Requirements in Postal Automation: a Case Study, *Proc. 4th IFAC Workshop on Algorithms and Architectures for Real-Time Control (AARTC'97)*, A.E. Ruano, P.J. Fleming (Eds.) (Pergamon Press, Amsterdam, The Netherlands), Vilamoura, Portugal, Apr. 1997, pp. 155-160.

[2] G. Deconinck, O. Botti, F. Cassinari, V. De Florio, R. Lauwereins, Stable Memory in Substation Automation: a Case Study, *Digest of Papers 28th Annual Int. Symp. on Fault-Tolerant Computing (FTCS-28)* (IEEE Comp. Soc. Press, Los Alamitos, CA), Munich, Germany, Jun. 1998, pp. 452-457.

[3] G. Deconinck, T. Varvarigou, O. Botti, V. De Florio, A. Kontizas, M. Truyens, W. Rosseel, R. Lauwereins, F. Cassinari, S. Graeber, U. Knaak, (Reusable Software Solutions for more Fault-Tolerant) Industrial Embedded HPC Applications, *Int. Journal Supercomputer* (ASFRA BV, Edam, The Netherlands) 69 (Vol. XIII, No. 3/4), 1997, pp. 23-44.

[4] Powell D. (Ed.), *Delta-4: A Generic Architecture for Dependable Distributed Computing*, ESPRIT Research Reports, Springer-Verlag, 1991.

[5] Barrett P.A. et al., The Delta-4 Extra Performance Architecture (XPA), *Proc. of the 20th Fault Tolerant Computing Symposium*, 1990, pp. 481-488.

[6] B. Randell, J.-C. Laprie, H. Kopetz, B. Littlewood (Eds.), *ESPRIT Basic Research Series: Predictably Dependable Computing Systems*, Springer-Verlag, Berlin, 1995.

[7] G. Deconinck, J. Vounckx, R. Cuyvers, R. Lauwereins, B. Bieker, H. Willeke, E. Maehle, A. Hein, F. Balbach, J. Altmann, M Dal Cin, H. Madeira, J.G. Silva, R. Wagner, G. Viehöver, Fault Tolerance in Massively Parallel Systems, *Transputer Communications*, Vol. 2(4), Dec. 1994, pp. 241-257.

[8] G. Agha and D.C. Sturman, A Methodology for Adapting to Patterns of Faults, G. Koob, ed., *Foundations of Ultradependability, vol. 1*, Kluwer Academic, 1994.

[9] D. B. Stewart, R. A. Volpe, P. K. Khosla, Integration of Real-Time Software Modules for Reconfigurable Sensor-Based Control Systems, *Proc. IEEE/RSJ Int.*

*Conf. on Intelligent Robots and Systems (IROS '92)*, Raleigh, NC, Jul. 1992, pp. 325-332.

[10] Y. Huang, C.M.R. Kintala, Software Fault Tolerance in the Application Layer, chapter of *Software Fault Tolerance*, M. Lyu (Ed.), John Wiley & Sons, Mar. 1995.

[11] M.R. Lyu (Ed.), *Handbook of Software Reliability Engineering*, McGraw-Hill, New York, 1995.

[12] V. De Florio, G. Deconinck, R. Lauwereins, Software Tool Combining Fault Masking with User-Defined Recovery Strategies, *IEE Proc. - Software, Special issue on Dependable Computing Systems* (IEE, London, UK), Vol. 145, No.6, Dec. 1998, pp. 203-211.

[13] G. Deconinck, M. Truyens, V. De Florio, W. Rosseel, R. Lauwereins, R. Belmans, A Framework Backbone for Software Fault Tolerance in Embedded Parallel Applications, *Proc. 7th Euromicro Conf. on Parallel and Distributed Processing (PDP'99)* (IEEE Comp. Soc. Press, Los Alamitos, CA), Funchal, Portugal, Feb. 3-5, 1999, pp 189-195.

[14] G. Efthivoulidis, E. Verentziotis, A. Meliones, T. Varvarigou, A. Kontizas, G. Deconinck, V. De Florio, Fault Tolerant Communication in Embedded Supercomputing, *IEEE Micro, Special issue on Fault Tolerance*, Vol. 18, No.5, Sep.-Oct. 1998.

[15] V. De Florio, G. Deconinck, M. Truyens, W. Rosseel, R. Lauwereins, A Hypermedia Distributed Application for Monitoring and Fault-Injection in Embedded Fault-Tolerant Parallel Programs, *Proc. 6th Euromicro Conf. on Parallel and Distributed Processing (PDP'98)* (IEEE Comp. Soc. Press, Los Alamitos, CA), Madrid, Spain, Jan. 1998, pp. 349-355.

[16] V. De Florio, G. Deconinck, R. Lauwereins, Recovery Languages: an Effective Structure for Software Fault Tolerance, Fast abstract at *9th Int. Symp. on Software Reliability Engineering (ISSRE'98)* (R. Chillarege and T. Illgen, New York), Paderborn, Germany, Nov. 1998, pp. 39-40.

[17] Anon., Parsytec CC Series — Cognitive Computing, *Parsytec GmbH*, Aachen, Germany, Jul. 1995.

[18] Anon., Parsytec CCi Series, *Parsytec GmbH*, Aachen, Germany, 1997.

[19] F. Cassinari, E. Birindelli, TEX User manual, *TXT Ingegneria Informatica*, Milano, Italy, 1997.

*Chapter 8*

# MEQA$^3$- A MULTI-END QOS APPLICATION ADAPTATION ARCHITECTURE

ATHANASIOS G. MALAMOS*, THEODORA A. VARVARIGOU**, ELIAS N. MALAMAS* AND CHI-HSIANG YEH***

* Dept. of Electronics and Computer Eng.,
Technical University of Crete,
University Campus, GR-731 00, Chania,
GREECE
*tmalamos@electronics.tuc.gr, emalamas@dilos.systems.tuc.gr*

** Dept. of Electrical and Computer Eng.,
National Technical University of Athens,
Eroon Polytechniou 9, GR-157 73, Zographou, Athens,
GREECE
*dora@telecom.ntua.gr*

*** Dept. of Electrical and Computer Eng.,
Queen's University,
Kingston, ON K7L 3N6,
CANADA
*yeh@ee.queensu.ca*

*Abstract:* We present MEQA$^3$ application adaptation architecture. MEQA$^3$ manages QoS in two different points of the service activity, 1) the setup/initialisation period and 2) the service period. During the initialisation phase, the system performs an overall optimal QoS to application allocation considering the user requests, the estimated service requirements and the resource constraints. However, during the service time a resource overloading may occur either by bad initial estimation of application requirements or by some unexpected event that limits its performance. Thus, MEQA$^3$ monitors the QoS of the applications on the user's side and if this exceeds the user specifications then dynamically adapts applications to the current situation. We demonstrate by a videoconference example that MEQA$^3$ is an easy to implement low complexity architecture.

*Key-Words:* Quality of Service (QoS), QoS management, multimedia services, application adaptation, user profile

# 1 Introduction

Multimedia services have imposed new requirements in the system design. In the "traditional" network services, such as e-mail, ftp and WWW the goal was to deliver the information in acceptable time. In the multimedia network services the goal is to deliver information with acceptable quality. This implies that when a user requests for a multimedia service, he has Quality of Service requirements. The Quality of the Service that the user experiences is related to the QoS characteristics of the service that the system delivers. Such QoS characteristics might be frame rate and resolution for video, volume and sampling rate for audio. The QoS characteristics are related to the performance of the resources of the system infrastructure. Thus, efficient management of the system resources is essential to provide QoS management. Multimedia services may differ extremely in their requirements for quality and resource utilisation. Users, on the other hand, vary in the way they perceive quality and tolerate a multimedia service that is degraded. This becomes very important in the light of the fact that resource availability, in the present networks, changes dynamically causing problems to the delivery of the information and degradation of the quality of the service that is provided to the user. Therefore, in order to achieve maximum user satisfaction, multimedia services have to be customisable in order to be easily adaptable to the user needs and resource availability. An effective QoS management scheme has to manage QoS in an overall-service fashion, controlling the QoS throughout the levels of a service, from the user level to the network, considering the performance, the dependencies and the relationships of all the individual parts of the system. Moreover, in the present distributed service environment with the multi-user services where each service consists of several fundamental applications, a multi-user and multi-application QoS management seems to be more appropriate.

Research on Quality of Service for multimedia applications has gained much attention during the last few years. There is a lot of research that has been carried out in the area of the QoS resource management [1-3], where many QoS architectures have been designed and many protocols have been presented. Most of this research has focused on the link, transportation (protocols) and network infrastructure of the system. Researchers, usually consider QoS performance characteristics such as throughput, delay, delay jitter, probability of losses, etc. These QoS parameters are fundamental in QoS control. However they are rarely understandable by the user of the services. To overcome this difference between the characteristics that are used to control QoS and the characteristics that a user understands, usually, these architectures include negotiation mechanisms. These mechanisms provide the user with the ability to choose a set of QoS requirements that fits to his preferences and the QoS management seeks to make the appropriate arrangements (routing, reservations, resource allocation) in the network level of the system in order to fulfil them. However, in general the existing networks are not compatible to those architectures. Thus, the implementation of these QoS architectures requires a significant reconfiguration of the existing network infrastructure, which leads to increased costs. There are other architectures that manage QoS by using resource reservations over the existing networks (RSVP), which are hardly implemented in service networks since they lead to poor utilisation of the network resources.

Recent research has introduced QoS management frameworks network application development schemes [4-7] that considers QoS characteristics related to the upper layer (User, application) of the service such as video quality characteristics, audio quality characteristics, intra-media and inter-media delay, etc. These frameworks are user oriented and use utility functions to express the relation between the user satisfaction and QoS expressed in the traditional sense (throughput, delay, etc.). The use of utility functions leads to formulation of the resource allocation as an optimisation problem. However this problem is proven to be a NP-Hard problem [5], thus the solutions are either heuristics or approximations and are not appropriate for real-time control of QoS.

Application adaptation has also earned much attention from the research community since it provides a solution to the dynamic varying environment of service networks. This approach manages QoS at the application level rather than the network level. It adjusts the application needs according to the dynamic network situation instead of changing the network configuration to meet the strict application requirements. Application adaptation modifies the application characteristics in such a way to provide a service acceptable to the user. Application adaptation is suitable mostly for "best effort" networks like the Internet, although there are cases, like system failure or resource insufficiency, where application adaptation can be implemented in networks that provide resource reservation. Some of the research in this area uses application level characteristics (media characteristics) to express QoS [8] while other are system oriented [9-11].

In this paper, we present an architecture that manages QoS of a multi-user multimedia service. In order to realise QoS management, we analyse the service to the fundamental applications consists of. In order to map QoS parameters of the individual parts of a multimedia service, we introduce a model that relates application QoS characteristics, resource parameters and the user's QoS profile. The QoS architecture manages QoS in two different points of the service activity, 1) the setup/ initialisation period and 2) the service period. During the initialisation phase of the multimedia service, the architecture performs an overall optimal QoS to application allocation considering the user requests, the service requirements and the resource constraints. By this calculation, the architecture computes per application and per user the QoS that the system is a-priory able to guarantee given the user QoS profile and application requirements. During the service time, the system monitors the QoS that the users experience. If the observed quality reaches a value less than the user specified minimum then the QoS assigned to the applications is re-calculated on-line by a polynomial time algorithm.

# 2 Architecture Fundamentals

A typical multimedia service (i.e. video on demand, teleconference, etc.) consists of a set of fundamental multimedia applications. Consider for example a videoconference that consists of video, audio, messaging and file transfer applications. The performance of these applications will affect the QoS that the users experience. A system that supports multimedia services has to manage efficiently all types of applications, supporting QoS with respect to the user requirements. As far as temporal requirements are concerned, multimedia applications may be distinguished into three major classes: a) continuous-media applications (CM) (presentation of video, audio, animation data etc.) b) aperiodic applications with real time constraints (presentation of photos, graphics, text, etc.) and c) aperiodic applications without real time constraints (file transfer, message-exchanging etc.). In this work we focus on the continuous- media applications, since they have the most delicate requirements from the QoS management architectures and influence the user satisfaction the most.

Every application has an upper limit on quality that is able to provide. This upper limit on quality is independent of the network or other temporal characteristics of the communication infrastructure and depends on the application and the service provider. When a user refers to quality, he/she implies a portion of the best quality that the application can support.

**Definition 1:** *In this architecture, when we refer to quality (q) of an application, we mean the real number in the [0,1] interval, which expresses the fraction of the optimal quality that the application and the provider may provide.*

When quality (q) is equal to one, then the user experiences the maximum quality that the service can provide. When quality (q) is forced to zero, the user does not get any service at all.

The part that affects crucially the performance of the system is the resources. The parameter that characterises the resource performance is the resource-utilisation. Utilisation of a resource is usually expressed through a utilisation constraint. If a set of applications fulfils the utilisation constraint of the resource then no temporal violation or overloading occurs. In this framework, we consider two types of resources: 1) the processing resources and 2) the network resources.

## 2.1 The Processing Resources

For the processing resources, the parameter that is usually considered in the utilisation constraint is the processing rate of the application (R). The processing rate of the application is referred to the ratio of the processing time (P) per period and the period (T) of the application.

$$R = \frac{P}{T} \tag{1}$$

Consider, for example, a video presentation application. Processing time (P) is related to the frame size in pixels (S) that the application delivers to the resource at every period and the time interval that is required to processes a single pixel of the application. Period (T) is related to the frame rate (f) of the video. In the case of the video application, equation (1) is defined as:

$$R = \frac{P}{T} = \frac{\text{frame size(in pixels)} \times \text{proc. time per pixel}}{\frac{1}{\text{frame rate}}} = \text{frame size(in pixels)} \times \text{proc. time per pixel} \times \text{frame rate} \tag{2}$$

In the light of quality, processing time and temporal constraints (period) are related to the quality of the application. In the video example, the larger the frame size (S) and the frame rate (f) that the user experiences the more the quality of the video.

$$R(q) = \frac{P}{T} = \frac{S(q) \times \text{proc. time per pixel}}{\frac{1}{f(q)}} = S(q) \times \text{proc. time per pixel} \times f(q), \quad \begin{cases} S(q) : \text{frame size (pixels)} \\ f(q) : \text{frame rate (frames/sec)} \end{cases} \tag{3}$$

Consequently, the more the quality (q) of a continuous-media application, the more the processing rate[2] (R) that is necessary to achieve it. In our approach, we assume that, if a multimedia application is of quality q then it requires processing rate R(q) equal to the q-th portion of the processing rate of the same application in the maximum quality (q=1). Hence,

---

[2] This assumption stands only for uncompressed continues media. For compressed information, such as MPEG video or audio the assumption stands for the worst-case processing rate.

$$R(q) = \frac{P(q)}{T(q)} = a \cdot q \tag{4}$$

In (4), q is the quality of the service and a is a constant which expresses the processing rate of the multimedia application when the quality is maximum (q=1). It is obvious that for a specific processing resource, like a CPU, there is a set of frame-size and frame-rate pairs that may correspond to the same processing rate. From all these sets the user should be able to choose the set of the format characteristics/parameters that fits to his requirements. In our approach this is achieved via the user profile.

In Fig.1, there is an illustrative example of the graphical representation of the relation between format characteristics (frame size and frame rate) and the processing rate performance of a video in a specific processor. The curves in Fig.1(b) correspond to different processing rates. Every point into a specific curve performs the same processing rate produced by different media format (frame-size, frame-rate). For the rest of this paper, we will refer to these curves as the iso-rate curves. In order to achieve a direct relation between quality and format characteristics of the media we have to consider the user preferences. The dotted curve in Fig.1(b) is expressing the user preferences[3]. That is the way that the user understands quality. Every point in the dotted curve relates quality to a specific video format. The intersection between an iso-rate curve and the user-profile expresses the specific video format, the corresponding computation rate and the quality it is assigned to this service. In order to achieve user profile we use the following methodology. The user is provided with media (i.e., video) in various formats but with the same processing rate. From all these media presentations, the user chooses the one with the format characteristics that satisfy him most. We assign to the media with the specified format characteristics the corresponding quality q. We repeat the above procedure for some other processing rate and quality q, until we achieve a suitable set of media format characteristics and the corresponding qualities. We generate the user profile by interpolation in the set produced by the user.

[3] In the rest of this paper we will refer to this curve as the user-profile

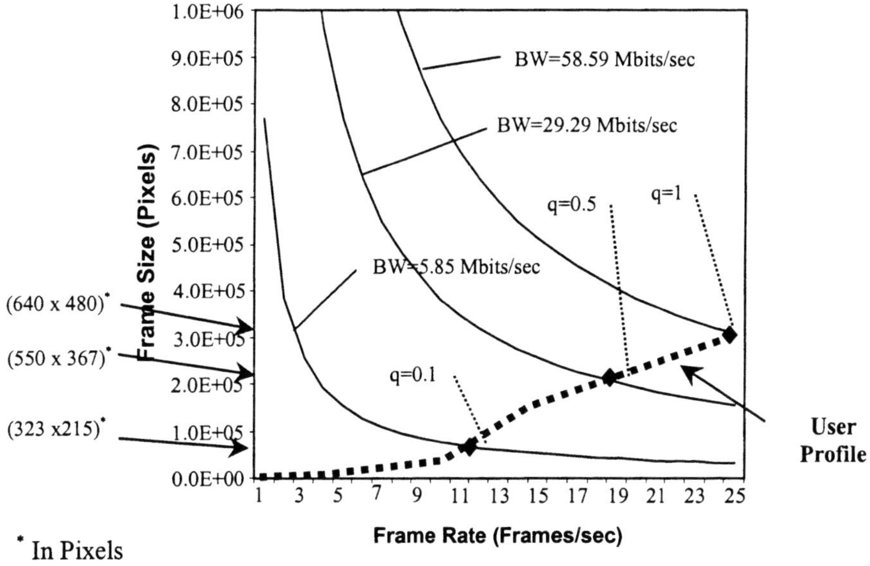


(a)

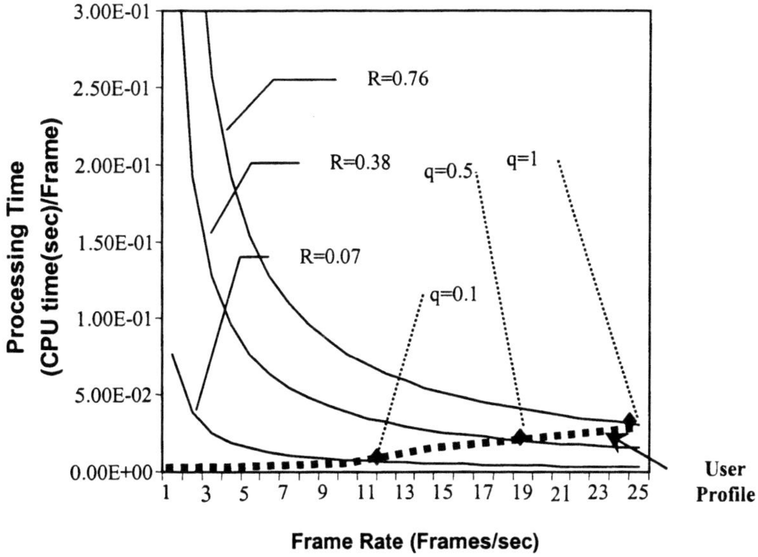


(b)

Fig.1. The iso-bandwidth and iso-rate curves of a NTSC video

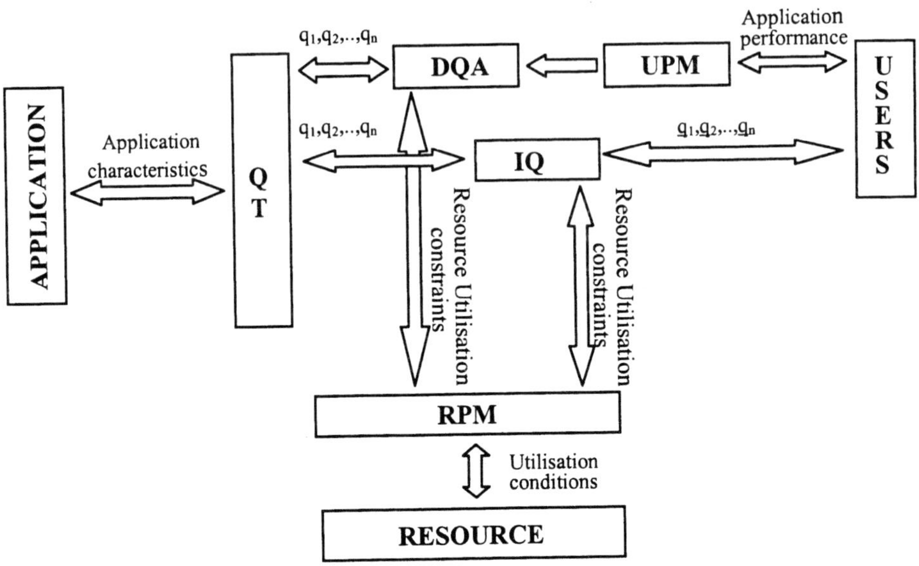


Fig.2. The MEQA[3] architecture overview

## 2.2 Network Resources

For network resources (i.e., transmission lines, switches, etc.) performance is related to architectural and industrial bandwidth specifications, consequently the resource utilisation is referred directly to the size of information as well as to temporal characteristics such as period.

The necessary bandwidth may be formulated similarly to the processing rate.

$$BW(q) = \frac{S(q)}{T(q)} = b \cdot q\,, \tag{5}$$

where S is the size per period (in bits) and T is the period of the application. The parameter b is a constant related to the application and expresses the maximum necessary bandwidth in the highest quality. Obviously, the curves computed for the case of the processing resources may be used to formulate QoS mapping curves appropriate for the network infrastructure. In this case we consider the iso-bandwidth curves (Fig.1(a)). The user-profile, in the case of bandwidth, is extracted by calculation over the user-profile produced for the same application in the case of the processing resource.

## 2.3 Application Importance

All the applications that are involved in a multimedia service are not of the same importance. Thus, considering user and service requirements, QoS management has to embed mechanisms that support importance gradation, among services. In our model, weights are assigned to applications to scale the influence of individual multimedia services on the overall quality.

**Definition 2:** *Every application is assigned a weight (w), that is a constant can be specified by both provider and user and expresses the importance of the corresponding application to the performance of the entire multimedia service.*

Two parameters, that determine the user satisfaction, are delay and frame losses. Delay may be distinguished into the intra-media and the inter-media delay. Intra-media is the delay that is observed between frames of the same media, for example between frames of the same video. Inter-media is the delay that is observed by the synchronisation error between different media, for example a video and the corresponding voice. In addition, frame losses are responsible for the discontinuity and the glitches that are observed in a media presentation. If resource utilisation constraints are met then the user does not experience any degradation of the application in terms of delays and frame losses. Since the application characteristics are fixed, overloading (utilisation constraint violation) of some resources leads to increase of delay and frame losses which appear in the user side as intra-media delay, inter-media delay and glitches. Thus, the applications should be reconfigured and adapted to the performance of these resources. In our work, we use delay and frame losses to monitor the performance of the system and to trigger the reconfiguration mechanisms for re-computing qualities in respect to resources utilisation.

# 3 The MEQA³ Architecture

In order to realise QoS management we introduce the Multi-End QoS Application Adaptation Architecture (MEQA³) (Fig.2) which consists of:

- The QoS Translator (QT) which through the iso-rate curves, iso-bandwidth curves and the user profile achieves mapping among quality q, format characteristics (frame-size and frame-rate) of the multimedia applications and resource utilisation
- The Initial QoS Allocator (IQA) which through an allocation algorithm assigns quality to the applications, considering user preferences, the application requirements and the resource utilisation constraints.
- The Resource Performance Monitor (RPM) which monitors the performance of each individual resource by periodically inspecting if the corresponding

utilisation constraint for a processing resource or bandwidth constraint for a network resource is fulfilled.

- The User-side QoS Monitor (UQM) which examines at the user-end the cycle-time and the frame sequence of the media delivered. UQM extracts the intra-media delay and the frame losses of the media delivered to the user and estimates QoS degradation in the user side.
- The Dynamic QoS Allocator (DQA) which is responsible of adapting the quality of the applications, whenever the utilisation constraints of one or more resources are violated.

MEQA$^3$ manages QoS in two different phases of the service activity, 1) the initialisation (setup) period and 2) the service period. During the initialisation period (Fig.4(a)), the MEQA$^3$ performs, through the Initial QoS Allocator (IQA), an overall QoS allocation that assigns quality to the applications of all the concurrently arrived user requests. IQA performs this calculation considering the user and the service requirements, specified by the QoS Translator (QT), and the resource constraints specified by the Resource Performance Monitor (RPM). During the service time (Fig.4(b)), the Resource Performance Monitor (RPM) monitors the performance of each individual resource and the User-side QoS Monitor (UQM) observes the quality the user experiences. If the observed quality drops below the user tolerance then the system locates through RPM the "problematic" resource and the Quality of the service is re-calculated by the Dynamic QoS Allocator (DQA) according to the constraints of this particular resource. From a topological point of view, the individual components of MEQA$^3$ architecture may be host by different physical and logical processing units. RPM may be part of the resources since it must be aware of the resource availability. UQM should be hosted in the user side machine. QT, IQA, and DQA, depend on the service type and the development strategy whether they will be hosted in a centralised (in the service provider side) or in any of the user side machines. In the following subsections we present in detail the key components of the MEQA$^3$ architecture, namely the QT, the IQA, and the DQA and we describe the corresponding algorithms.

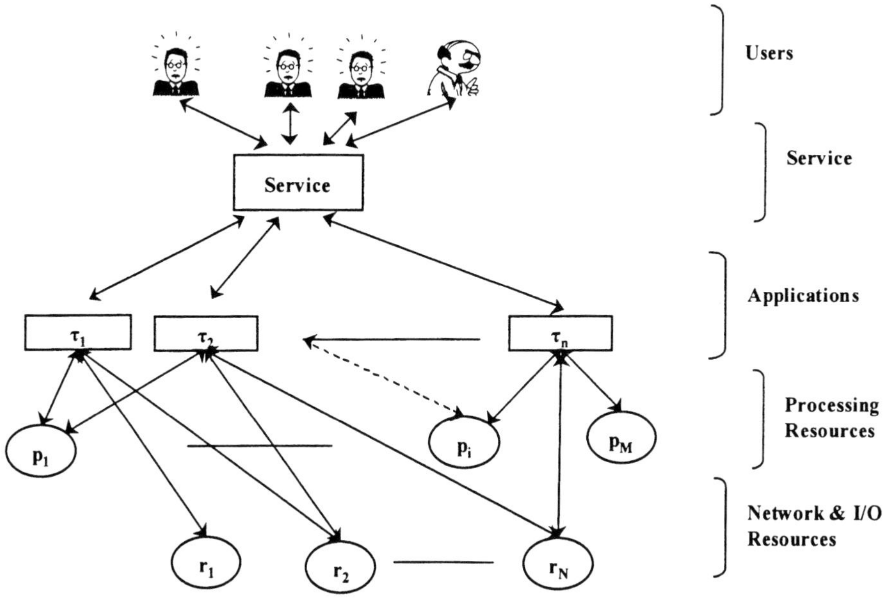


Fig.3. The individual parts of a network service

## 3.1 The QoS Translator (QT)

QoS Translator (QT) uses the iso-rate and iso-bandwidth curves to map quality (q) to the values of the format characteristics (frame-size and frame-rate) of the continuous media applications and the corresponding resource utilisation. During the service time, the system adapts the quality of the applications according to the network and processing resources availability. The QoS Translator (QT), through the user profile (Fig.1), assigns the computed quality to the corresponding processing rate, frame size and frame rate of the application. The mathematical formulation of QT is as follows:

$$R(q) = S(q) \cdot (\text{processing time/size unit}) \cdot f(q) = a \cdot q \Rightarrow$$

$$S(q) = \frac{a \cdot q}{(\text{processing time/size unit}) \cdot f(q)} \quad : \text{Processing rate} \quad (6)$$

$$S(f, q) = F(f(q)) \quad : \text{User -profile} \quad (7)$$

Where in (7), F is the user profile function, which is produced by the interpolation of the user preferences as explained in section 2. Equations (6) and (7) are a system of equations with input parameter the quality (q) and solutions the size S and the frame rate f of the application. From these application parameters, considering that the format of a media frame is specified (i.e., horizontal to vertical ratio and colour depth per pixel for a video), QT is able to compute the horizontal and the vertical resolution of a video or the sample resolution of an audio media as well as the bandwidth requirements of the application.

## 3.2 The Initial QoS Allocator (IQA)

The initial QoS allocator performs an optimal assignment of quality to applications, considering the user, the application and the resource constraints. The computation of the application parameters, given the quality q is done by QT as explained above.

IQA carries out a double task (Fig.4(a)). At the same time, it admits user requests for service and also computes the quality with which these requests will be executed. The QoS allocation task may be formed as an optimisation problem. In general, optimisation is a task of high computation complexity. However, in the case of linear equations with continuous variables, solutions can be achieved in acceptable time, with the Simplex algorithm [12]. Moreover, the idea of optimisation process is more realistic, if one considers that it takes place only once, in a multimedia service session, during service initialisation.

### *3.2.1 Formulation of the QoS Allocation Problem*

Assume (Fig.3) that a system of M processing $\{p_i, i=1..M\}$ and N network resources $\{r_j, j=1..N\}$ (see Table 1). This system has to service n multimedia applications $\{\tau_k, k=1..n\}$ (Fig.3). Each task $\tau_k$ is assigned a maximum processing rate $a_{ki}$ for every processing resource $p_i$ (i=1..M) and a maximum necessary bandwidth $b_{kj}$ for every network resource $r_j$ (j=1..N). If $\tau_k$ has no processing requirements on $p_i$ then $a_{ki}=0$, also if $\tau_k$ has no throughput requirements on $r_j$ then $b_{kj}=0$. Each processing resource $p_i$ has upper bound of utilisation $\underline{U}_i$ and each network resource $r_j$ has available bandwidth $\underline{BW}_j$. Each application $\tau_k$ is assigned an importance $w_k$. For each application $\tau_k$ there is a lower bound of quality $\underline{q}_k$. In this paper, we study the application adaptation problem, thus we assume that the assignment of applications to processing and network resources has been done prior to IQA (the application assignment task belongs to the area of resource management). We seek to find the optimal quality levels $(q_1, q_2,..,q_n)$ of the multimedia applications, so that no multimedia application will violate any period or deadline and to maximise the weighted overall quality (8) that the system provides.

$$Q = \sum_{k=1}^{n} w_k \cdot q_k \; . \tag{8}$$

In order to admit and schedule task on the processing resources of the system, we consider two very popular optimal scheduling algorithms, the Earliest Deadline First (EDF) for pre-emptive dynamic priority scheduling and the Rate-Monotonic algorithm (RM) for fixed priority scheduling. However, our model is general and can be applied with other schedulability conditions and performance guarantees. The schedulability conditions of the EDF and the RM algorithms for each one of the processing resource have been presented in [13] and are expressed as follows.

Table 1. Notation.

| **Parameter** | **Comments** |
|---|---|
| $\tau_k$ | k-th application |
| n | The number of applications |
| $p_i$ | i-th processing resource |
| M | The number of processing resources |
| $r_j$ | The j-th network resource |
| N | The number of network resources |
| $R_{ki}$ | Processing rate of k-th application into the i-th processing resource |
| $P_{ki}$ | Processing time of the k-th application to the i-th processing resource |
| $T_k$ | Application period |
| $a_{ki}$ | Maximum processing rate of the k-th application into the i-th processing resource |
| $b_{kj}$ | Maximum bandwidth requirements of the k-th application on the j-th network resource |
| $q_i$ | quality of the i-th application |
| $\underline{q}_i$ | required quality of the i-th application |
| $w_k$ | Application importance |
| $U_i$ | Utilisation of the i-th processing resource |
| $\underline{U}_i$ | The available utilisation (resource capacity) of the i-th processing resource |
| $BW_j$ | Bandwidth requirements of the applications from the j-th network resource |
| $\underline{BW}_j$ | Available bandwidth of the j-th resource |

$$U_{EDF} = \sum_{k=1}^{n} \frac{P_k}{T_k} \leq 1, \text{ for n applications} \tag{9}$$

$$U_{RM} = \sum_{k=1}^{n} \frac{P_k}{T_k} \leq n(2^{1/n} - 1), \text{ for n applications} \tag{10}$$

Using (4) these conditions becomes as follows:

$$U_i(q) = \sum_{k=1}^{n} R_{ki} = \sum_{k=1}^{n} \frac{P_{ki}}{T_k} = \sum_{k=1}^{n} a_{ki} \cdot q_k \leq \underline{U}_i, \quad \left( \underline{U}_i = \begin{cases} 1 & ,\text{EDF} \\ n_i(2^{1/n_i} - 1), \text{with} \quad n_i = \left|\{k : a_{ki} \neq 0\}\right| & ,\text{RM} \end{cases} \right), \tag{11}$$

Where $n_i$ in (11) is the number of applications with nonzero maximum processing rate ($a_{ki} \neq 0$) in the i-th processing resource.

According to (5) the utilisation constraints of the network resources can be expressed as functions of quality in a manner similar to that of processing resource utilisation. Thus for the j-th network resource the utilisation constraint becomes:

$$BW_j(q) = \sum_{k=1}^{n} \frac{S_k}{T_k} = \sum_{k=1}^{n} b_{kj} \cdot q_k \leq \underline{BW}_j, \tag{12}$$

User preferences of quality are expressed through the lower bound on quality of the corresponding application.

$$\underline{q_k} \leq q_k \leq 1, \quad k = 1..n \tag{13}$$

Hence the IQA problem becomes equivalent to the following optimisation problem:

$$\text{Find } q_k, \text{ k=1..n that maximise } Q = \sum_{k=1}^{n} w_k \cdot q_k \tag{14}$$

given conditions

$$\begin{cases} U_i(q) = \sum_{k=1}^{n} a_{ki} \cdot q_k \leq \underline{U}_i, \quad \forall i \in \{1,\ldots,M\} & (15) \\ BW_j(q) = \sum_{k=1}^{n} b_{kj} \cdot q_k \leq \underline{BW}_j, \quad \forall j \in \{1,\ldots,N\} & (16) \\ \underline{q_k} \leq q_k \leq 1, \quad \forall k \in \{1,\ldots,n\} & (17) \end{cases}$$

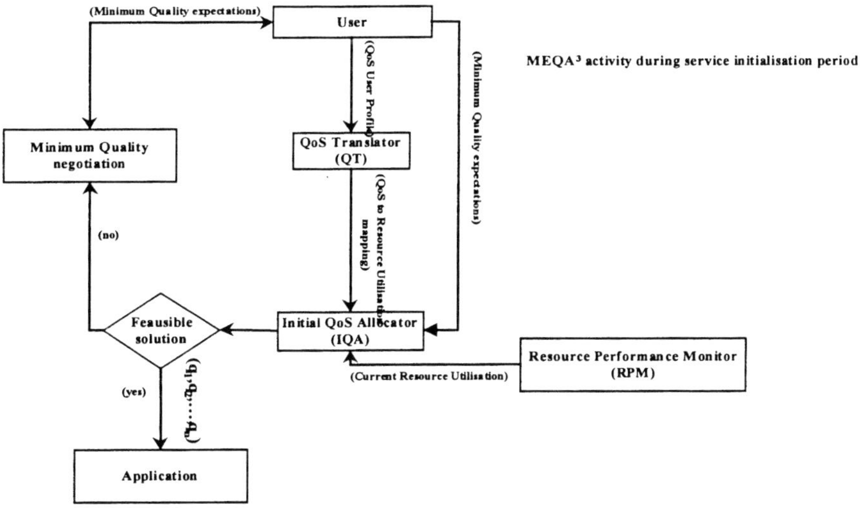


(a)

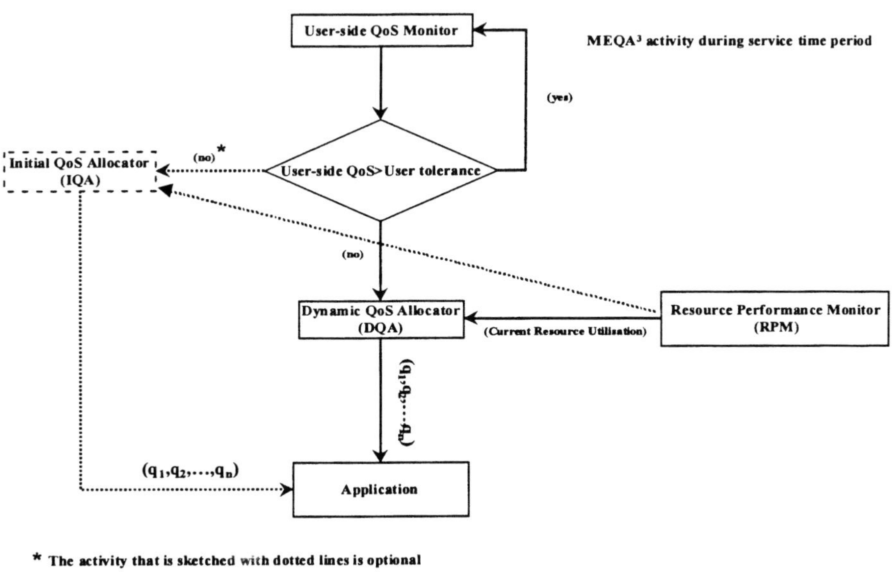


(b)

Fig.4. (a) The IQA algorithm. (b)The DQA algorithm.

Thus the quality allocation problem becomes an optimisation problem that can be solved with Simplex linear programming algorithm. A detailed example with simulation results can be found in section 4.

After the quality allocation procedure completion, IQA informs the network manager and the users, about the quality levels that can be admitted and the users can either accept or reject the offer. If scheduling of a set of applications is not feasible then the system starts a renegotiating procedure, where users should either reduce their minimum preferences ($\underline{q}_k$) of quality or withdraw their requests.

## 3.3 Dynamic QoS Adaptation

During the service time, the Resource Performance Monitor (RPM) monitors the performance of each individual resource by regularly applying the corresponding utilisation test, for processing (18) or network resources (19).

$$U_i(q) = \sum_{k=1}^{n} a_{ki} \cdot q_k \leq \underline{U}_i, \quad \forall i \in \{1,\dots,M\} \tag{18}$$

$$BW_j(q) = \sum_{k=1}^{n} b_{kj} \cdot q_k \leq \underline{BW}_j, \quad \forall j \in \{1,\dots,N\} \tag{19}$$

A resource overloading may occur either by bad initial estimation in the processing rate of an application or by some unexpected event that limits the performance of the resource. In addition, in the user-end the User-side QoS Monitor (UQM) examines the cycle-time and the frame sequence of the media delivered. From the above examinations the UQM extracts the intra-media delay and frame losses of the media delivered to the user. During service time we might have to optimise again, if RPM signals performance degradation. However, IQA is computationally expensive, thus DQA performs an optimised procedure, individually to each overloaded resource, which is faster than the IQA. During DQA procedure we reallocate $q_i$'s to the applications and drop some of the applications whose quality requirements cannot be met. Thus, If RPM observes an overloaded resource and UQM observes that delay and/or frame losses exceed user tolerance then the system applies the Dynamic QoS Allocator (DQA) to adapt quality levels of the applications under the overloaded resource utilisation constraint. If the achieved quality levels do not satisfy users then the system re-executes the IQA. For a specific resource the optimisation problem that the DQA is solving is a subproblem of the overall IQA which is of linear complexity and can be expressed as follows:

For the i-th processing resource ($p_i$), we are looking for $q'_k$ to

maximise $$Q = \sum_{\{k:a_{ki}\neq 0\}} w_k \cdot q'_k + \sum_{\{k:a_{ki}=0\}} w_k \cdot q_k , \tag{20}$$

given conditions

$$\begin{cases} \sum_{\{k:a_{ki}\neq 0\}} a_{ki}\cdot q'_k \leq \underline{U_i}, & (21)\\ 0 \leq q'_k \leq q_k,\ (k: a_{ki}\neq 0), & (22)\end{cases}$$

where $q_k$ is the quality assigned to the application by the IQA.

For the j-th networking resource ($r_j$), the DQA problem is expressed as:

$$\text{maximise} \qquad Q = \sum_{\{k:b_{kj}\neq 0\}} w_k\cdot q'_k + \sum_{\{k:b_{kj}=0\}} w_k\cdot q_k, \qquad (23)$$

given conditions

$$\begin{cases} \sum_{\{k:b_{kj}\neq 0\}} b_{kj}\cdot q'_k \leq \underline{BW}_j, & (24)\\ 0 \leq q'_k \leq q_k,\ (k: b_{kj}\neq 0). & (25)\end{cases}$$

The DQA problem is equivalent to the Knapsack problem with real variables. In [14], there is the Knapsack problem declaration as well as the proof of the optimality of the greedy algorithm we use to solve the DQA problem. In this algorithm, quality is assigned with respect to the weight w and processing ratio R of the application. Applications are sorted into non-increasing order of the ratio w/R. Starting from the first application in the non-increasing order, the algorithm assigns the maximum allowable quality to the applications, which is the quality the IQA had assigned to the application. This procedure is repeated until the resource utilisation reaches the upper limit.

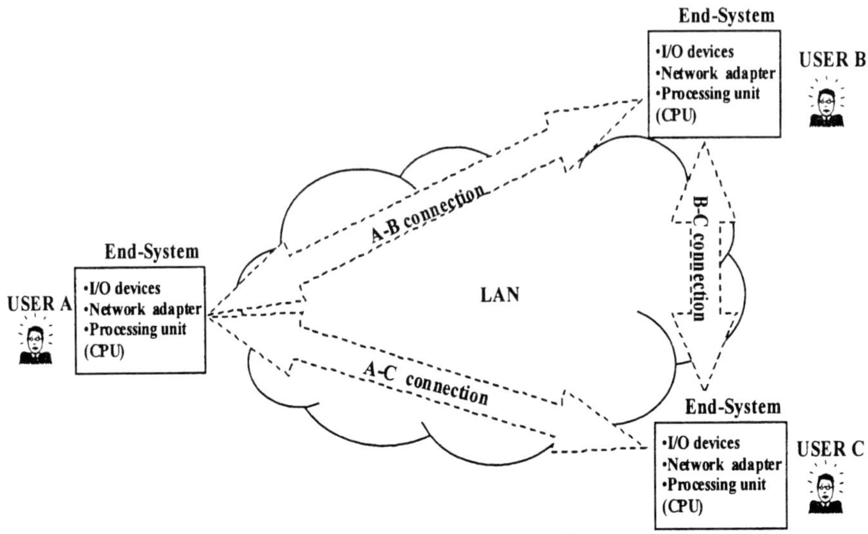


Fig.5. A videoconference scenario

More specifically, the algorithm we use to solve the DQA problem is as follows:

```
Q(1..n)  // solution vector
q(1..n)  // vector of qualities were calculated by the IQA
α(1..n)  // maximum resource utilisation (rate or bandwidth)
W(1..n)  // vector of applications weights (importances)
// applications ordered so that W(i)/α(i)>= W(i+1)/α(i+1)
Q:=0                    // initialisation
RU:=U                   // remaining resource utilisation RU equals to the
                           available resource utilisation U
for i:=1 to n do
  {if α(i)>RU then exit endif
   Q(i):=q(i)
   RU:=RU-α(i) }
if i<=n then Q(i):=q(i)*(RU/α(i))
```

# 4 Simulations

At this point we will give a simple but illustrative example of the Initial Quality Allocator (IQA) functionality. Assume a videoconference service (Fig.5) that exchanges video and audio among the three users A, B and C. These three users communicate with each other through a network infrastructure (i.e., assume a TCP/IP LAN). At any instance of the service we may assume three virtual connections, A-B connection with current bandwidth capability $\underline{BW}_{AB}$, A-C with current bandwidth capability $\underline{BW}_{AC}$ and B-C connection with current bandwidth capability $\underline{BW}_{BC}$. Users A, B use videoconferencing end-systems (i.e., workstations) whose operating system employs EDF algorithm to execute the applications, while the end-system of user C employs RM algorithm. In this example, there are three applications executed at each end-system in order to handle the videoconference, one video capture and two video displays (displaying video captured and sent by the colleagues) applications. Thus, there are nine applications that must be served by the system. For simplicity, we assume that the quality that the video will be displayed is equal to the quality it was captured (i.e., if user A captures video with quality $q_A$ then users B and C will display this video in the same quality). The users A, B, C introduce minimum expectations for the quality of the video application $\underline{q}_A$, $\underline{q}_B$ and $\underline{q}_C$ respectively. Each application is assigned a weight $w_k$ (k=1..9), an integer in [1,10], that indicates the importance of the application. For simplicity, we assume that video and audio are interleaved in the same media. Finally, we do not consider other applications that the user may execute in his workstation at the same time. Table 2 presents the notation details of the videoconference example.

IQA formulates an optimisation problem that considers the service, the users and the infrastructure constraints.

Maximise $$Q = \xi_A(w,q) + \xi_B(w,q) + \xi_C(w,q) \quad (26)$$

$$\xi_A(w,q) = w_1 q_A + w_2 q_B + w_3 q_C \quad (27)$$

$$\xi_B(w,q) = w_4 q_B + w_5 q_A + w_6 q_C \quad (28)$$

$$\xi_C(w,q) = w_7 q_C + w_8 q_A + w_9 q_B \quad (29)$$

given that

$$U_A(q) = a_1 \cdot q_A + a_2 \cdot q_B + a_3 \cdot q_C \le 1 \quad (30)$$

$$U_B(q) = a_4 \cdot q_B + a_5 \cdot q_A + a_6 \cdot q_C \le 1 \quad (31)$$

$$U_C(q) = a_7 \cdot q_C + a_8 \cdot q_A + a_9 \cdot q_B \le 3 \cdot (2^{1/3} - 1) \quad (32)$$

$$BW_{AB}(q) = b_2 \cdot q_A + b_5 \cdot q_B \le \underline{BW}_{AB} \quad (33)$$

$$BW_{AC}(q) = b_3 \cdot q_A + b_8 \cdot q_C \le \underline{BW}_{AC} \quad (34)$$

$$BW_{BC}(q) = b_6 \cdot q_B + b_9 \cdot q_C \le \underline{BW}_{BC} \tag{35}$$

$$\underline{q_A} \le q_A \le 1 \tag{36}$$

$$\underline{q_B} \le q_B \le 1 \tag{37}$$

$$\underline{q_C} \le q_C \le 1 \tag{38}$$

Table 2 Videoconference example parameter specification.

| **Problem Parameter** | **Value** | **Comments** |
|---|---|---|
| $W_1$ | 4 | Importance of capturing video of User A |
| $W_2$ | 4 | Importance of displaying video sent by User B in User's A end-system |
| $W_3$ | 4 | Importance of displaying video sent by User C in User's A end-system |
| $W_4$ | 4 | Importance of capturing video of User B |
| $W_5$ | 4 | Importance of displaying video sent by User A in User's B end-system |
| $W_6$ | 4 | Importance of displaying video sent by User C in User's B end-system |
| $W_7$ | 4 | Importance of capturing video of User C |
| $W_8$ | 4 | Importance of displaying video sent by User A in User's C end-system |
| $W_9$ | 4 | Importance of displaying video sent by User B in User's C end-system |
| End-System processing time/video pixel | 0.1μsec | The necessary time for the end-system to process a pixel of a video application (assumed common between capturing and displaying applications).<br><br>In this example we assume that all end-system has the same video processing performance. |

| Best quality video specifications | 640X480 pixels/frame<br><br>25 frames/sec | NTSC quality video |
|---|---|---|
| $b_j$ , j=1..3 | 7680000 X 8 bits/sec<br><br>Color depth =8bits/pixel | Maximum necessary video Bandwidth (best quality) |
| $a_i$ , i=1..9 | 7680000 pixels X 0.1 μsec | maximum processing rate (q=1) |
| $\underline{BW}_{AB}$ | 24 Mbits/sec $< \underline{BW}_{AB} <$ 60 Mbits/sec<br><br>Fig. 6(a) (Randomly generated) | Available bandwidth in A-B connection |
| $\underline{BW}_{AC}$ | 24 Mbits/sec $< \underline{BW}_{AC} <$ 60 Mbits/sec<br><br>Fig. 6(b) (Randomly generated) | Available bandwidth in A-C connection |
| $\underline{BW}_{BC}$ | 24 Mbits/sec $< \underline{BW}_{BC} <$ 60 Mbits/sec<br><br>Fig. 6(c) (Randomly generated) | Available bandwidth in B-C connection |

To evaluate the performance of our architecture, we performed a number of simulations where we considered the videoconferencing example. For simplicity, we assume that all videoconference end-systems are of the same processing power. Due to network traffic, we assume that bandwidth availability varies randomly in a way that is consistent to the real network bandwidth variations (Fig.6). For simplicity, we assume that all the applications are of the same importance (identical weights). In Table 2, there are the numeric values of the problem parameters we assume in this simulation. Simulations performed in a simple Intel-Pentium based personal computer with the MAPLE program and we explored the dynamic behaviour of IQA algorithm. For the problem stated above and the computer described, the IQA algorithm performed about 10msec CPU-time for a complete computation of the optimisation problem with the Simplex algorithm. Simulation results are presented in Fig.7. In Fig.8 there is a graph that focus on a small area of the results, where the qualities computed by the IQA algorithm are presented. It is clear that the quality values (Fig.8) are modified according to the network availability (Fig.9). In Fig.9 there is the total necessary bandwidth ($BW_{AB}$) (dashed line) as well as the available bandwidth $\underline{BW}_{AB}$ (solid line) of the A-B connection resource. Bandwidths were computed by (33) for the quality values of Fig.8. Notice that the necessary bandwidth follows the random variations of the available bandwidth ($\underline{BW}_{AB}$) and its value is always less or equal to the available. Similar results were produced for the rest of the connections. The simulations show that the $MEQA^3$ adapts properly the quality values of the applications under the system infrastructure constraints.

# 5 Conclusions

In this work we present $MEQA^3$ application adaptation architecture. The architecture performs an overall QoS adaptation management of a multi-user multimedia service. In order to realise QoS management, the service is analysed to its minimal applications and through a model that relates QoS characteristics, resource parameters and the user's QoS profile, the system maps QoS parameters of the multimedia service. $MEQA^3$ manages QoS in two different points of the service activity, 1) the setup/ initialisation period and 2) the service period. During the initialisation phase, the system performs an overall optimal QoS to application allocation considering the user requests, the service requirements and the resource constraints. By this calculation, the architecture computes the QoS that the system is a-priory able to guarantee given the user QoS profile and application requirements. During the service time, the system monitors the QoS of the applications on the user's side. If this quality is becoming less than the user-specified minimum then a dynamic fast algorithm adapts the applications configuration according to the constraints of the resources that produce this QoS degradation. We explored the behaviour of our approach by extended realistic simulations on a videoconference scenario and as we present in the corresponding section, $MEQA^3$ architecture performed appropriately.

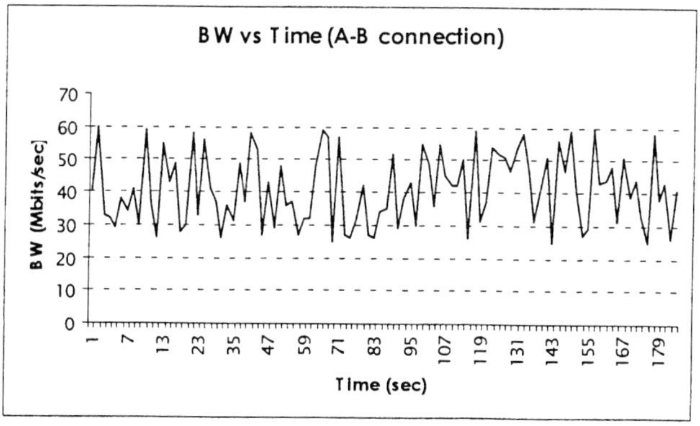


(a)

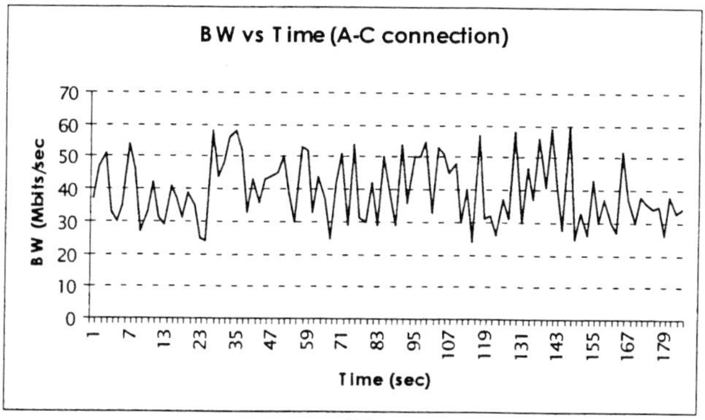


(b)

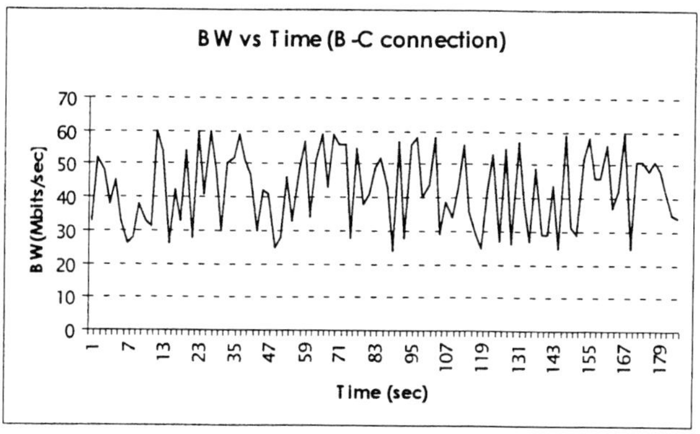


(c)

Fig.6. Bandwidth availability of the simulation scenarios

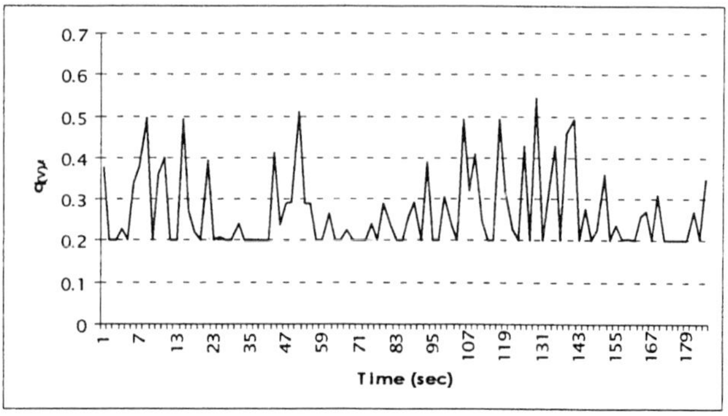


(a)

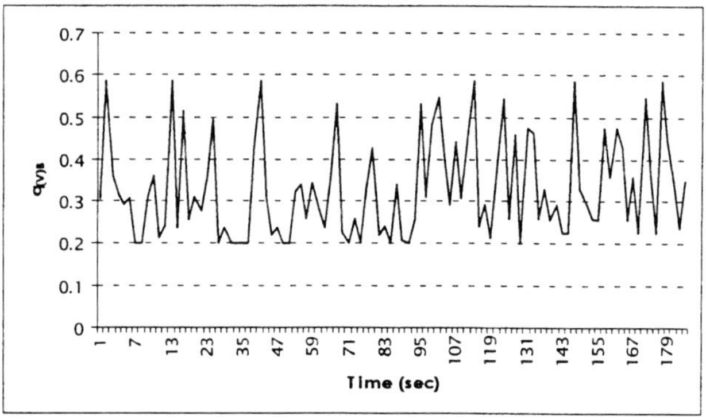


(b)

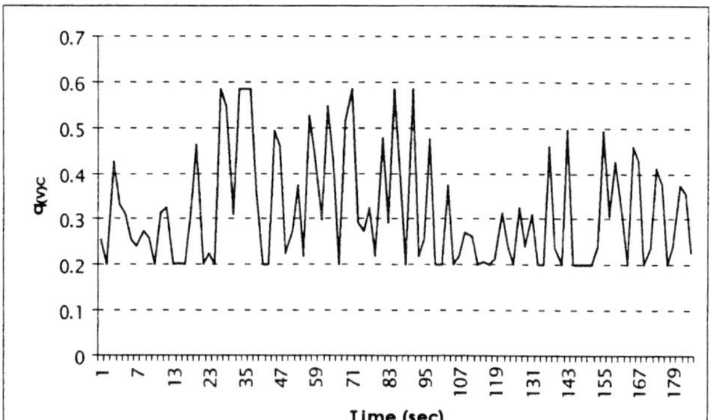


(c)

Fig.7. Qualities computed by IQA algorithm for the simulation scenario

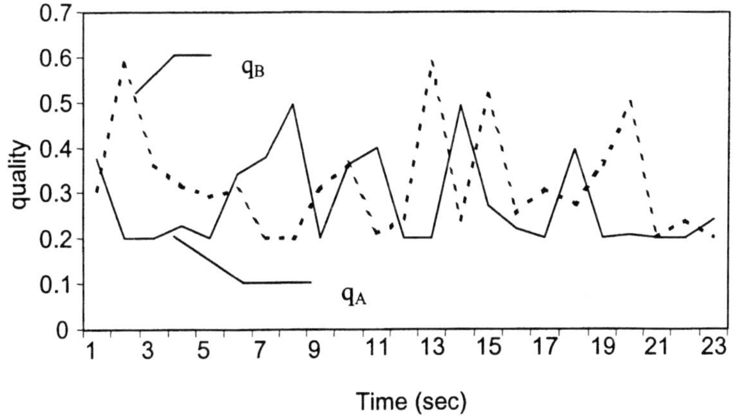


Fig.8. A more detailed view of the results

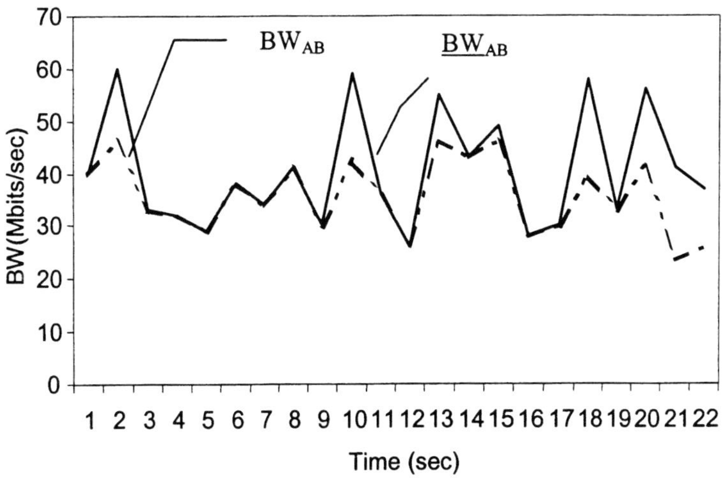


Fig.9. Bandwidth variations during the first 23 sec of the simulation.

# References


[1] A. Vogel, B. Kerhervé, G.V. Bochmann and J. Gecsei, "Distributed Multimedia Applications and Quality of Service- A Survey," *IEEE Multimedia*, vol. 2, no. 2, Summer 1995, pp. 10-19.

[2] G.V. Bochmann and A. Hafid, "Some principles for quality of service management", *Distributed Systems Engineering Journal* , vol. 4, no. 1, 1997, pp. 16-27.

[3] C. Aurrecoechea, A.T. Campbell, and L. Hauw, "A Survey of Quality of Service Architectures," *Multimedia Systems Journal* Special Issue on QoS Architecture, May 1998.

[4] R. Rajkumar, C. Lee, J. Lehoczky and D. Siewiorek, "A Resource Allocation Model for QoS Management," *IEEE Real-Time Systems Symposium* , December 1997.

[5] R. Rajkumar, C. Lee, J. Lehoczky and D. Siewiorek, "Practical Solutions for QoS-based Resource Allocation Problems," *IEEE Real-Time Systems Symposium* , December 1998.

[6] C. Lee, J. Lehoczky, R. Rajkumar and D. Siewiorek, "On Quality of Service Optimization with Discrete QoS Options," *5$^{th}$ IEEE Real-Time Technology and Applications Symposium*, June 1999, Vancouver, Canada.

[7] J. Bolliger and T. Gross, "A Framework-Based Approach to the Development of Network-Aware Applications," *IEEE Trans. Software Engineering*, Vol.24, May 1998, pp 376-390.

[8] G.A. Rovithakis, A.G. Malamos, T.A. Varvarigou and M.A. Christodoulou, "Quality Assurance in Networks – a High Order Neural Net Approach," *37$^{th}$ IEEE Conf. On Decision and Control CDC'98*, Florida, Dec. 1998.

[9] A. Hafid and G.V. Bochmann, "Quality of Service adaptation in distributed multimedia applications," *Multimedia Systems J.*, Vol.6, no.5, 1998, pp. 299-315.

[10] A.T. Campbell and G. Coulson, "A QoS Adaptive Multimedia Transport System: Design, Implementation and Experiences," *Distributed Systems Engineering J.*, Special Issue on Quality of Service, 1997

[11] C. Cowan, S. Cen, J. Walpole and C. Pu, "Adaptive Methods for Distributed Video Presentation," *ACM Computing Surveys,* 27, 1995, pp. 580-583.

[12] C.H. Papadimitriou and K. Steiglitz, *"Combinatorial Optimization-Algorithms and Complexity,"* ED. Prentice-Hall 1982

[13] C.L. Liu and J.W. Layland, "Scheduling Algorithms for Multiprogramming in a Hard-Real-Time Environment," *J. of the Ass. for Computing Machinery*, vol. 20, no. 1, January 1973, pp. 46-61.

[14] E. Horowitz and S. Sahni, *"Fundamental of Computer Algorithms,"* ED. Computer Science Press, 1984

# INDEX

## A



## B



## C

# P



# Q



# R



# S

## T



## U



## V



## W



## X